Spinoza, Ecology and International Law

This book addresses the use of Benedict Spinoza's philosophy in current attempts to elaborate an ecological basis for international environmental law. Because the question of environmental protection has not been satisfactory resolved, the legal debate concerning our responsibility for the environment has – as evidenced in the recent UN report series Harmony with Nature – come to invite calls for a new eco-centric, rather than anthropocentric, legal paradigm. In this respect, Spinoza appears as a key figure. He is one of the few philosophers in the history of western philosophy who cares, and writes extensively, about the roots of anthropocentrism; the core issue of contemporary normative debates in ecology. And in response to the rapidly developing ecological crisis, his work has become central to a re-thinking of the human relationship with nature. Addressing the contention that Spinoza's ethics might provide a useful source for developing a new, eco-centred framework for environmental law, this book elaborates a more nuanced understanding of Spinoza's philosophy. Spinoza cannot, it is argued here, simply be reduced to an eco-ethicist. That is: his metaphysics cannot be used as the basis of an essentially naturalised or extended human morality. At the same time, however, this book argues that the radicality of Spinoza's naturalism nevertheless offers the possibility of developing a more adequate ecological basis for environmental law.

Moa De Lucia Dahlbeck is a postdoctoral researcher at the department of law at Gothenburg University and a member of the Spinoza Research Group (Grupo de Investigación sobre Spinoza y el spinozismo) at the Faculty of Philosophy and Arts, Buenos Aires University.

Law, Justice and Ecology

Series editors
Anna Grear, *Law School, Cardiff University*, UK

For information about the series and details of previous and forthcoming titles, see https://www.routledge.com/Law-Justice-and-Ecology/book-series/LAWJUSTECO

A GlassHouse Book

Spinoza, Ecology and International Law

Radical Naturalism in the Face of the Anthropocene

Moa De Lucia Dahlbeck

Routledge
Taylor & Francis Group
LONDON AND NEW YORK

First published 2019
by Routledge
2 Park Square, Milton Park, Abingdon, Oxon OX14 4RN

and by Routledge
52 Vanderbilt Avenue, New York, NY 10017, USA

First issued in paperback 2020

Routledge is an imprint of the Taylor & Francis Group, an informa business

A GlassHouse book

British Library Cataloguing-in-Publication Data
A catalogue record for this book is available from the British Library

Library of Congress Cataloging-in-Publication Data
Names: De Lucia Dahlbeck, Moa, 1981- author.
Title: Spinoza, ecology and international law radical naturalism in the face of the anthropocene / Moa De Lucia Dahlbeck.
Description: Abingdon, Oxon ; New York, NY : Routledge, 2019. | Series: Law, justice and ecology | Includes index.
Identifiers: LCCN 2018025590 | ISBN 9781138038684 (hbk)
Subjects: LCSH: Environmental law, International—Philosophy. | International law—Philosophy. | Spinoza, Benedictus de, 1632-1677—Influence.
Classification: LCC K3585 .D4 2019 | DDC 344.04/6—dc23
LC record available at https://lccn.loc.gov/2018025590

ISBN 13: 978-0-367-66551-7 (pbk)
ISBN 13: 978-1-138-03868-4 (hbk)

Typeset in Galliard
by Taylor & Francis Books

For Sofia and Ona

Contents

Acknowledgements

First and foremost I would like to thank my brother Johan Dahlbeck for your comments and questions on the work. Our conversations have been absolutely essential for developing my understanding of Spinoza and for finding the arguments about Spinoza and normativity presented in this book. I would also like to thank Gregor Noll and Lena Wahlberg. Their support during my doctoral studies encouraged me to deepen my interest in the metaphysics of international environmental law and to extend my studies into the realm of philosophy. Finally, I thank the wonderful scholars of the Spinoza Study Group at Buenos Aires University (Grupo de investigación sobre Spinoza y el spinozismo) who all have contributed to my understanding and love of Spinoza's writings.

Editions used and abbreviations

Descartes, R.

The Geometrical Demonstration of Meditations on First Philosophy (Med); Principles of Philosophy (Principles); Discourse on the Method. References to Descartes' works as found herein use the pagination of the Adam and Tannery volumes (AT), *Oeuvres de Descartes*, 11 vols. The citations give volume and page numbers. The Cottingham, Stoothoff, Murdoch and Kenny translation, *The Philosophical Writings of Descartes*, 3 vols, has been used; it shows the AT pagination in the margins.

Spinoza, B.

Ethics, Treatise on the Emendation of the Intellect (TdIE) and Letters (Ep.): 1–84; Theological-Political Treatise (TTP); Political Treatise (TP) – Curley, E. (ed. and trans.) *The Collected Works of Spinoza* vols I and II. 1985 and 2016. Princeton, NJ: Princeton University Press.

Abbreviations for Spinoza's works

TdIE Tractatus de Intellectus Emandatione [*Treatise on the Emendation of the Intellect*]
TP Tractatus Politicus [*The Political Treatise*]
TTP Tractatus Theologico-Politicus [*The Theological-Political Treatise*]
Ep. Epistolae [Letters]

Abbreviations for the geometrically ordered passages from Spinoza's *Ethics*

E Ethics
a axiom
c corollary
d (before proposition) definition
d (after proposition) demonstration
L lemma

p proposition
post postulate
s scholium
exp explanation

Example: *E*2p7s = Part 2, Proposition 7, scholium.
References to the non-geometrically ordered passages from the *Ethics*, as well as references to the *TdIE, TP* and *TTP* are supplemented by references to Gebhardt's edition *Spinoza Opera* (4 vols 1925. Heidelberg: Carl Winter), according to the following form:
G II/208/25–30 = Gebhardt, Vol. 2, page 208, lines 25–30.

Introduction

How is the philosophy of a seventeenth century philosopher relevant for the contemporary legal project of navigating an ongoing global ecological crisis? This book is an attempt to answer that question by way of reconstructing a recent argument within instances of both legal and philosophical scholarship which implies the use of the philosophy of Benedict Spinoza (1632–1677) as a means to combat the practical consequences of the problem of nature. As will become evident shortly, contemporary commentators on Spinoza and nature/law argue that his philosophy is being vindicated by new scientific findings related to the Anthropocene.[1] In this context, the Anthropocene is understood as the ultimate empirical and physical upshot of having constructed and adhered to a modern episteme which is both ontologically erroneous and providing epistemological support for an unlimited exploitation of nature. As such, the Anthropocene is highlighted as a natural phenomenon that demonstrates the relevance of Spinoza's critique of Descartes' metaphysical explanation of the human being as a 'dominion within a dominion' and his own alternative explanation based on substance monism, philosophical naturalism and strict determinism.

Arguments indicating Spinoza's relevance for the problem of nature are not only useful as vantage points from where to begin a study of recent developments within discourses concerned with the normative protection of the natural environment, they can also serve as incentives for an independent reflection on Spinoza's responses to the philosophical issues underscored by the problem of nature taken on its own. To this end, this book is intended to work on two parallel levels. It can be read as an analysis of the contemporary legal project to combat the physical effects of our traditional way of understanding the human–nature relationship and the problem of nature. It can also be read, however, as a study of Spinoza's conceptualization of that relationship and problem.

The problem of nature and a normative call for a new metaphysics

The birth of a global concern for nature is usually dated to the 1970s. Different suggestions of how to make international environmental law able to meet the requirements of that global concern have been put forward regularly ever since (see e.g. Speth, 2002, 12). Following the law-making tradition of international law, these suggestions initially revolved mainly around treaty-making, methods of harmonization, implementation techniques and compliance mechanisms (Palmer, 1992, 259–283). However, because none of these suggestions has been considered entirely successful the normative debate has come to involve arguments other than those dealing with the content, form and scope of international environmental law (Speth, 2002, 11–30; Palmer, 1992, 271).

One such argument is put forward by the United Nations' report series entitled *Harmony with Nature: Report of the Secretary-General* (henceforth the Reports). The aim of the Reports is to envision a truly uniform and holistic approach to the problem of nature so that the world becomes prepared to take on any one of its different potential effects: be it of economic, legal, educational or other nature. The method settled on by the Reports for taking on this task spells a change in the theoretical framework under which human interactions with nature are evaluated. In essence, the envisioned plan implies that if we can alter the premises determining how we think about and relate to nature – from a utilitarian, anthropocentric perspective to a naturalistic scheme – then, our normative framework for protecting nature will become more effective because legislation will proceed according to nature's perspective and states and people will naturally comply with protective laws as nature's wellbeing will be thought of as part and parcel of their own.

In a way then, we may understand the changed direction taken by the normative debate as stemming from a critique of the theoretical basis of contemporary international environmental law: a critique that portrays that law as being anthropocentric and therefore biased. As such, the argument that we are interested in links metaphysics (understood as a paradigm of thought) to legal theory and normative practices in that it holds that an anthropomorphic explanation of value and wellbeing leads to an anthropocentric morality and if we manage to change that anthropomorphic basis then nature will naturally be given both legal and moral standing (United Nations). Thus, the Reports' call for action connects the normative problem of environmental protection with those underlying thinking patterns allegedly responsible for our understanding of value. Understood this way, we can isolate and identify the same call in a variety of discourses within the normative debate on environmental protection: a call for a new paradigm of thought; for a change in basic values; and for a new foundation of right and wrong (cf. Adetunji, Price, Fleming and Kemp, 2003, 169; Peet and Bossel, 2000, 225; Burns and Witoszek, 2012, 159; Latour, 2010).

It is noteworthy that the call for a new theoretical framework is not only visible within normative discourses, as a suggested means for tackling the problem of insufficiency surrounding traditional approaches to the legal problem of protecting nature. In this book I will highlight the fact that the same call is also being independently sustained by scholars in other disciplines – such as, but not limited to, philosophy, ecology and ethics. In these contexts the call appears as a suggestion for a better explanatory framework of the powers causing our rapidly deteriorating natural environment (cf. Guilherme, 2011, 60–78; Kober, 2013, 43–66; Gamlund, 2007, 3–27; Sharp, 2011a, 185–220; 2011b, 48–68; 2016, 272–281; Mack, 2011). This book focuses on the specific formulation of the argument for a new metaphysics that is provided by the Reports because, as I will outline shortly, although it is merely one of many similar formulations of one and the same argument (and to some extent seems to be constructed as a generic compilation of various disciplinary takes on one basic argument), the Reports' formulation is special in that it is explicitly concerned with the normative upshots of this argument. This makes the Reports interesting from the point of view of international (environmental) law in so far as they serve as a good empirical basis for an evaluation of the conceptual conditions involved in a project aiming at protecting nature through turning to a new paradigm of thought.

The Reports series currently comprises seven separate reports. The initiative to author and disseminate them was taken by the United Nations General Assembly in 2009. The history of the Reports starts with the General Assembly Resolution A/RES/63/278 in which the UN proclaimed 22 April to be 'International Mother Earth Day'. According to the United Nations' webpage on the chronology of the Reports, it was the Plurinational State of Bolivia that initiated negotiations on the principles of harmony with nature. Shortly after Bolivia initiated these negotiations, the first resolution on harmony with nature was adopted by the General Assembly. Through this resolution, the Secretary-General was requested to issue a first Report on the theme (A/RES/64/196). According to the description of the so-called harmony with nature process on the UN website, the Reports aim to 'devise a new world'. The same webpage elaborates:

> Since 2009, the aim of the General Assembly, in adopting its five [*sic*] resolutions on 'Harmony with Nature', has been to define this newly found relationship based on a non-anthropocentric relationship with Nature. The resolutions contain different perspectives regarding the construction of a new, non-anthropocentric paradigm in which the fundamental basis for right and wrong action concerning the environment is grounded not solely in human concerns.
> (United Nations, quotation marks in original)

I take as one of my points of departure in this book that the theoretical implications of the Reports' call for 'a new, *non-anthropocentric paradigm* in which the fundamental basis for right and wrong action concerning the environment is grounded not solely in human concerns' can be traced and investigated if connected to a broader theoretical discourse (ibid., my emphasis). For this task, I will rely on some of the other just mentioned versions of the argument in favour of a new metaphysics. Another point of departure is the premise that the Reports' formulations of this argument constitute illustrative examples of the way by which certain formulations in the contemporary environmental discourse imply, without properly following through on its consistent application, the need to rely on a new non-anthropocentric paradigm of thought. It is thus the principal aim of this book to render these implications explicit so that they can be carefully considered in light of the question of how the international community wishes to organize international law. For this reason, the book includes a careful reading of the Reports as well as, in the last chapter of the book, a cross-reading of their formulations with an especially elaborate example of a similar argument within the discipline of philosophy, all in light of my review of Spinoza's philosophy as a whole.

The principal aim emerges from considering statements in the Reports, like the following, which hint at the normative power of acquiring new thinking patterns:

> Education is critical if people are to be motivated and informed to take the necessary actions to mend the damage already incurred and avoid further damage to the Earth and its ecosystems. The focus on environmental education has been on teaching a respect of nature. However, *such respect alone has clearly not changed society's destructive behavior.* Respect and appreciation are the first steps toward developing environmentally aware citizens. *Effective learning should manifest itself in changes in values and behavior.*
>
> (Rep. I, para.46, my emphasis)

> [C]hanging how we behave on the planet will require a major shift in values.
>
> (Rep. II, para.78)

As mentioned, the reason for focusing on the Reports is rather straightforward considering their affinity with the discourse on international law. The Reports' outline of a theoretical framework apt for dealing with the global environmental concern is different in relation to similar calls visible within other discourses concerned with the problem of nature in so far as it is relatively more concrete and explicit in detailing the normative upshots connected with a new metaphysics. To this end, the Reports provide an opportunity to study what otherwise appears to be too elusive for investigation. For instance, the Reports describe not just what basic assumptions and intuitions must change if we want to create a new, environmentally friendly ethics but also how these changes will affect law-making and law practices. This renders it possible to investigate the normative implications of the argument for a new metaphysical understanding of value as a response to the problem of how to make environmental protection more effective and truly global. Also, in so far as ethical arguments always are central for legal claims, the Reports' outline of the argument for a new metaphysics is important in and of itself as it clearly is grounded on ethical concerns. This is especially so because of the similarity between the Reports' request – understood in the way that I will suggest we understand it – and the recent tendency within other disciplines to argue for a relationship between a certain metaphysical outlook and a successful combat of the rapid deterioration of the global natural environment (cf. Taylor, 2000, 248–250; Stenmark, 2007, 37–50; and Sharp, 2011a).

The Reports, non-anthropocentrism and Spinoza

For a considered reflection of the argument that a change in the direction suggested by the Reports will effectuate a change in normative ethics and law, it is necessary to insert the Reports' arguments into a theoretical framework that explicates and elaborates on the conceptual conditions at work. I suggest, as indicated initially, that one possible way of evaluating the Reports' arguments is by reading them in the light of Spinoza's early modern philosophy. I base this suggestion on two motives. First, that the Reports' substantial claims about the requirements of the called-for new metaphysics, ethics and moral theory demonstrate a semantic similarity with many of Spinoza's central doctrines. Second, that this apparent similarity between the Reports and Spinoza's philosophy is supported not only by the texts themselves but also by a certain eco-ethical reading of Spinoza's philosophy in so far as this is read as a philosophical and conceptual explication of the main argument of the Reports. In order to flesh out the Reports' sketchy and eclectic arguments I will therefore turn to this reading of Spinoza and use it as a more elaborate design of the Reports' main philosophical ideas and normative propositions, before analysing the feasibility of the Reports' argument. Spinoza's philosophical structure is suitable to perform the function of theoretical blueprint for the Reports' claims and arguments since it contains all of those metaphysical premises being highlighted by the Reports – and as elaborated by the eco-ethical reading – as necessary for the construction of a new kind of normativity: a normativity sensitive to the needs and wellbeing of nature. Assuming a tangible similarity between the Reports' formulations and Spinoza's metaphysics, I will use the latter as a means for analysing the Reports' argument. I believe this analysis is facilitated by understanding the normative claims of the Reports as grounded in this eco-ethical reading of Spinoza. Establishing a framework of evaluation this way, I will proceed to consider the feasibility of the Reports' substantial normative suggestions in light of the normative consequences deduced from a study of Spinoza's political philosophy against the background of his metaphysics.

As Chapter 1 will show, the semantic similarity between the Reports and Spinoza's philosophy can be grouped in three main categories. The first is constituted by arguments in the Reports that pose a conceptual link between a shift in basic thinking patterns – our current paradigm of thought – and a new definition of value and normative ethics. This group of arguments points to Spinoza's philosophy in so far as the latter arguably is one of the few philosophical systems in the history of philosophy that is grounded on the very metaphysical premises that are being detailed by the Reports and that furthermore connects these premises to a formal moral theory and normative ethics. The second group is of a more nominal nature and it consists of arguments which feature one of the following two characteristics: a) explicit mentioning of Spinoza as a figure opposing the powers responsible for an erroneous anthropocentric understanding of nature and b) references to readings of Spinoza's philosophy within studies of ethics and/or philosophy which make the explicit link between Spinoza's metaphysics and a new kind of political and normative theory; one that reconfigures the human responsibility for nature's wellbeing. With respect to this group, it is especially interesting to note the Reports' explicit references to the work of Arne Naess, who is perhaps the first in the history of ecological thought to connect Spinoza to a new ecological normativity. The third category, finally, consists in arguments outlining the substance of the called-for new metaphysics, or paradigm of thought. Although the Reports draw from a variety of theoretical sources, as already mentioned, the result of their mixed and eclectic references is a metaphysical explanation of the world, existence and human nature which is strikingly similar to the one provided by Spinoza in the first three parts of his principal work the *Ethics*. There are simply not that many advocates of substance monism and philosophical naturalism (which essentially is what the Reports call for) to be found in the history of philosophy to begin with. Even less so, a metaphysics that combines substance monism with radical naturalism in a way that effectively erases any qualitative differences between species and individuals; that neutralizes and relativizes the concept of value; and that intertwines human destiny with that of nature (Melamed, 2011, 207–208). This motive for connecting the Reports to Spinoza becomes even more forceful if we consider it in the light of the conceptual context to which the Reports pertain. Because, from the perspective of a rational tradition of thought, which arguably is the tradition to which we associate ourselves when talking about the modern idea of the nation-state and international law, Spinoza appears to be the *only* one arguing for a substance monistic ontological explanation.

One of the presumptions that can be deduced from the Reports is that a new normative relationship between humanity and the rest of nature will emerge *naturally* as soon as we manage to alter our most fundamental patterns of thinking and basic presumptions about nature. Thus, the Reports argue for a direct link between altering our metaphysical understanding and a new understanding of value and desire. Because Spinoza's philosophy, as mentioned and as will be elaborated further, can be regarded as a study essentially concerned with the normative aspects of the human condition following from a rarely seen systematic reconsideration of human nature, and because of the fact that the Reports arguably position their called-for new metaphysics very close to that reconsideration, his philosophical structure makes for an excellent evaluative tool of the Reports' main argument (cf. Kisner and Youpa, 2014, introduction, 1).

Methodological challenges and points of departure

Before embarking on an analytical project such as the one undertaken in this book there are a few methodological challenges to contemplate. To begin with it should be noted that while one of the book's aims is to affirm a similarity between the Reports and Spinoza's philosophy, its main objective is to carefully consider and evaluate the Reports' specific and concrete normative suggestion in the light of Spinoza's philosophy and by doing this contribute to the understanding of that philosophy as such. To this end, there is a secondary object of the book which deserves to be noted. So, apart from aiming to contribute to the development of a considered theorization of the scope of international environmental law, it aims to partake in the debate on how to 'use' Spinoza's philosophy in a contemporary and empirical context.

This second object requires methodological considerations of a different character than those related to deducing a semantic similarity between two unrelated texts. The book's second object requires a methodological sensitivity to problems internal to the study of Spinoza's philosophy. It has, for instance, been suggested that a problem of connecting Spinoza's metaphysics with practical and normative practices emerges due to the apparent paradox between the normative ideas represented in the *Theological-Political Treatise* (*Tractatus Theologicus-Politicus* [*TTP*], 1670) and the posthumously published, unfinished *Political Treatise* (*Tractatus Politicus* [*TP*], 1677), and, the strictly naturalistic ontology and metaphysics of the *Ethics* (*E*, 1677) (cf. Steinberg, 2008, 249). Arguably, this paradox results in the difficulty to attribute one coherent view to Spinoza with regard to empirical and practical disciplines such as legal and political theories. As mentioned, this opens up a methodological discussion of a different character than the one prompted by the principal empirical problem of this book.

The *TTP* is organized in two parts; each with a specific scope and each providing a different philosophical critique. The first part is directed towards the question of interpretation of Scripture and the theological discourse, and the other part is directed towards the question of political organization and political freedoms (*TTP* preface [8], G III/7). It is not strange that most investigations of Spinoza's conception of law, for instance, have been focused on the second part of the *TTP* (cf. Melamed and Rosenthal, 2010, introduction, 3). Scholars trying to unpack Spinoza's concept of law have thus traditionally focused on reading and commenting on Chapter 16 of the *TTP*: 'On the foundation of the state, on the natural and civil right of each person, and on the authority of sovereign powers' and Chapter 3 of the *TP*: 'The right of the state' (cf. Lauterpacht, 1927, 89).[2]

Now, the naturalness and exclusivity of this focus has recently been questioned by scholars who suggest an integrated approach to the understanding of Spinoza's doctrines and ideas. Whereas Spinoza's philosophy previously has been studied in a piecemeal fashion, according to the formal epistemological pertinence of each section studied – be it metaphysics, ethics, psychology or physics – this approach has more and more become replaced by the aim of achieving a coherent and overall understanding of the political aspects of the philosophy in light of the metaphysics and vice versa. It is argued that the explicit political ideas of the *TTP* and the *TP* cannot fully be comprehended unless read in light of the *TTP*'s methodological critique against classical theology and Scripture interpretation *as well as* in light of the first three metaphysical parts of the *Ethics* (cf. Melamed and Rosenthal, 2010, introduction, 3; Batnitzky, 2003–2004, 508). This way, convincing arguments are being forwarded as to what we should reconsider to be the natural scope of investigation when it comes to studies aimed at clarifying specific aspects of Spinoza's philosophy. Yitzhak Melamed and Michael Rosenthal enumerate the following arguments in favour of extending the scope for studies concerned with Spinoza's political philosophy. First of all, they write, the *TTP* was not developed in an intellectual vacuum, Spinoza wrote in constant dialogue with Jewish philosophy as well as the Dutch and other European early modern rational tendencies (cf. Melamed and Rosenthal, 2010, introduction).[3] Second, there is a clear conceptual inter-dependence between many key notions of the *TTP* and the *TP* on the one hand and the *Ethics* on the other. The full picture is thus best created by regarding specific political and normative doctrines of the *TTP* and the *TP* in light of their metaphysical conditions as presented therein, in the *Ethics*, or in some of Spinoza's earlier works on methodology, Cartesian metaphysics and human nature (Melamed and Rosenthal, 2010, introduction). The principal lesson to learn from this methodological debate is that for a considered understanding of Spinoza's normative position, it is not sufficient to look at his metaphysical structure alone *or* his explicit expression of a political philosophy. A considered understanding depends on a careful parallel and integrated reading of both.

For this reason, I will first delineate the basis of Spinoza's metaphysics and then continue with an outline of the relevant aspects of Spinoza's political philosophy, focusing not only on those parts that are concerned explicitly with the concepts of law, the state and international relations but also on the metaphysical premises underpinning those parts. Based on the image of Spinoza's political philosophy that will emerge this way, I will approach the book's main objective: to evaluate the Reports' argument for a new metaphysics as a means to establish an alternative and radically ecological normative ethics. Assuming that a contemporary take on Spinoza's philosophy functions as a foundation for that argument's conceptual premises (which, as mentioned, will be inferred from a cross-reading of the Reports and a specific reading of Spinoza), I will analyse whether the Reports' call with respect to the normative framework of a global concern for nature is feasible or not.

Chapter outline and structure of arguments

The book is structured as follows. In Chapter 1, I give an overview of the Reports and their arguments for turning to a radically different metaphysics in the face of an imminent environmental crisis. I organize the Reports' arguments according to a division between a) arguments that point to Spinoza's philosophy as their source of inspiration and b) arguments about the normative consequences that will flow from adhering to the called-for new metaphysics. As mentioned, after having established a semantic similarity between the Reports and Spinoza's metaphysics, I will suggest that this similarity can be substantiated and supported by a trending reading of Spinoza that expands on the potentiality of his philosophy as a ground for a new kind of politics. This suggestion will be introduced in Chapter 1 in connection with the Reports' argumentation and then picked up again in a separate section of Chapter 6, where the aim is to provide the Reports' implicit use of Spinoza a concrete and more explicit content.

As I have already indicated, the book's main concern requires a thorough and careful review of Spinoza's entire philosophical system. The main thrust of the book is therefore dedicated to providing the building blocks of Spinoza's metaphysical and normative philosophies in order to prepare for an evaluation of a normative reading of Spinoza's metaphysics in line with the Reports' call and argument for a change in basic thinking patterns. Chapter 2 provides an outline of Spinoza's metaphysical and ethical structure so that the foundation of the implications of the Reports' arguments can be established. For the sake of simplicity and clarity, this outline is focused on those of Spinoza's metaphysical doctrines and ideas that are being highlighted by either the Reports themselves or the reading of Spinoza which I will argue can be regarded as an elaboration and clarification of the Reports' arguments.

Chapter 3 is dedicated to the aspects of Spinoza's political philosophy that are concerned with the conceptualization of the notion of law. Chapter 4 discusses how Spinoza frames the concept of the state and focuses specifically on the notions of sovereignty and governance. Chapter 5 concludes the review of Spinoza's philosophy with a discussion of the implications of Spinoza's political philosophy for the theorization of international law and international relations.

After having juxtaposed the Reports' and Spinoza's respective metaphysical and normative claims and arguments, the book is concluded with a twofold analysis of the implications for normative thought and practice of relying upon Spinoza's philosophy. To this end, Chapter 6 aims at providing answers to the two main objectives of the book: to evaluate the feasibility of following through on the normative structure that is extractable from the Reports in so far as there is a resemblance between this and Spinoza's philosophy, as well as to answer the question of reconciliation between Spinoza's metaphysics with his explicit normative doctrines about law and the state in order to discuss how Spinoza's philosophy can be used in a contemporary and empirical context. In order to fulfil the second of these objectives, and because of the role played by the eco-ethical reading of Spinoza in providing a concrete content of the Reports' calls, Chapter 6 will start with a preliminary outline of the main features of this reading. Based on this outline, the implications for legal theory of adhering to the Reports' call will be investigated through a comparison between the understanding of Spinoza's political philosophy as sketched out in Chapters 2, 3, 4 and 5, and the understanding suggested by the eco-ethical reading.

The final conclusion will outline why Spinoza's conceptualization of nature, human nature, morality, ethics and law, taken together, makes it abundantly clear that there is no viable argument for subsuming nature to a human moral order as requested by the Reports and the eco-ethical reading. The final conclusion will also contain an explanation of why the fusion called for between human and natural needs is not only inconsistent with Spinoza's philosophy but undesirable given its overall normative goal.

Notes

1 The notion of the Anthropocene is usually understood as representing our present geological epoch as being defined more by human actions than by (other) natural phenomena and changes. It is for instance debated in a special theme issue of *Philosophical Transactions of the Royal Society A* (2011) entitled: 'The Anthropocene: A New Epoch of Geological Time?'

2 It is relevant to note that *TP* 3, which is the most commonly used reference when it comes to stating the *TP*'s account of law, often is described as being a more or less literal repetition of *TTP* 16 (cf. Lauterpacht, 1927, 89 n1).

3 For an interesting discussion about the issue of external influences on Spinoza's political theory see Antonio Negri, 2008, chap. 1.

References

Adetunji, I., Price, A., Fleming, P. and Kemp, P. 2003. 'The Application of Systems Thinking to the Concept of Sustainable Development', in Greenwood, D.J. (ed.), 19th Annual ARCOM Conference, 3–5 September 2003, University of Brighton, Association of Researchers in Construction Management vol. 1: 161–170.

Batnitzky, L. 2003–2004. 'Spinoza's Critique of Miracles', in *Cardozo Law Review* 25: 507–518.

Burns, T.R., Witoszek, N. 2012. 'Brundtland Report Revisited: Toward a New Humanist Agenda', in *Journal of Human Ecology* 39(2): 155–170.

Gamlund, E. 2007. 'Who Has Moral Status in the Environment? A Spinozistic Answer', in *The Trumpeter* 23(1): 3–27.

Guilherme, A. 2011. 'Metaphysics as a Basis for Deep Ecology: An Enquiry into Spinoza's System', in *The Trumpeter* 27(3): 60–78.

Kisner, M.J. and Youpa, A. 2014. 'Introduction', in *Essays on Spinoza's Ethical Theory*, Kisner, M.J. and Youpa, A. (eds). Oxford: Oxford University Press.

Kober, G. 2013. 'For They Do Not Agree in Nature: Spinoza and Deep Ecology', in *Ethics and the Environment* 18(1): 43–66.

Latour, B. 2010. 'An Attempt at a "Compositionist Manifesto"', in *New Literary History* 41: 471–490.

Lauterpacht, H. 1927. 'Spinoza and International Law', in *British Yearbook of International Law* 8: 89–106. Oxford: Oxford University Press.

Mack, M. 2011. *Spinoza and the Specters of Modernity*. London: Continuum.

Melamed, Y. 2011. 'Why Spinoza is not an Eleactic Monist (Or Why Diversity Exists)', in *Spinoza on Monism*, Goff, P. (ed.): 206–222. London: Palgrave.

Melamed, Y. and Rosenthal, M. (eds) 2010. *Spinoza's Theological-Political Treatise: A Critical Guide*. Cambridge: Cambridge University Press.

Negri, A. 2008 (1981). *The Savage Anomaly: The Power of Spinoza's Metaphysics and Politics*. Hardt, M. (trans.). Minnesota: Minnesota University Press.

Palmer, G. 1992. 'New Ways to Make International Environmental Law', in *American Journal of International Law* 86: 259.

Peet, J. and Bossel, H. 2000. 'An Ethics-Based System Approach to Indicators of Sustainable Development', in *International Journal of Sustainable Development* 3(3): 221–238.

Sharp, H. 2011a. *Spinoza and the Politics of Renaturalization*. Chicago: The University of Chicago Press.

Sharp, H. 2011b. 'Animal Affects: Spinoza and the Frontiers of the Human', in *Journal for Critical Animal Studies* 9(1/2): 48–68.

Sharp, H. 2016. 'Endangered Life: Feminist Posthumanism in the Anthropocene?', in *Feminist Philosophies of Life*, Sharp, Hasana and Taylor, Chloë (eds): 272–281. Quebec: McGill-Queen's University Press.

Speth, J.G. 2002. 'The Global Environmental Agenda: Origins and Prospects', in *Global Environmental Governance: Options & Opportunities*, Esty, D.C. and Ivanova, M.H. (eds): 11–30. New Haven, CT: Yale School of Forestry & Environmental Studies.

Spinoza, B. 1985. *Ethics; Treatise on the Emendation of the Intellect (TdIE) and Letters (Ep.):1–28*. Curley, E. (ed. and trans.), *The Collected Works of Spinoza*, vol. I. Princeton, NJ: Princeton University Press.

Spinoza, B. 2016. *Theological-Political Treatise (TTP); Political Treatise (TP) and Letters (Ep.)*. Curley, E. (ed. and trans.). *The Collected Works of Spinoza*, vol. II. Princeton, NJ: Princeton University Press.

Steinberg, J. 2008. 'On Being Sui Iuris: Spinoza and the Republican Idea of Liberty', in *History of European Ideas* 34(3): 239–249.

Stenmark, M. 2007. 'Ethics, Sustainable Development and the Millennium Declaration', in *Sustainable Development and Global Ethics*, Grenholm, C.H. and Kamergrauzis, N. (eds): 37–50. Uppsala: Uppsala Universitet.

Royal Society. 2011. 'The Anthropocene: A New Epoch of Geological Time?', *Philosophical Transactions of the Royal Society A* 369(1939) (Theme Issue).

Taylor, P. 2000. 'Heads in the Sand as the Tide Rises: Environmental Ethics and the Law on Climate Change', in *UCLA Journal of Environmental Law & Policy* 19(1): 247–280.

United Nations/Harmony with Nature/Chronology of Harmony with Nature. www.harmonywithnatureun.org/chronology.html, accessed 16 April 2018.

1 The *Harmony with Nature* Reports and the call for non-anthropocentrism as a response to the environmental problem

The review of the Reports that I will undertake in this chapter will be structured thematically. In a first part I will discuss the literal expressions pointing towards Spinoza within the Reports. After having roughly presented their background, political context and chronology, I will discuss the Reports' main arguments for a new metaphysics and ethics in accordance with four categories, or kinds of argument: arguments about the need for change at the most fundamental level of thought; arguments describing the metaphysics that arguably is responsible for our current wanton destruction of nature; arguments describing what the old metaphysics must be replaced with; and finally, arguments about the ethical and normative consequences that the author(s) of the Report hope for if their call for change is being respected and adhered to. Then, in a second part, I will emphasize that one of the Reports' theoretical references is worthy of special attention in so far as their conceptual dependence on Spinoza's metaphysics is concerned. To this end, the Reports' references to and affirmation of Arne Naess' justification of the so-called deep ecology movement establishes a direct link between the Reports' call for a new paradigm of thought and Spinoza's metaphysics. I will describe this justification and how it is framed in Spinozistic terms.

Part I: the Reports

To date, the United Nation's initiative concerned with 'life in harmony with nature' has resulted in seven reports with the title *Harmony with Nature: Report of the Secretary-General* (see Harmony with Nature/Chronology; UNGA Res. A/64/196).[1] They were published between 2010 and 2015. The first report was instigated by a General Assembly resolution in 2009 which is also entitled *Harmony with Nature*. This resolution was adopted unanimously (A/64/196). Each Report has been included in the General Assembly's yearly session agenda as a sub-item called *Harmony with Nature* under the permanent main item of *Sustainable Development*. The 2009 resolution calls upon the Secretary-General to express his view on the subject of 'life in harmony with nature' as well as to provide a summary of the inputs received from states and selected regional and major groups on the same matter (Rep. I para.2). He responds by writing the Reports and hosting live interactive dialogues on the same theme to which he invites not only state representatives but also scientists, scholars and interest groups. In addition to the six reports authored by the Secretary-General, a seventh *Experts' Summary Report on Harmony with Nature* (A/71/266) was published 1 August 2016. This report draws on the outcomes of the first *Virtual Dialogue of the General Assembly on Harmony with Nature*, which was hosted at the Harmony with Nature website, and specifically dedicated to the discussion of so-called 'Earth jurisprudence'.

The Reports, as well as their accompanying interactive dialogues, were initiated to form parts of the UN lead preparation for the second environment and development summit held in June 2012 in Rio de Janeiro, Brazil (Rio+20). The summit was organized to commemorate the twentieth anniversary of the 1992 Rio Conference on Environment and Development. On the website giving information about a second interactive dialogue on the theme of harmony with nature, the dialogue's host Ban Ki-moon describes his position as follows:

> Designing and implementing sustainable development policies that are truly in harmony with nature implies *profound changes* in consumption and production patterns, energy and material use and *lifestyle aspirations*. Such *deep changes* would require promoting major shifts in *attitudes*, behaviour and education, as well as changes in public policy and consensus-building at all levels, through inclusive processes that respect national sovereignty and the rights of individuals.
>
> (UNSG, 2011, my emphasis)

This excerpt nicely demonstrates, I think, the common thread which runs throughout all of the seven Reports produced so far. Ban Ki-moon's statement indicates that the change needed is one that will have a broad impact and affect economic, scientific, as well as ethical knowledge. This is so at least in so far as consumption and production patterns could be said to qualify as economic knowledge; energy and material issues as concerning scientific knowledge; and the notion of lifestyle aspirations as ethical knowledge. As we see in the second sentence of the above-cited excerpt, the enforcement of this wide wave of changes is thought to be linked to 'major shifts in attitudes, behaviour and education'.

As mentioned in the Introduction, there are a few things about the Reports that make them stand out in relation to similar calls for action. First, it is noteworthy that they are explicitly presented as being developed from the collected impressions of listening to various traditions of thought and voices speaking from very different positions within a long, widespread and diverse debate (see e.g. Rep. I, paras1 and 2; Rep. II, para.2; Rep. III, para.1; Rep. IV, para.1). The seventh report is in itself a product of such cooperation. Second, and of even more importance for the purposes of this book, it is noteworthy that the Reports appear unique in the sense that they actually ground their arguments about a new ethical and moral attitude in a metaphysical outline. In this chapter, I will explore both of these aspects in a condensed manner. In the end, my argument is that the Reports represent and bring together a wide variety of views in order to encircle an ethical position which can be understood in light of the eco-ethical reading of Spinoza's philosophy that was presented in the Introduction.

Scope and sources

The report series is based on a multitude of sources, originating from very different areas of the very wide-ranging discourse related to the concept of sustainable development. The Reports draw on the views of state representatives, civil interests groups and specialists within scholarly disciplines as diverse as biology and philosophy when sketching an outline of a new eco-ethical paradigm of thought.[2] For instance, the series opens with an overview of existing global legislation on environmental protection. This overview ends by emphasizing the global consensus on supporting sustainable development which was reached in Rio in 1992. In connection with the conclusion that sustainable development constitutes the tool *par excellence* for global environmental protection, the first Report argues that the inability to achieve an effective and global protection of the natural environment is the main problem of the international community today (Rep. I, para.15). The answer to this problem spells, according to the same Report, a new metaphysics, and normative ethics guiding our decisions about nature (ibid. para.16).

In sketching the basis for a new normativity, the Reports refer to groundbreaking environmental essays like Rachel Carson's *Silent Spring* and to Nobel laureate Eric Chivian's view on biodiversity and human health issues. They also draw from the views of Mohammad Yunus (yet another Nobel laureate) and Josef Stieglitz on social and economic issues. The Reports furthermore find support for their position with respect to the issue of the need for a new normative ethics in standard legal agreements concerned, at least partially, with sustainable development (Rep. I, paras3, 12–14 and 48). They refer to the ideas of the World Commission on Environment and Development (WCED), as expressed in the *Our Common Future* document (ibid., para.11). Two major fields of historical study are described as presenting arguments for the need of a shift in ethics. The first is the history of traditional medicine and theology, and the second is the history of political philosophy. In their description of the second field, the Reports focus on how nature has been conceptualized within, on the one hand, the dominant philosophical tradition (represented by Cartesian dualism) in the western hemisphere, and, on the other, one of its opposing traditions represented by Spinoza's broadening of the notion of mind and Aldo Leopold's development of an environmental ethics proper in *A Sand County Almanac* (Rep. II, paras18–19 and 38). The seventh Report is, in its entirety, a product of inputs of different 'experts on Earth jurisprudence' with the vision 'to inspire citizens and societies to reconsider how they interact with the natural world in order to implement the Sustainable Development Goals in harmony with nature' (Rep. VII, para.1). The group of international experts (120 in total, of 33 nationalities) who communicate their common opinion in the seventh Report do so from eight different disciplinary perspectives: Rights of nature, ecological economics, education, ethics, philosophy, holistic science, media, and Earth jurisprudence (Rep. VII, para.8).

Among the more contemporary events reviewed in the Reports, educational research is highlighted, as is progressive national legislation that recognizes the rights of nature (Rep. I, paras46–66; Rep. II, paras73–75; Rep. VII, paras1 and 36). Consumerism, development, human cognition, economy and, of course, ethics, are other epistemological fields which all are drawn on in the discussions (Rep. II, paras59–63; Rep. III, para.38; Rep. VII, para.8). Two theorists are especially highlighted by the Reports as important sources of inspiration for the paradigm of thought sought after. These are Arne Naess, philosopher and environmental ethicist, and system theorist Donella Meadows, along with their respective fields of study. According to the Reports, these two stand out as individuals and efforts particularly suited to inspire the concretization of the ethical ideal that the Reports are asking us to seek (Rep. II, para.62; Rep. IV, paras16–17). I place emphasis on this as the reference to Arne Naess establishes a direct link between the Reports' argumentation and Spinoza's metaphysics.

Taken together, and considering how the Reports' recommendations are based on these voices and many more, the Reports come across as a rather diplomatic product of a careful search for the lowest common denominator within a multifaceted context. The fact that a clear ambition – which is to respond to the threat of nature's degradation by way of reformulating our moral theory – shines through in the Reports despite the heterogeneity of their sources, is interesting to note as it speaks in favour of this ambition being an important and central idea within the current discourse on the global problem of environmental degradation. Having concluded this, let us turn now to the way by which the Reports provide for an outline of *how* our current, basic thinking patterns must change in order to incorporate an environmentally more sound definition of value and moral right and wrong, in short: a new ecological morality.

Key concepts and chronology

One of the key notions for the Reports' argument about a viable path towards a new kind of environmental care and protection is the concept of *holism*. Holism is portrayed as promoting a balanced relationship between human beings and the Earth (Rep. I, para.45). For the Reports, holism stands for the idea of understanding the function of a part by attending to the whole (ibid. para.38). The first Report argues that the balanced relationship which is promoted by holism is present in many indigenous cultures as well as in ancient western traditions but that it has been lost in the transition to modernity[3] and that it may be regained by revisiting the common basis of various 'indigenous beliefs and traditions' which all have 'an inherent holistic vision' (Rep. I, paras6, 16 and 47). In order to contribute to the preparatory process of the 2012 Rio+20 conference, the second and third Reports add more specific information about the scholarly and scientific development of a holistic understanding of the world (Rep. II, para.3; Rep. III, para.2). The fourth Report, written after the +20 conference, looks ahead and draws on the outcome document of that conference as well as a third interactive dialogue held on the International Mother Earth Day. Accordingly, this Report aims at providing 'inputs for discussion of the post 2015 development agenda' (Rep. IV, para.1). The same goes for the fifth, sixth and seventh Reports. They focus on the normative adaptation of the specific physical and metaphysical understanding of the world which is to ground the new normative ethics in demand (Rep. V, paras2, 11 and 12; Rep. VI, paras2 and 5; Rep. VII, paras15, 16 and 18).

Specifically, the first Report begins by establishing that it aims to highlight the implicit holistic meaning of sustainable development. According to this Report the implicit holistic meaning places a special emphasis on the environmental pillar of the concept of sustainable development (Rep. I, para.4).[4] Paragraphs 15 and 16 of the first Report explain the problem connected to the realization of the environmental (holistic) aspect of sustainable development:

> Since UNCED [United Nations Conference on Environment and Development in Rio 1992], sustainable development has become part of the international lexicon. The concept has been incorporated in many UN declarations and its implementation, while complex, has been at the forefront of the world's institutions and organizations working in the economic, social and environmental sectors. However, they all recognize how difficult it has been to grant the environmental pillar the same recognition enjoyed by the other two pillars despite the many calls by scientists and civil society signalling the vulnerability and precariousness of the Earth since the 1960s.
>
> An explanation for this dilemma may be found in the *relationship* that civilizations over the course of centuries *have had with the Earth* and also *with their own existence*, particularly since the industrial revolution.
>
> (My emphasis)

We see in this argument how the first Report couples the lack of efficiency of our current legal protection of nature with the way we, who live in the aftermath of the industrial revolution in the western hemisphere, relate to (i.e. understand and value) the world and being. Thus, from this we may conclude that already at the outset of the Reports it is clear that it is the basic, philosophical foundation of modern societies that is the root of unsustainability and that a different kind of such foundation is needed in order to remedy our destructive relationship with nature.

The second Report picks up and develops this argumentation by explaining just where in the history of philosophy our understanding of existence and the world went wrong and why we began to allow for a wanton destruction of nature (Rep. II, paras8–34). The second Report, then, can in a way be read as developing the conceptual framework around a philosophy of holism as well as explaining why this philosophical position never gained a foothold in the history of western philosophy. To this end, it begins by describing the relationship between humankind and nature as a relationship that needs to be studied within the realm of 'philosophy and religion' (ibid., para.8). The Report argues that the relationship between humankind and nature lies at the heart of all ethical investigations concerned with the issues of the meaning of life and happiness (ibid.). By the end of the second Report, the notion of holism (which in the first Report was revealed as central for the discovery of a new, environmentally friendly ethics) is connected with a change to a new paradigm of thought. A paradigm the central tenet of which is the idea of the world as a single and connected whole in accordance with philosophical accounts found in ancient eastern wisdom; traditional medicine; indigenous forms of relating to nature; as well as in ancient western definitions of natural law (Rep. II, paras79–80).

The third Report focuses more narrowly on the particular philosophical explanation of the world which grounds western modern science and, by extension, the ethical relationship with nature emerging from this tradition. Specifically, it argues for the view that modern science is based on a mistaken metaphysical conception of pre-scientific concepts like nature and individuality. To this end, the Report traces the ways in which current economic, legal and social orders affirm a now arguably outdated explanation of existence and being (Rep. III, paras34–38). In doing so, the third Report probably provides us with more concrete information about the metaphysical grounding of the needed new ethics than any of the other Reports.

The fourth Report continues and deepens the discussion instigated by the third Report. It points to the inherent vagueness of the concept of nature and how this vagueness has political and normative consequences in that any given intuitive and metaphysical representation of nature necessarily affects, not only the scientific (causal) explanation of things in nature but also, the understanding of wellbeing and the concept of need. It argues that the scientific paradigm which emerged with Cartesian rationalism and became dominant after the industrial revolution has steered society towards an erroneous economic paradigm which, in turn, has been allowed to set the agenda for normative ethical decisions in favour of an irresponsible use of natural resources (Rep. IV, paras12, 18, 60 and 64). Like the third Report, the fourth Report places the metaphysical explanation of the human–nature relationship right at the centre of the global environmental problem.

According to its opening section, the fifth Report follows the trajectory laid out by the fourth one. Thus, just like the fourth, it is to be treated as 'an input for the discussion of the post-2015 United Nations development agenda' (Rep. V, para.1). The fifth Report is important in that it explicitly ties the conclusions about metaphysics and science, of the previous Reports, to concrete social practices such as law. To this end it calls 'Earth system science' the preferred paradigm, which would result from coherently applying the metaphysical and scientific conclusions laid out in the previous Reports. Earth system science, according to the fifth Report, is characterized by the assumption that 'the Earth is a holistic system, in which no single element takes precedence over another, a system that is *indivisible*, in an *endless continuum*' (Rep. V, para.11, my emphasis). It is not until the fifth Report that we get to see the full metaphysical implications of the concept of holism which has been referred to continuously throughout the Report series. The fifth Report addresses, for instance, how understanding the world around us according to the assumption of the holistic 'Earth system science' will come to affect the normative dimensions of sustainable development (ibid.). Accordingly, it sets out to describe the components of 'Earth system governance, Earth-based law and Earth-based economics' (Rep. V, para.12).

The sixth Report highlights the normatively important concept of intrinsicality which is said to follow from holism. It states for instance that it is necessary to understand the intrinsic link between humankind and nature in order to determine the effective use of scientific resources for protecting nature (Rep. VI, para.5). In emphasizing the need to turn to so-called traditional knowledge in 'cogenerating' an appropriate knowledge about nature, it defines traditional knowledge as stemming from traditions that do not distinguish between 'the physical' and 'the spiritual' (Rep. VI, para.35).

The seventh Report clarifies even further the metaphysical basis sought for when it claims that there is consensus among its participating authors about the importance of 'recogniz[ing] the *intrinsic value of nature* and the need to shift our perceptions, attitudes and behaviours from anthropocentric or human-centred, to non-anthropocentric or Earth-centred' (Rep. VII, para.5, my emphasis). Normatively speaking, to develop this recognition means, according to the seventh Report, to regard the world *not* as 'an inanimate object to be exploited, but as our common home, *alive* and subject to a plethora of dangers to its health'. Furthermore, to regard the world this way 'requires a *serious reconsideration of our interaction* with nature' (Rep. VII, para.6, my emphasis).

As a preliminary conclusion we may say then – as is clearly indicated also by the titles of the Reports – that the Reports' overall approach is one wherein the overarching question of effectiveness in relation to environmental protection is being treated as a question of normative ethics: as a question of understanding wellbeing as 'harmony with nature'. We may also conclude that a successful search for this harmony must start in understanding nature according to a philosophical order that conceives of the world as an interconnected whole wherein the parts are intrinsic to the whole, physically as well as metaphysically speaking. The seventh and most recent Report expresses this position with absolute clarity when it states that '[e]xperts in philosophy and ethics emphasize the need for a new paradigm that allows humanity to repair its current destructive relationship with the Earth' and:

> [i]n order to forge a balanced and healthy relationship between human activity and the Earth, there is an urgent need for society to *replace the current anthropocentric worldview* with a holistic system of governance, in which humanity plays a different role in *how it perceives* and interacts with the natural world. In the new role, humanity would *accept the reality* that its well-being is derived from the well-being of the Earth.
>
> (Paras15 and 16, my emphasis)

That the change towards the so-called Earth jurisprudence will alter our deepest philosophical conceptions is clear from the way in which the same Report defines this jurisprudence as 'imply[ing] wholeness, and a complex and deeply interdependent life-support network that rejects the logic that gives priority to the "part" as distinct from the whole, whether it is the individual versus the community or the state versus the world' (para.19, quotation marks in original). From the quoted passage it is reasonably clear, I think, that normatively speaking the Report connects the holistic sentiment implied by Earth jurisprudence with a holistic way of governing. It clearly implies, for instance, an incentive to blur the line between natural and civil law; that it would be fruitful to make and enact civil laws as continuations of natural laws.

> Earth jurisprudence recognizes the Earth as the source of *natural laws that govern life*. It provides a cohesive framework that underpins many disciplines, weaving them together to create a more *effective, holistic governance approach*, reflecting the integrated nature of the world in which we live.
>
> (Rep. VII, para.17)

Overall, the structure of the Reports' arguments promotes a very specific understanding of holism as inherent to the concept of sustainable development. The following final couple of excerpts from the Reports about holism show how their use of the term revolves around the notions of one-ness and intrinsicality.

In the first Report, South African statesman Jan Christiaan Smuts is referred to when defining holism as 'a philosophical position that was directed towards an understanding of whole systems rather than particular events or phenomena. It carries the synergetic understanding that wholes are greater than the sum of their parts' (Rep. I, para.38). The third Report states that the '*renewed recognition* of the relationship between humankind and the Earth reaffirms that *human existence is inextricably part* of nature, and sets a path towards action based on that belief' (Rep. III, para.3, my emphasis). Descriptions of this kind with regard to holism are explicated by utterances like the following:

> physical substances work and exist in terms of highly complex, interdependent, and changeable contexts and relationships. Scientists have therefore embraced a holistic view of the Earth system, *in which* all the elements are interconnected and changes in any one single element affects the functioning of the others in countless and, more often than not, in unknown ways.
>
> (Rep. III, para.30, my emphasis)

And:

> Experts from around the world working in the natural and social sciences and members of the Harmony with Nature Knowledge Network participating in the virtual dialogue recognize the need for a *holistic worldview rooted in* respect for Nature and the *interdependence* of humankind and the Earth. They believe that humanity, which is *inextricably part of the community of life on*

> *Earth*, cannot continue to override the *laws that maintain the homeostatic balances* of the Earth system.
>
> (Rep. VII, para.12, my emphasis)

And, finally:

> The philosophy of Earth jurisprudence can be formulated under four main principles: subjectivity: the *Universe is a holism*, with values and rights; community: *everything is related and coexists* with everything else; lawfulness and order: there are *organizing patterns* in the Universe and in the Earth community that we can detect and understand; and wildness: the *order* and lawfulness in the *Universe* remains *dynamic, mysterious and unpredictable.*
>
> (Rep. VII, para.20, my emphasis)

All in all, then, it seems pretty clear that the Reports connect the concept of holism to a kind of general principle of causality; that is, to a metaphysical position answering the question of how the things that form a system are connected. Holism, according to Smuts, describes interconnected individual things as inextricable parts of an individual that is greater – something more – than the sum of the things that constitute it (1927, 88). Relying on Smuts, all individual things in the world can be said to be connected, according to the Reports, because they all constitute one coherent 'Earth system' (cf. Rep. VII, para.19).

Another noteworthy aspect of the Reports' chain of arguments about holism is the outline it gives of the ethical implications of holism. Shortly, we will see examples from the Reports pointing to the affirmation that a) 'Nature and her intrinsic value *must be* revered and honoured' (Rep. II, para.79, my emphasis) as well as b) 'Deep ecology' is to be preferred, as this 'is rooted in the basic concept that every living thing, animal and plant, has an equal right to live and flourish' (Rep. IV, para.17). In a way, the entire Report series functions as an explication of the claim about the connection between holism as a metaphysical point of view on the one hand, and, between holism and a new ethical relationship between nature and human kind as a means towards the goal of sustainable development, on the other. It is the new ethics, the Reports argue, that will make us care more for and protect nature.

In what remains of this chapter I will demonstrate how a careful study of the Reports' specification of the philosophical conditions of holism allows us to connect the Reports' call for a new ethics to an eco-ethical reading of Spinoza's philosophy in accordance with the reading briefly described in the Introduction. To this end, I will highlight the core concepts in the Reports' description of holism and sketch out how these concepts together constitute a metaphysical outline of the world that resembles Spinoza's metaphysics in such a significant way that it is difficult to ignore.

Arguments about change in thought at the metaphysical level

The need for change at the most basic level of thought is – as mentioned – clearly stated throughout the entire Report series. In the second Report we can read for instance that '[i]f we are to avoid catastrophe, current world conditions leave no doubt that a major change is required in the way that human beings *relate* to the three pillars of sustainable development: environmental, social and economic' (Rep. II, para.72, my emphasis). In so far as the word relate in this quote may be conceived of as 'to understand', the change called for by the Report is a change in the way by which we understand nature, ourselves and our values. Given that the notions listed by the Reports seem to be of a preliminary nature with regard to ethical inquiries, the understanding sought after seems to go beyond ethics.

The same Report also establishes that '[a]s we prepare to convene the United Nations Conference on Sustainable Development, changing how we behave on the planet will require a *major shift in values*. Our survival depends on the wise choices of how we coexist with Mother Earth' (Rep. II, para.78, my emphasis). It also argues that '[a]long with reverence for nature as our guide, it is to *our spirit* that we must turn in order to advance in our journey towards sustainable development. We must look at the *bedrock* of our intrinsic human values, at *the intentions behind* our actions' (Rep. II, para.80, my emphasis).

First of all it could be argued that in making reference to the bedrock of our intrinsic human values, the second Report is making reference to our metaphysical starting points. Alternatively, it can be regarded as posing the question of sustainable development as a question of teleology. As such, it is a question that clearly intermingles with metaphysics in so far as the purpose(s) that things serve is interrelated to the question of what they *are*. First, the Report establishes that in order to change our behaviour we must change our values – this is a question of ethics. Then, however, it associates the desired ethical change to a study of the bedrock of intrinsic human values; that is, a study of that within us which makes us act the way we do. Arguably then, the second Report proposes that we do not properly understand either our own cognitive foundation or our purposes ('bedrock of our values'). Regardless of what position one takes in relation to the question of cognitive foundation and purposes – whether all things happen for natural ends or whether ends instead necessarily are perspectival interpretations – the question itself requires considerations of a metaphysical nature.[5] In other words, the study of human intrinsic values (to which the second Report refers) requires considerations of the kind that focus on the nature of intentionality, the human mind, nature and final ends. To this end, the study requested by the second Report requires considerations which all seem to involve metaphysical arguments (cf. Chase, 2011, 517; Cameron, 2010, 1097 and 1099; Tahko, 2008, 53–63; Idalovichi, 1992, 86).

An even clearer formulation of the call for a new metaphysics is found in the following two quotes from the second Report. First: 'Environmental scientist and system analyst Donella Meadows has explained that the most effective leverage point for changing a system is to change its paradigm, that is to say, the *shared ideas and assumptions* around which the system functions' (Rep. II, para.62, my emphasis). A little further down we read that, 'it is necessary to change our current paradigm, which is grounded on the false *premise* that nature is an object that can be appropriated and exploited' (Rep. II, para.66, my emphasis). In the first quote we see the term paradigm being specified as those ideas and assumptions around which a system functions. Given that the system in which the Reports take a special interest is the system organizing our perception and evaluation of nature, the basic shared ideas and assumptions that seem to be in question here are those used in explaining individuality, nature and the relationship between humans and nature. In short, it would seem that the paradigm which the same Report refers to as outdated in the next quote is our currently governing metaphysical paradigm. The paradigm which the Report seeks to change is a paradigm based on the allegedly false premise that nature is an object that can be 'appropriated and exploited'; that is, something that exists outside the human self, on whose existence the human sense of a self does not depend. This is clearly a premise of a metaphysical nature.

That a change at the metaphysical level of thought is required to bring about changes in our way of acting (and, by extension, our way of making laws) is absolutely clear from how the seventh Report first emphasizes 'the need for a *new paradigm that allows* humanity to repair its current destructive relationship with the Earth' and then connects this paradigm to metaphysical propositions (Rep. VII, para.16, my emphasis). The connection is established by describing Earth jurisprudence (the term the Report uses as a label for the new paradigm) as the recognition of 'Earth as the source of *natural laws that govern* life'; as 'a cohesive framework that underpins many disciplines, weaving them together'; and as 'the understanding that human governance systems must be derived from the laws of the Earth and be in compliance with them' (Rep. VII, para.17, my emphasis).

Description of the outdated metaphysics

As a first concrete variable of the metaphysical scheme which we ought to leave behind, the first Report posits the idea that we are independent beings in relation to Nature. It reads:

> The report provides an overview of how the lifestyle of the 21st century, through its consumption and production patterns, has severely affected the Earth's carrying capacity and how human behaviour has been the result of a *fundamental failure to recognize that human beings are an inseparable part of Nature* and that we cannot damage it without severely damaging ourselves.
>
> (Para.6, my emphasis)

This allegedly erroneous separation between man and nature stems from, according to the same Report, a more general misunderstanding of substance which, apart from the conceptual separation of man from nature, also leads to the separation within man of the mind from the body. The Report describes this erroneously perceived ontological division between humankind and nature as deriving from the piecemeal method of modern medicine. Modern medicine, it argues, also reflects the equally false metaphysical assumption of a division between mind and body. The Report refers both modern medicine and the division of mind and body to a common philosophical basis, as is aptly demonstrated by the following passage:

> The roots of conventional medicine, that is the drug- and surgery-based mainstream medical procedure that came into dominance in the early 20th century, can be traced back to the time of René Descartes (1596–1650), the scientist and philosopher whose work led certain of his followers to develop Cartesianism, a philosophy characterized by its rationalistic, dualistic world view. A consequence of Cartesianism was the separation of the 'mind' from the body.
>
> (Rep. I, para.31)

Then, in the second Report this position is substantiated by the following explanation:

> In the evolution of medical science that took place in the seventeenth century, vivisection was widely used to study the workings of the body. The practice angered early humanitarians, and vivisectionists turned to René Descartes (1596–1690) to justify their research methods. A celebrated mathematician, physiologist and psychologist, Descartes provided *a general philosophy of the irrelevance of ethics to the relationship between man and nature.*
>
> Animals, according to Descartes, were insensible and irrational creatures, living things with no sensation of pain: lacking minds, they could not be harmed, did not suffer and had no consciousness. Humans, on the other hand, had souls and minds. Thinking, in fact defined the human organism. '*Cogito ergo sum*' (I think, therefore I am) was Descartes' basic axiom. This dualism, the separation between human beings and nature, justified vivisection and *any human exploitation of the environment.* Descartes left no doubt that people were the 'masters and possessors of nature'. Descartes believed that the objectification of nature was an important prerequisite for the progress of science and civilization.
>
> (Rep. II, paras8–19, parenthesis in original, my emphasis)

These paragraphs are referred to again later in the Report series when Descartes' dualism is explicitly denounced as erroneous. To this end, the third Report states that the two previous Reports have established the historical origins of a 'masters of the planet' doctrine (which, as we just have seen, they do while referring specifically to Descartes' dualism) and that modern scientific discourse now admits that 'this 300-year-old scientific doctrine is too simplistic'. The passage in question reads in its entirety:

> There is a long-held viewpoint concerning human–environmental relationships, namely the *human exemptionalism paradigm*, in which human beings are seen as being separate from the environment, and as *masters* of the planet.

> The origins of the doctrine have already been addressed in detail in the two previous reports of the Secretary-General on Harmony with Nature [the two quotes provided above]. Today scientists are admitting that this 300-year-old scientific doctrine [Descartes'] is too simplistic (…) (Rep. III, paras29–30, my emphasis)

In subsequent phrasings, the third Report refers continuously to Descartes' philosophical paradigm by calling it interchangeably 'exemptionalism' (para.36) and a 'domination paradigm' (para.55). In paragraph 44 it reaffirms that this paradigm of thought is based on the 'false assumption that the natural world is property to be manipulated for human benefit'. In short, the second and third Reports together plainly state that Descartes and Cartesianism are to blame for us getting the nature of things wrong.

On the basis of these quotes we can conclude that the Reports establish a link between what they argue are two basic misconceptions. The mistaken conception of the human being as an entity made of two substances (mind and body) is what has allowed us, falsely, to treat nature as an object to possess and appropriate. According to the Reports, then, it is because of the misconception of our own constitution that nature has erroneously been associated with the physical part of the human being, that is, the part which Cartesian metaphysics tells us has no sensibility and therefore cannot suffer as the human mind suffers when its body is hurting. The first Report stipulates that:

> The failure to do so [i.e., recognize that nature is also connected to the mental sphere of the human being] has created serious ecological imbalances and environmental degradation. Ultimately, environmentally destructive behavior is the result of a failure to recognize that human beings are an inseparable part of Nature, and that we cannot damage it without severely damaging ourselves.
>
> (Rep. I, para.44)

The link between the emergence of modern science and a mistaken conception of the essence of nature is rendered explicit in the following statement:

> The present technological age has seen an impoverishment in the historical relationship between human beings and Nature. Nature has been treated as a commodity that exists largely for the benefit of people, and all environmental problems as solvable with a technological fix.
>
> (Rep. I, para.101)

The allegedly erroneous metaphysical perspective is even further substantiated in one of the second Report's discussions. Here, the erroneous perspective is referred to as anthropocentrism (see Rep. II, para.23). Anthropocentrism is further defined as a perspective that posits a) the Earth as the centre of the universe, b) nature as depending on humans, c) the human being as the entity which orders and makes sense of otherwise wild, untamed nature, d) the purpose of nature's existence as its usefulness to human beings, and finally e) human beings as masters of nature, who exist outside the rules and laws of nature (ibid.).

Later on in the same Report, it is explained that many of the variables of the anthropocentric paradigm still govern our current economic system, although scientific discoveries in relation to nature have begun to motivate scepticism towards it. Thus, paragraph 62 reads:

> In the case of the consumerist paradigm, the assumptions *that need to change* include that more goods make people happier, that perpetual growth is good, *that human beings are separate from nature*, and that *nature is a stock of resources to be exploited for human purposes.*
>
> (My emphasis)

Later on in the same Report, the need to change our metaphysical paradigm is similarly connected to the error of believing that 'nature is an object that can be appropriated and exploited' (Rep. II, para.66). Then, in the fourth Report, it is stated that there is a connection between the post-industrial, modern world-view (defined by the Reports as modernism) and the erroneous utilitarian conception of nature as a commodity for us to use. It reads:

> The environment is a relatively recent concept, dating to the early years of the nineteenth century with the growth of industrialization and the modernization of the world economy. In this view, nature and the resources it provides, are seen in a utilitarian fashion, as raw materials for our use.
>
> (Rep. IV, para.18)

In the seventh Report the call for a new metaphysical paradigm is for the first time presented as a remedy for the negative effects of the epoch of the Anthropocene. The Anthropocene is explained as an epoch in which 'a collaborative relationship between human activity and its natural surroundings' is not being advanced by 'philosophy, ethics, theology and spirituality'. The Report states that 'the major challenge' of philosophy, ethics, theology and spirituality 'is to fashion an Earth-centred jurisprudence that can reshape the dominant model' (Rep. VII, para.28).

There is one last, important thing to note in relation to the Reports' description of the role played by Cartesian metaphysics for the modern, mistaken relationship with nature. As evident from the following passage, the fifth Report establishes that the new normative ethics ('Earth system science') should be a development of Cartesian thought. The fifth Report states that:

> Earth system science *has evolved from Cartesian*, cause-and-effect, duality science to a form of study that embraces the complexity of life. It has informed and given place to Earth system governance, which draws upon the holistic scientific knowledge provided by the Earth system science to evolve laws and

> policies that better manage human behaviour in light of the interconnections among people and nature.
>
> (Rep. V, para.50, my emphasis)

Apparently, then, everything in the Cartesian system is not to be rejected even though it is portrayed as the main cause of the modern, erroneous human–nature relationship. This is important to keep in mind in so far as the question of affinity between the Reports and Spinoza is concerned. This is because it is a well attested fact that Spinoza stands out in the history of philosophy as one of few metaphysicians who radically opposes many of the Cartesian conclusions while departing from the same basic premises (cf. Della Rocca, 2003).[6]

In sum, the Reports' outline of the erroneous, but hitherto dominating, metaphysical explanation of nature can be summarized as follows: It begins in a general ontological assumption that the world is divided into two substances. It stipulates that because there are two substances at work in the human being – mind and body – there must be two substances in general. This metaphysics has led us to the Anthropocene which is defined as the epoch 'in which many geologically significant conditions and processes are being profoundly altered by human activity' (Rep. VII, para.28, fn 5). The anthropocentric (Cartesian) metaphysics responsible for the Anthropocene posits that because humans are alone in having mind-substance, we are separated from and superior to other things in the totality. Thus, the proposition about two separate substances in the world and in the human being quickly leads, according to the Reports, to positing an anthropocentric perspective on morality and normativity. The Reports could not be clearer in denouncing this perspective as false.

Specifically, the Reports position the erroneous metaphysics as erroneous in so far as it presumes that the natural world is different from the human (constructed) world – the natural world is organized without the interference of the mind-substance whereas the human mind can create artefacts and artificial worlds. This presumption, then, is what constitutes the basis for a relationship with nature where the human being understands herself as residing outside the domain of the rest of the natural world. The Reports denounce this relationship as the exemptionalist paradigm because it allegedly takes as its starting point the view that humans are separate from – and therefore do not abide by – the laws of nature. As such, exemptionalism, according to the Reports, has given rise to an economic perspective which is characterized by its affirmation and approval of human beings' appropriation and exploitation of nature. This is what the Reports call 'the domination paradigm'.

With the coining of this term we have, according to the Reports, finally reached a position which may explain our habit of wantonly destroying nature. As we have seen, nature is, because of the allegedly erroneous metaphysics' arbitrary differentiation between nature and humankind, perceptible only through a concept of utility. Nature has been considered as existing only as a resource for our human benefit because whereas humans are endowed with a mind, nature is not. We are, thus, special in relation to nature.

Arguments about the conceptual conditions of the new metaphysics

As well as the description of the metaphysics that we ought to leave behind, we also find references in the Reports to the sought after metaphysical structure: the one that allegedly holds the key to a better – truer – relationship with nature, which automatically will lead to an effective protection of it. As such, it is the metaphysics that emerges once all the errors of the counter-image are corrected. The first Report states that:

> [p]erhaps the greatest lesson to be learnt from the wisdom of sacred traditions is also the simplest; to honor creation by nurturing a *kinship with nature*. This assertion is most revealing in how ancient civilizations viewed the human body in relation to Mother Earth and how harmony with nature was the essence of good health.
>
> (Para.23, my emphasis)

According to the same Report, because the erroneous image of nature (the one that ultimately leads to a validation of wanton destruction) is directly connected with an erroneous understanding of the human being, our conceptual re-ordering must begin with a new understanding of the human being. So, in paragraph 28 of the first Report we find that:

> Greek doctors took a holistic view of their patients, who were seen as the *embodiment of natural forces* that operated harmoniously in states of health but could fall out of balance in disease states. This holistic view meant the whole was greater that [*sic*] the sum of its parts.
>
> (My emphasis)

Likewise, in the subsequent paragraph it is stated that '[p]eople accepted that the physical, mental, emotional, and spiritual elements of the body are interconnected as one whole' (Rep. I, para.29).

As already mentioned, holism is consistently portrayed as a form of causal integration that must be accepted as a bearing principle of our understanding of pre-scientific concepts such as nature and individuality if we wish to see a change in our treatment of the natural environment. To this end we find the seventh Report stating that the called-for new philosophical paradigm 'Earth jurisprudence' 'implies wholeness, and a complex and deeply interdependent life-support network that rejects the logic that gives priority to the "part" as distinct from the whole [i.e. holism]' (Rep. VII, para.19, quotation marks in original). It also states that a change towards this jurisprudence 'can reshape prevailing models' that oppose the 'Earth-centred model' consisting in 'a culture of partnership wherein the central values are equity, cooperation, dialogue, inclusion, comprehension, agreement, respect and co-inspiration' (ibid.).

At the end of the first Report, two other specifications of the Reports' understanding of holism are presented. First, that the new metaphysics must embrace 'a holistic approach to healing the world, which, like holistic medicine, addresses *causes rather than symptoms*' and then, that the philosophy of holism 'rests on an understanding that all things are *interconnected* and that nothing occurs in isolation' (Rep. I, paras88 and 102, my emphasis). In the seventh Report this interconnectedness is explained further, as we just saw, as a 'life-support network that *rejects the logic that gives priority to the "part" as distinct from the whole*' (para.19, quotation marks in original, my emphasis). According to these statements, holism requires that things are explained by their causes, as opposed to merely their appearances, and that these causes should be looked for, not in the things themselves, but in the whole, which is nature.

The seventh Report develops the idea of holism even further when it establishes four main principles of the so-called philosophy of 'Earth jurisprudence'. In a passage which I have already mentioned, the Report states that this philosophy rests on the principles of subjectivity; community; lawfulness and order; and wildness. Taken together these principles explain the universe as 'a holism with values and rights' where 'everything is related and coexists with everything else' and follow 'organizing patterns [...] that we can detect and understand' but which appears to us as 'dynamic, mysterious and unpredictable' (Rep. VII, para.20). It is a significant feature of the desired new metaphysics then that everything, in fact, is governed by the same set of rules. It is only us humans who, from our limited perspective, are ignorant of these rules and perceive events as mysterious and unpredictable.

The outline of a new, more adequate, metaphysics which we find in the seventh Report is carefully being prepared by the previous Reports. To this end the second Report connects modern western and anthropomorphic epistemology to a 'dangerous indifference' towards the problem of nature. An indifference which could have been avoided had humanity been more attentive to eastern, traditional philosophy. From eastern thought traditions, the second Report gives one holistic example of a remedy for the western erroneous understanding of nature: the realization that there is 'no sharp divide between creator and created animals, between human and gods' (Rep. II, para.9). Moreover, from the 'cultural practices and thought systems in China', the same Report affirms 'uphold[ing] the belief that reality consists of countless manifestations of one unbroken continuum' which led the Chinese philosophy to 'the assertion of a fundamental unity of all things in their essential aspects' (para.10). However, it is not only in a culturally distant knowledge tradition (from a western perspective) that keys to a better representation of nature and the human being can be found according to the second Report. The same wisdom actually resided in the history of western culture and philosophy as well. The second Report states:

> In the Western tradition, Greek and Roman philosophers had a clear concept of the laws of nature, as opposed to man-made law. Recognizing that people existed prior to the establishment of civil order and government, they made a

clear distinction between natural law (*jus naturale*) and common law (*jus commune*).

(Para.14, emphasis in original).

From this last passage we may conclude that the lawfulness which the seventh Report highlights as one of the bearing principles of a correct metaphysical representation of the world, nature and individuality is present also in the platform of the very same western tradition of thought which later on, according to the Reports, comes to propagate a false representation of nature. It is here – right after having highlighted western epistemology's origin in a truthful representation of the relationship between humans and nature – that the second Report raises the issue of Cartesian responsibility for what has gone wrong in our modern conception of the world. As mentioned, it is important to remember that the Report in this context refers to Spinoza as someone who to some extent both continues the correct ancient tradition and simultaneously opposes Descartes' ideas (see Rep. II, para.20). The twentieth paragraph of the second Report describes Spinoza's most pertinent opposition to Descartes as holding 'that nature and the wilderness were imbued with spiritual values, and that humans could not, therefore, be separated from nature' (ibid.).

Later in the same Report, the anti-Cartesian conception of nature is again referred to when establishing the need of a new economic order. The statement in question reads: '[w]e need to accept nature as our source of guidance to create an economic system that is both morally and scientifically sound'. The necessity expressed in this statement clearly supports the idea which we have seen being indicated in the first and seventh Reports about there being no ontological difference (the same general laws apply), and hence a possible communication, between human nature and the rest of nature (Rep. II, para.79). This is so in so far as the statement about change in the economic system in the second Report implies that (what we know about the laws of) nature should 'guide' the formulation of a new economic system. Were human nature not following the same kind of laws as nature in general does, it would be pointless to regulate human behaviour based on information and knowledge about nature. This position is affirmed in the seventh Report's discussions about Earth jurisprudence and ways to combat the Anthropocene. We have already seen how that Report emphasizes the lawfulness of nature as a criterion for a correct conception of the world. It then 'underscores the urgency of reconstructing civilization on ecological principles of sustainable development' clearly hinting that once understood, nature's laws should also be used for directing our behaviour (Rep. VII, paras19 and 22). In a section dedicated to 'Earth-centred law' the Report renders explicit this hint when it states that nature 'regarded as the source of basic "Earth rights" cannot be validly circumscribed or abrogated by human jurisprudence' (para.36). We should rather, according to the same paragraph, 'include the rights of Nature into our governance systems' (ibid.). By this statement, the seventh Report clearly confirms the position that since human nature is governed by the same laws as every other thing in nature these laws should be incorporated into our human governance systems rather than the other way around.

The third Report also concerns itself with the issue of practical, action-guiding consequences of the ontological and epistemological unity implied by holism. In a vivid argument, it states that:

> In the current scientific view, influenced by quantum mechanics, the cosmos is seen as a *seamlessly interconnected and complex whole, in which everything is quite literally connected with everything else. Any sense we may have* that the collections of particles we think of as our individual selves are isolated and alone is an *illusion fostered by a lack of understanding of the nature of reality.*
>
> In the current thinking in the field of biological science, the system of life on Earth is seen as being *self-organizing* on the molecular, cellular and embryological levels, and interactions between organisms regulate the atmospheric gases and sustain conditions that perpetuate the existence of the whole.
>
> (Rep. III, paras32 and 33, my emphasis)

Taken together, these two paragraphs indicate that if we want to correct our mistaken approach to nature, we should understand the world as a totality in which everything is literally connected with everything else. What is more, we should recognize that any sense we have of specialness – indeed any sense of true individuality – which we might feel tempted to reflect in our understanding of things around us, is an illusion due to an inadequate understanding of the totality. The adequate way to conceive of reality, then, is to see it as a totality that is self-organizing in all of its aspects including its organization of us humans.

This position is confirmed by the fourth Report, as it plainly states that '[a]ny ontological difference between what was once called the mineral kingdom, the plant and the animal kingdom and the kingdom of man has vanished: the scope of the idea of ecology is universal' (Rep. IV, para.15). It continues by stating that '[m]oreover, in accepting nature as a source of life, *as* life itself, we might be brought to realize that it cannot be protected in a piecemeal fashion' (Rep. IV, para.19, my emphasis). I think it is fair to say that these quotes create an image of human nature as an entirely integrated part of nature as a whole, as well as an image of the totality as one single, uniform substance. These two images, in turn, render the human sphere – the human kingdom – understandable by the same laws and principles as everything else. What is more, they render the human being understandable *as* nature, not as a special substance within nature. As we shall see in Chapter 2, the overall image of nature, human nature and the human relationship with nature which emerges from these passages resembles (to a not insignificant degree) the central tenets of Spinoza's metaphysics. As such, the Reports depict nature, human nature and the human–nature relationship in a way that sits well with the eco-ethical reading of Spinoza's commitment to philosophical naturalism which I have mentioned in the Introduction to this book and which I shall return to in the final analysis of the feasibility of the call for grounding a new normative ethics on Spinoza's metaphysics.

Continuing the theme of linking the Reports to a (particular reading of) Spinoza's metaphysics, the fourth Report is worthy of special attention. In outlining a new economical paradigm it stipulates that such paradigm:

> must go beyond neoclassical and environmental economics and learn instead from the concepts of *deep ecology*, the rights of nature and systems theory. Serving nature and recognizing *its inherent significance* should be part of the foundation of a new economic model that ought to factor into the complex dynamic interplay between all key drivers of sustainability, including justice, equity and the rights for all the citizens of the world, and for the natural world from which they derive their existence.
>
> (Para.64, my emphasis)

This is a very interesting statement for several reasons. First, it draws a direct link between the metaphysics claimed to be needed and deep ecology. Deep ecology, in turn, constitutes an explicit attempt to extend Spinoza's normative ethics – a set of protective imperatives – to include nature and 'natural' entities (Naess, 1977, 45). It is also an interesting statement in that it affirms the dissolution of a separate set of laws governing human beings in relation to the laws of the totality. Just what does it mean to recognize the 'inherent significance' of nature as a foundation for 'a new economic model factoring into the interplay between justice, equity and the rights for all of the world's citizens and for the natural world', if not that nature is to provide us with the rules for our understanding of ourselves and other social phenomena?

The idea that there is a normative impulse inherent to the concept of metaphysical interconnectedness is also visible in the sixth Report. It states in its fifth paragraph:

> Raising awareness of sustainable development, which includes recognition of the *intrinsic link* between human beings and nature *in order* to *foster* a mutually beneficial relationship, is *essential for achieving* a transformative post-2015 development agenda that will *preserve* the Earth for present and future generations.
>
> (My emphasis)

This last excerpt demonstrates that the kind of holism which is being outlined by the Reports, in addition to being a principle of causality on the ontological level (i. e., concerning what things are), is directly responsible for developing new and specific normative results in the fields of economy, social development and law.

Arguments about the called-for new ethics

The last group of arguments which I would like to discuss before turning to Spinoza's metaphysical structure is the group of arguments that is related to the ethical position which allegedly will be the result of following through on the metaphysical re-thinking suggested by the Reports. The resulting, normative ethics already begins to emerge in the second Report when the premises of the new metaphysics are discussed. The connection between the old metaphysics and an erroneous definition of value is described in paragraphs 34 and 35 of the second Report as follows. First, the change in metaphysical understanding is clarified:

> Whereas in the nineteenth century, environmental protection was largely advanced for *utilitarian purposes*, be it for food, timber, shelter, *the scientific basis* for the need to protect the environment and its natural resources gained significant ground in the twentieth century. Scholars and scientists developed *new concepts describing the interconnectedness* and the balance of life on Earth.
>
> (Rep. II, para.34, my emphasis)

Having established this, the Report then establishes a link between a new moral theory and the new scientific description of 'life on Earth' with the words '*because of* the holistic orientations of their discipline, these early ecologists frequently *connected their scientific research to moral philosophy*' (Rep. II, para.35, my emphasis).

A few paragraphs later, the same Report gives some examples of the ecologists mentioned in the passage just quoted. In that paragraph, support is also provided for a connection between investigations of metaphysical questions and a resulting normative ethics.

> Philosophy and theological inquiry also informed environmental conservation ethics. Nobel Laureate Albert Schweitzer (1875–1965) considered that a reverence for life was a sufficient rationale for valuing the environment. [...] Alfred North Whitehead added to this idea, contending that the identity and purpose of every object in the universe arose from its relationship to everything else. Every organism, indeed every atom, had *intrinsic value* if only for the contribution it made to the ongoing reality of the interlocking pieces that make up the world.
>
> (Rep. II, para.37, my emphasis)

We see in the last quote how perhaps the most central of all the ethical consequences that will derive from the new metaphysics, begins to emerge. Value, it is argued, is to be defined as something that pertains to existence. It is something that resides within all things as an intrinsic aspect of them.

In the second half of the second Report, its author discusses the direction which a future law-making process ought to take if it is to follow the ethical path indicated by the new metaphysics. The Report gives a few examples of progressive laws, which it defines as respectful of the new metaphysics' conditions on the notion of value. To this end, the second Report mentions that in 'New Zealand's Environmental Act of 1986, the essential value of nature was specified, as follows: "Ensure that, in the management of natural and physical resources, full and balanced account is taken of the intrinsic values of ecosystems"' (Rep. II, para.73, quotation marks in original). It also highlights Sweden's Environmental Code of 1999 and its statement that 'Biological diversity must be protected since the natural environment is *worth protecting for its own sake*' (Rep. II, para.74, my emphasis). Lastly, it makes reference to the recently (2008) adopted constitution of Ecuador, which it describes as stating that 'the *rights of nature* should be taken into account in all planning activities' (Rep. II, para.75, my emphasis). In the same spirit as these legislations, the Report itself claims that 'Nature and *her intrinsic value* must be revered and honoured' (Rep. II, para.79, my emphasis).

Then, in the third Report, the Ecuadorian example of recognizing the rights of nature is recalled as a natural consequence of reaffirming the metaphysical understanding that human beings form an inextricable part of nature (Rep. III, para.3). According to the view expressed in this Report, a recent increase in a more general affirmation of this inextricability has led to the fact that:

> [n]umerous scientists, economists and legal experts, as well as members of civil society, have decried the escalating destruction of the Earth's natural systems and called for a *rights-based* movement for nature in order to recognize our dependence and interconnectedness with the natural world.
>
> (Rep. III, para.3, my emphasis)

It is interesting to note, in relation to this quote, that the said rights-based movement is portrayed as an aspect of recognizing our dependence and interconnectedness with the natural world. Thus, due to the way in which the quoted paragraph is phrased, one is prone to think that interconnectedness and rights of nature are two sides of the same coin. The latter follows as a consequence allegedly naturally from the first.

On a more general level, the third Report explains that the consequence of changing our way of understanding nature in accordance with the Reports' prescriptions will be that 'the rule of law, science and economics would be grounded in concern for the Earth' (Rep. III, para.45). Arguably then, the goal is to enable global governance to affirm and further the new metaphysical ideas. Precisely how the new metaphysics, assuming for the sake of argument that it is Spinoza's metaphysics to which the Reports' refer, is apt to alter our conception of the rule of law will be discussed extensively in the coming discussion of Spinoza and international law (Chapter 5). For now, however, let us take a closer look at how the third Report develops the idea of a naturalized rule of law. Paragraph 46 reads:

> A key challenge in developing a global governance system *built on the rule of ecological law* is reinvigorating a transformed sense of democracy, in which individuals and communities embrace their ecological citizenship in the world and act on their responsibility to *respect the complex workings of the Earth system.* Such a system would reconnect people to the ecological foundations

> that sustain them, and would recognize and enable maintenance of those connections in good working order over the long term.
>
> (My emphasis)

Judging by all the passages from the Reports reviewed in this section, it is clear that a transformation of state practices and state policy hinges upon a definition of value as intrinsic. This is so, first of all, because all things in nature are naturally good and, second of all, because they are so in themselves – from the mere fact of existing. Nature is therefore not to be treated as a human commodity because all natural entities are inherently good in themselves, in the same sense as are human beings.

The notion of intrinsic value is perhaps most clearly emphasized in the fourth and fifth Reports. In the fourth, it is recalled together with an argument that '*Nature is the locus and nutrient of our physical lives*, providing transcendental value in what may seem otherwise transient and dead' (paras12 and 13, my emphasis). Next, the Reports reflect on what kind of moral theory is able to transfer the idea of nature as our common locus and nutrient into the reality of governance. To this end, the Reports once again draw on Arne Naess and deep ecology. The fourth Report's choice to rely on Arne Naess and deep ecology when conceptualizing a morality that can accommodate new metaphysical ideas within a normative setting is reiterated in the fifth Report (Rep. V, para.20). The fifth Report does so before discussing, in more detail, just what the social and legal consequences of the new metaphysics would be.

Describing deep ecology, the fourth Report posits it as the opposite of the anthropocentric ecological movement which is chiefly concerned with 'pollution, the depletion of natural resources and the usefulness of the Earth for humans' whereas the former is concerned 'with the richness, diversity and intrinsic value of all the natural world' (Rep. IV, para.16, citing Naess, 1973, 95–100). In relation to the question of how deep ecology will manage to turn environmental protection into something radically different from the ecology concerned with pollution, depletion of natural resources and the usefulness of Earth for humans, the fourth Report places emphasis on the fact that deep ecology is rooted in the 'basic concept that every living thing, animal and plant, has *an equal right to live and flourish*' (Rep. IV, para.17, my emphasis). The concept of intrinsic value is thus, once again, emphasized as being central for rendering protection of the environment better. In other words, understanding value as intrinsic in the sense that all things are good within themselves is what will make us *care* for nature, according to the Reports. Again, it is interesting to note that the Reports refer to the roots of deep ecology as that which will bring the change forwards. This is interesting as a part of these roots, according to the founding father of deep ecology himself and as already mentioned, is constituted by Spinoza's metaphysics.

The Report goes on to quote Arne Naess saying that:

> We are living on an incredibly beautiful little planet, but our human existence is threatened. If we are to survive we have to learn to think differently. The

> thinking for the future has to be loyal to nature. It must encompass all humans and all living creatures, *because everything alive, in itself, has a value*.
>
> (Rep. IV, para.17, citing Naess, 2007. My emphasis)

In its conclusions, the fourth Report affirms the position taken by Naess by arguing that because the world has come to recognize that 'the supreme value of the human person did not originate in the decision of a worldly power, but rather in the fact of existing' we must also 'recognize the *supreme value and rights of the natural world as arising from the fact of existing*' (Rep. IV, para.70, my emphasis). Thus, in addition to being intrinsic, value is also arguably equal for all, because it is connected to existence – which all things on the Earth share equally. To judge from the fourth Report, then, the concept of value that corresponds to the new metaphysical structure is clearly based on the notion of intrinsicality. Such, then, is the understanding of value that according to the Reports we are to live by if we are serious about our wish to protect the environment better than we do now. It is argued that if this conception of value is transported into our moral theory, it will make us defend nature's rights as if they were of personal and individual interest to us.

As mentioned, this position is confirmed and elaborated even further in the fifth Report. This Report argues that the shift in law towards this conception of value has already begun. 'Hence, a legal system based on recognizing that ecosystems, in all aspects, have inherent rights to health, prosperity and evolution is gradually becoming the norm' (Rep. V, para.58). In connection to this statement, the fifth Report also posits that the new objective for the international legal community should be 'a legal system founded on equal rights and responsibilities – one that reflects and *implements the mutually enhancing relationship that exists among humans and the natural world*' (Rep. V, para.59, my emphasis).

Taken together, the Reports make clear that the new ethical attitude, which arguably originates in the specific metaphysical understanding of the world as one single corpus of interconnected things, can *and should* function as a new basis for moral and social efforts (like laws) to protect nature. To this end, it is stipulated in the third Report, for instance, that 'there is a basis for believing that, as members of the human family and the commonwealth of life, we have *a duty* to use our foresight and empathy for *their benefit*' (Rep. III, Para.34). Likewise, it is stated that:

> [h]umanity needs to recognize that it is time to *serve the planet* rather than using the planet to serve our economic goals. When science is taken into account, it is clear that damaging the environment to serve the needs of the human economy only serves to damage ourselves.
>
> (Rep. III, para.37, my emphasis)

In light of statements like this, the following quote from the fifth Report firmly establishes the Reports' overall goal as being one of ensuring that a perception of nature as something beyond a human commodity can be duly administered by a traditional understanding of law. The fifth Report states that:

> The objective is a *legal system* founded on equal fundamental rights and responsibilities – one that *reflects and implements the mutually enhancing relationships that exist among humans and the natural world*. What is needed is a corpus of Earth law *integrating* modern science and ethical awareness of our responsibilities as humans. If we are to survive as an ethical and physical species, we must *legislate* a system of Earth-based law to *mirror* our expanding *scientific and ethical 'awareness'* and our place in the Earth community.
>
> (Rep. V, para.59, my emphasis, quotation marks in original)

In sum, it is the conceptual basis of the so-called 'Earth-based law' which the Reports argue is necessary to fuse with international environmental law in order to enhance that law's protective qualities. As we have seen, the seventh Report clarifies that this conceptual basis amounts to the framework of Earth Jurisprudence: a framework of knowledge which, if incorporated into 'mainstream philosophy and ethics':

> removes the artificial difference between humans and Nature, creating a world in which children are raised to believe that to love Nature is to love one's self, in which all people are compelled to consider the consequences of this entwined reality in their economic and political interactions.
>
> (Rep. VII, para.23)

Part II: from the Reports' concept of holism, via Arne Naess and deep ecology, to Spinoza

There are today – notwithstanding the Reports – very few attempts to prescribe a new human relationship with nature which move *beyond* merely calling for a new ethics. To this end, the Reports appear to provide us with a unique opportunity to study the metaphysical premises necessary for the ethics called for. Still, the specific formulation of this metaphysical foundation such as it stands to be found in the Reports alone is not sufficient to explain all of the metaphysical premises and the normative implications of the call. In order to do so, we need to look beyond the Reports and into the wider historical and conceptual context with which they may be associated. Only this way can we achieve a considered understanding of the normative implications that their call bring about.

The Reports, because they are authored by the UN Secretary-General and endorsed by the General Assembly by way of resolution, clearly form part of the international legal discourse on environmental protection. In this chapter we have seen how the Reports approach the question of protection of nature from the perspective of ethics and basic thinking patterns. This might seem surprising considering that they clearly form part of a legal initiative, and that such initiatives usually approach the question of protection more instrumentally, from the perspective of legal techniques and measures. However, taking into account – as we will in this part of the present chapter – how the discourse of legal protection of nature has developed, the Reports' turn to ethics stands out as fairly consistent.

For some time now, there has been a broad consensus among international environmental legal scholars about 'nature as a whole' becoming an independent and major area of interest for the international community. This consensus is usually explained as originating in the publication of the 1987 World Commission on Environment and Development's (WCED) benchmark report *Our Common Future*[7] (cf. Redgwell, 2010; Birnie, Boyle and Redgwell, 2009; Morrow, 2011).

Emphasizing the inter-generational aspect of environmental protection, *Our Common Future* or the Brundtland report seeks to show that the environment should not only be conceived of as one variable out of many affecting humans, but as the actual basis to human life and wellbeing. Nature will always therefore 'outlive' the present generation and affect the lives of coming generations. For this reason, *Our Common Future* is often described as marking a shift in the standard conception of international environmental law: this is when law moves from being triggered when – and only to the extent that – particular cases of human wellbeing are negatively affected by specific environmental degradation, to being a global and pro-active law geared to the protection of the whole of nature (Birnie and Boyle, 2002, 82–83). Before the Brundtland report, the international legal community spoke of 'the human environment' (cf. United Nations, 1972); after Brundtland it speaks of the 'environment and development' (cf. United Nations, 1992).

Legal scholar Christina Voigt points out that many doctrinal analyses argue that this shift in language demonstrates how the Brundtland report has participated in turning nature into an independent object of law, making it constitute something like a new basis for the entire field of international environmental law (2009, 16). In line with Voigt's argument, it has been suggested that 'The human environment', which constituted the object of the first global conference dedicated to environmental issues, is thought to represent the natural environment as first and foremost a human (or state) commodity to be used as a variable in international negotiations between developing and developed states (Najam, 2005, 308). Conversely, 'Environment and development', which became the leading theme after the WCED report in 1987, tends to represent nature, it is argued, as an independent (global) entity which is to be *weighed against* all human activities and needs (Najam, 2005, 310; Hopwood, Mellor and O'Brien, 2005, 40; Birnie and Boyle, 2002, 82–83). The impact of this shift in language, which allegedly was instigated by the Brundtland report, has arguably been beyond comparison in relation to previous attempts to develop a coherent and general understanding of international law concerned with the natural environment (Cordonier Segger and Khalfan, 2004, 20). This is for instance visible in the way by which its principal concept, sustainable development (establishing the importance of considering nature in all decisions concerning development), quickly became and remains by far the most reiterated goal within legal regulations and issues dealing with human activities with potential negative effects on nature (Birnie and Boyle, 2002, 84).

Sustainable development as an expression of holism

It is well known that the concept of sustainable development – which was highlighted and popularized by the Brundtland report – was discussed during the 1992 UN conference in Rio as an emerging principle of international law (Sands, 2003, 252–257). It was included, for instance, as a goal in relation to Principles 4, 5 and 8 of the *Rio Conference Declaration of Principles* (*Rio Declaration*). However, the spirit of sustainable development can be sensed in the formulation of other principles therein too, such as Principle 3. Sustainable development was also referred to as a principle – together with some of the *Rio Declaration*'s other concepts – in both of the two global environmental treaties which the participating states negotiated during the conference.[8] Likewise, it was referred to in the subsequently concluded (1994) *Convention to Combat Desertification*, which drew on guidelines from the conference's major policy document: *Agenda 21* (United Nations, 1992).

All in all, the events in Rio have come to be regarded as a consolidation of sustainable development as a legal principle relevant to international environmental law. It is reasonable to believe, therefore, that the concept, albeit not immediately, acquired the position of being a norm of customary international law in the interval between the conference and the present. In any case, most environmental legal scholars seem to think, as argued by Bosselmann and Voigt, that even if the formal legality of the concept may still be contestable, it is hardly controversial today to claim that the concept produces legal impacts and effects of *some* kind (Bosselmann, 2008, 23; Voigt, 2009: 24).

In so far as the precise meaning of sustainable development is concerned, it is notable that there is no specific mention of a holistic understanding of it, either in the Brundtland report or in the documents produced at the 1992 conference in Rio. However, according to Gro Harlem Brundtland, environmental problems are to be dealt with together with economic and social issues: 'Ecology and economy are becoming more and more interwoven – locally, regionally, nationally and globally – into a seamless web of causes and effects (WCED, 1987, 5). This and similar signs of an integral approach that we find within the earliest expressions of the concept of sustainable development do not, perhaps, allow for any far reaching conclusions about an early ethical approach to the problem of nature. They do, however, clearly demonstrate that already at the outset of the discourse the problem of nature was considered as one that reached far beyond the traditional realms of international law. The Brundtland report indubitably argues that if we want to understand the full extent of the global problem of ecology, we must include in this understanding knowledge about social and economic factors. So, sustainable development seems to have always (that is, from its emergence as a concept in global discourse of law and policy) contained a holistic feature of some kind, even though it is not certain that this notion refers to precisely the same metaphysical and ethical content as do the Reports' use of the term.

The Brundtland report formally defines sustainable development as 'development that meets the needs of the present without compromising the ability of future generations to meet their own needs' (WCED, 1987, 43). In the final preambular considerations of both the Climate Change Convention and the Biodiversity Convention the parties declare their determination to protect the climate system and conserve biodiversity respectively, for both present and future generations (UNFCCC, 1992, final preambular paragraph; UNCBD, 1992, final preambular paragraph). The *Biodiversity Convention* also emphasizes a sustainable use of natural resources as something that will strengthen international peace (UNCBD, preamble, para.21). The same convention opens its preamble with a statement claiming that its state parties recognize the intrinsic value of biodiversity (UNCBD, preamble, para.1). The *Biodiversity Convention* does not explicate, however, the metaphysical basis or further implications of this moral proposition. In the *Rio Declaration*'s preamble it is however stipulated that states signing the declaration recognize 'the integral and interdependent *nature* of the Earth, our home' (Preamble, para.4).

In light of this brief survey of the use of the concept of sustainable development in the international environmental legal discourse, we may establish that one of the major problems that has occupied environmental jurisprudence since the late 1980s has been to trace and identify an operational sense of the concept's rather ambiguous definition. This problem, in turn, is of course related to the wider problem – around which this book revolves – of not being able to establish the means by which to globalize and render more comprehensive international environmental protection. As mentioned, the Brundtland report itself is not of much assistance in either of these exercises as it merely provides the very general definition of sustainable development as 'development that meets the needs of the present without compromising the ability of future generations to meet their own needs' (WCED, 1987, 43).

After Brundtland: towards a normative ethics based on the concept of sustainable development as a response to the global problem of nature

Despite the fact that doctrinal analyses of environmental law have not been particularly successful in working out *how* to achieve sustainable development, there have been remarkably few objections to the importance of the concept as such for international law and policy. It has even been claimed that the vague definition of the concept is what makes it powerful in relation to law and policy, because it is what makes law and policy transformable, dynamic and adaptive to diverse contexts (Hajer, 1995, 14). Thus, we can conclude that it is rarely contested that sustainable development expresses a well-established and valid ambition. The third chapter of the Brundtland report includes an example that refers to this ambition and suggests a tangible content to it. A participant in one of the WCED Commission's hearings is cited as saying: 'we have to find a new *ethic* that will include the relationship between man and nature above all' (WCED, 1987, Part I, Ch.3, my emphasis).

In the wake of the Brundtland report, many have expressed variations of this ambition, noting the need to respond to nature's needs by way of ethics and giving suggestions as to what this response – more precisely – should mean. We find, for instance, environmental policy scholar Andrew Jordan elaborating on the suggestion that the power of the concept of sustainable development lies in its ambiguous meaning. He argues that this power derives from the focus of the concept on *making us willing* to be governed in the name of the natural environment rather than on explaining the rationale of this governance (Jordan, 2008, 20). Jordan's comment can be understood as saying that the ambiguity of the concept of sustainable development is normative in itself – instead of demonstrating a lack thereof – in the sense that it produces an ability in human beings to appreciate legal measures aimed at protecting the natural environment. On this reading, the concept's nature, or essence, is normative.

A few more examples of discursive comments that take a similar position to the one taken by both Maarten Hajer and Andrew Jordan mentioned above, can be given. First, consider the following:

> To scan the now ubiquitous definition put forward by the Brundtland Commission is to realize that our construction of 'sustainability' is driven by a notion of *care – care for the nonhuman environment* enfolded with a concern for our human descendants. The rhetoric around our ideal response to climate change structures it as an *ethical response.*
>
> (Johns-Putra, 2013, 125, my emphasis)

The core premise of this statement, I would argue, is that the realization of sustainable development – whatever the operative meaning of the concept – depends on a change of the attitudes informing our ethical beliefs.

More or less the same argument is being communicated by former Swedish Minister for the Environment, Andreas Carlgren, when stating Sweden's political commitment as it stood in 2011. He argues in a debate article written together with the Minister for International Development Cooperation, the Chairman of the 3rd Nobel Laureate Symposium, and the Secretary of the Swedish Royal Academy of Sciences, that:

> The research on human interference on our environment unambiguously shows that the world *needs a new vision* for global sustainable development [...]
>
> Therefore, the division between environment and economic growth must be abolished.
>
> (Carlgren et al. 2011, my translation and emphasis)

Assuming that the terms environment and economic in the second sentence can be taken as references to the traditional nature/culture divide, we may conclude that Carlgren puts the achievement of sustainable development on a par with a state of affairs in which this divide is completely abandoned. Judging by the first sentence, such abandonment seems to be conditioned by a change in our current conception of ethical prescripts. This conclusion is indeed suggested by philosopher and sociologist Bruno Latour, in a piece on contemporary discourses on environmental policy (2010). According to Latour, the call for a new ethical attitude makes perfect sense considering how new laws and implementation techniques have proved to be insufficient for halting the rapid degradation of the global environment. They have been insufficient, he argues, because we now adhere to a view which places the root of the problem of the fragile natural environment in the 'abuse of reason' within traditional ethics, which has led to the establishment of an unnatural division between nature and culture (2010).

There is more support for the view that the required change – whatever its precise content – must take place at a level deeper than the political or legal. In 2012, in a paper entitled 'Brundtland Report Revisited: Toward a New Humanist Agenda', sociologists Tom Burns and Nina Witoszek take stock of achievements in sustainability after the report's publication. They suggest that:

> there is a need to redirect and transform our economic, political, scientific, and educational systems to protect our earth home and to translate the agenda of sustainable development from being an instrument of 'moral blackmail' deployed by governments to a 'culture' which is accepted by the world at large.
>
> (Burns and Witoszek, 2012, 159)

The cited passage is presented as a response to the following problem description: 'countless reports and statistics show how basic necessities of life provided by the earth such as food, water, clean air and an environment conducive to human health, are being harmfully affected by massive environmental destruction' (Burns and Witoszek, 2012, 155). From this problem description follows, according to the authors, 'an acute need for significant reforms of our ways of thinking, organizing, and acting' (ibid.). Judging by the passage cited above, the suggested response to this 'acute need for significant reforms' is thus a pervasive transformation of the human relationship with nature on an individual level. As is also evident from the quote, economics, politics, science and education must all contribute to this transformation so that a new 'general culture' can come to reign; a culture that makes us value and protect the natural environment. In specifying the components of this culture, Burns and Witoszek say that it must be built on a value platform that 'perceives nature as an active agent and asks humans to listen to, understand, adapt to, and "dance" with nature' (2012, 159, quotation marks in original). This indicates that Burns and Witozsek maintain, in common with Carlgren and Latour, that the change now requested is metaphysical rather than political in nature.

To end this discussion, let us look at two examples of analyses of environmental law which specify something of what the new normative ethics should be about. The first states that:

> The ethic, which we believe is clearly based on the *sustainability moral postulate*, implies human behavior standards that are different from those that the dominant mainstream political economy currently promotes, but which are still entirely sensible and reasonable for most people. Implications of the ethic are that people:
>
> - Share available resources equitably
> - Protect all unique systems for their *intrinsic value*
> - Give all subsystems the chance to contribute to the *development of the whole.*
>
> (Peet and Bossel, 2000, 225, my emphasis)

The second proposes that:

> Sustainability demands *a shift* to a new perspective; the need to: *recognize our place in the ecosystem* by living in harmony with nature; and integrate continuing socioeconomic development with environmental protection. This perspective is realized through the bridging of many ideas, traditional beliefs and religious views and disciplines. The Brundtland Report promotes a debate on this new perspective.
>
> (Adetunji et al., 2003, 169, my emphasis)

It is within a legal discursive context characterized by statements like the ones we have looked at here that we find the Reports. The Reports rely on views like these and add to them the *Biodiversity Convention*; the Swedish Environmental Code of 1999 and New Zealand's Environmental Act of 1986 as illustrations of how to make law approach a new basis of normativity. As we have seen, however, no legal document or discourse renders explicit the conceptual premises and philosophical foundation which surround and explain these calls for a new ethics, holism and intrinsic value. The answer to this question needs to be sought within the context of a wider discourse about the problem of nature.

Arne Naess and Spinoza

The next step, then, in the search for an explanation of the Reports' underlying metaphysical presumptions seems to be to turn to the source of the references made within the Reports to the philosophical grounding of the new ethics. In this context, the Reports' references to Arne Naess stand out. Arne Naess was a Norwegian philosopher and eco-ethicist who founded the philosophical and practical movement called deep ecology (Keller, 2008). As already mentioned, Naess' engagement with metaphysics in relation to environmental practices plays a decisive role for linking the Reports to Spinoza's specific metaphysical outline. This is because Naess explicitly grounds his own foundation of a deep ecological ethics (his 'ecosophy') in Spinoza's metaphysics. Thus, when the Reports affirm Naess' justification of a deep ecology they indirectly affirm the grounding of ethical concern in a philosophy inspired by Spinoza's metaphysics. And as we have seen, the Reports do rely on Naess' concept of deep ecology when specifying the paradigm upon which we should build a new world economy and governance (see Rep. IV). Naess is explicit in his acknowledgement of Spinoza as a source of inspiration for the development of an eco-philosophical (ecosophic) motivation of deep ecology. In an article entitled 'Spinoza and Ecology' he 'invites the reader to consider a set of hypothetic connections between Spinozist and ecological thought' (1977, 45). Naess dedicates this article to the evaluation of the connections between Spinozism and his own understanding of the philosophical basis of ecology. He goes through almost the entire Spinozistic metaphysical system, concept by concept, and reaches the conclusion that '[n]o great philosopher has so much to offer in the way of clarification and articulation of basic ecological attitudes as Baruch Spinoza' (1977, 54).[9]

Naess' approach has been inherited and maintained by a number of suggestions for the construction of a new, more environmentally friendly ethics. In addition to the plethora of literature on how to develop Arne Naess' deep ecological heritage and vision directly, independent work on environmental ethics generally also tends to affirm Naess' work on metaphysics and thus – indirectly – his decision to draw from Spinoza. There is, for instance, Freya Mathews' book *The Ecological Self* (1991) in which she refers her metaphysical arguments directly to Naess and thus indirectly to Spinoza. There is also Bruce Foltz who suggests a metaphysical grounding of environmental ethics in the philosophy of Heidegger (1995). Interestingly, the ethical position which Foltz considers to have most potential for effectively protecting nature and which he, therefore, considers as the one that will gain most in turning to Heidegger's philosophy is deep ecology. On the one hand, he characterizes deep ecology as the best ethics – in so far as granting nature a measure of self-standing – that environmental philosophy has come up with so far. On the other hand, his advice is to move deep ecology from its current philosophical grounding to a Heideggerian one (1995, 172). In so far as the characterization, upon which Foltz's recommendation builds, amounts to recognizing the philosophical merits of the conclusions drawn by Naess in terms of being the drafter of deep ecology, it shows that Naess' decision to draw on Spinoza's metaphysics when theoretically grounding the deep ecology platform seems to be generally respected within the discourse of environmental ethics. All in all, this goes to show that the Reports' implicit references to Spinozistic concepts and propositions (relying sometimes, as we have seen, on Naess in doing so) sit rather well with a more general trend within ethical studies.

In the final chapter of this book, when I have sketched the contours of Spinoza's entire philosophical structure – from metaphysics to normativity – I will return to the issue of the Reports' theoretical framework and argue that a considered evaluation of the Reports' arguments and claims can be facilitated by regarding them as being consistent with a more elaborated scholarly reading of Spinoza which argues for his eco-ethical potentiality. To this end, I will highlight how many of the Reports' Spinozistic arguments appear to be echoes of a more refined interpretation of Spinozistic doctrines about value, desire and naturalism for instance which can be found within Spinoza studies. In brief, my argument will be that this scholarly reading provides an explanatory framework to the Reports' claims that, a) anthropocentric thinking has caused what is commonly known as the Anthropocene, and that, b) a non-anthropomorphic metaphysics is best apt to practically aid us in combatting the effects of the Anthropocene. However, before we return to the Reports' arguments and the normative suggestion that is to be evaluated in the light of Spinoza's philosophy, let us take some time to familiarize ourselves with that philosophy. Let us therefore now turn to the metaphysical, moral, ethical and political upshots of Benedict Spinoza's rational naturalism.

Notes

1 The seventh Report is not, however, authored by the Secretary-General himself but rather a group of experts who were called upon to participate in the eight and most recently virtual dialogues held on the subject of harmony with nature.
2 It should be recalled that by drawing on such a variety of voices the author of the Reports departs from the traditional method of collecting and relying on state opinion which is usually employed by UN organs when drafting declarations, reports or directives. Instead he turned, as is evident, also to scientific and scholarly discourses. This goes to show the progressiveness of the final call for action which we find outlined and motivated in the Reports.
3 This concept is associated in the Reports to the emergence of a rational philosophy and the development of a scientific basis to a secularization and industrialization of the state.
4 Sustainable development is usually regarded as constituted by a social, an economic and an environmental pillar.
5 As is well known, Aristotle used the question of final ends – teleology – for explaining the nature of things. He argued that in order to give a full explanation of a thing one must consider, not only its efficient, formal and material cause but also, its so-called final cause (*the cause for the sake of which*). This he stated in relation to the physical as well as the metaphysical nature of things. Spinoza takes an opposing position towards the argument of natural ends – arguing instead for a mechanical explanation of the nature of things (see Aristotle, *Physics* II 8 and *Metaphysics* A 2. For translations into English see Ross, 1928, and see Don Garrett's essay 'Teleology in Spinoza and Early Modern Rationalism' (1999) for an extended discussion of Spinoza's position with regard to teleology).
6 I will develop this argument further in the next chapter.
7 The *Our Common Future* report is usually called the Brundtland report after the commission's chairperson Gro Harlem Brundtland.
8 The Climate Change Convention and the Convention on Biological Diversity (Biodiversity Convention).
9 In literature Spinoza is regularly referred to as either Baruch or Benedict (Benedictus). According to Steven Nadler, Spinoza figures in most documents and records contemporary with his years within the Portuguese Jewish congregation of Amsterdam as Bento, a Portuguese name meaning Blessed. On three occasions (in the membership roll of the Ers Chaim educational society, the book of offerings listing contributions to the congregation and in the *cherem* document by which Spinoza was expelled from the Jewish congregation of Amsterdam) his name instead appears in its Hebrew form Baruch (Nadler, 1999, 42). However, during his adult life (and probably as a way to distance

himself from the Jewish tradition into which he was born and mark his affinity with the rational tradition of thought), Spinoza himself used the Latin version of the name: Benedict or Benedictus (Melamed, 2013, 265).

References

International instruments and documents

United Nations. 1972. Report of the United Nations Conference on the Human Environment. A/CONF.48/14/Rev.1. United Nations publications: Sales No. E.73.II.A.14.

United Nations. 1992. United Nations Conference on Environment and Development (UNED). 14 June 1992. UN Doc. A/CONF/151/26 (vol. I)/31 ILM 874.

United Nations General Assembly (UNGA). 2009. *Harmony with Nature.* A/RES/64/196.

United Nations Secretary General (UNSG). 2010–2015. *Harmony with Nature: Report of the Secretary General I–VI.* Report I: UNGA Res. A/65/314; Report II: UNGA Res. A/66/302; Report III: UNGA Res. A/67/317; Report IV: UNGA Res. A/68/325; Report V: UNGA Res. A/69/322; Report VI: UNGA Res. A/70/268; Report VII: UNGA Res. A/71/266.

United Nations Secretary General (UNSG). 2011. *Harmony with Nature. Initiatives of the President of the 65th Session* – General Assembly of the United Nations. www.un.org/en/ga/president/65/initiatives/HarmonywithNature.html, accessed 16 May 2011.

World Commission on Environment and Development. 1987. *Our Common Future,* Report of the World Commission on Environment and Development. UNGA Res A/42/427, 4 August 1987.

Bibliography

Adetunji, I., Price, A., Fleming, P. and Kemp, P. 2003. 'The Application of Systems Thinking to the Concept of Sustainable Development', in Greenwood, D.J. (ed.), 19th Annual ARCOM Conference, 3–5 September 2003, University of Brighton, Association of Researchers in Construction Management vol. 1: 161–170.

Birnie, P. and Boyle, A. 2002. *International Law & the Environment* (2nd edn). Oxford: Oxford University Press.

Birnie, P., Boyle, A. and Redgwell, C. 2009. *International Law & the Environment* (3rd edn). Oxford: Oxford University Press.

Bosselmann, K. 2008. *The Principle of Sustainability: Transforming Law and Governance.* Aldershot: Ashgate Publishing.

Bruntland, G.H. 1987. *Presentation of the Report of the World Commission on Sustainable Development to UNEP's 14th Governing Council Session.* Nairobi, June 1987. www.regjeringen.no/upload/SMK/Vedlegg/Taler%20og%20artikler%20av%20tidligere%20statsministre/Gro%20Harlem%20Brundtland/1987/Presentation_of_Our_Common_Future_to_UNEP.pdf, accessed 14 December 2014.

Burns, T.R. and Witoszek, N. 2012. 'Brundtland Report Revisited: Toward a New Humanist Agenda', in *Journal of Human Ecology* 39(2): 155–170.

Cameron, R. 2010. 'Aristotle's Teleology', in *Philosophy Compass* 5(12): 1096–1106.

Carlgren, A., Carlsson, G., Rockström, J. and Normark, S. 2011. 'Sverige kan bidra till en ny vision för en hållbar värld'. Dagens Nyheter, electronic edition. www.dn.se/debatt/sverige-kan-bidra-till-en-ny-vision-for-en-hallbar-värld.shtml, accessed 16 May 2011.

Chase, M. 2011. 'Teleology and Final Causation in Aristotle and in Contemporary Science', in *Dialogue* 50: 511–536.

Cordonier Segger, M.C. and Khalfan, A. 2004. *Sustainable Development Law: Principles, Practices and Prospects*. Oxford: Oxford University Press.

Della Rocca, M., 2003. 'The Power of an Idea: Spinoza's Critique of Pure Will', in *NOÛS* 37(2): 200–231.

Garrett, Don. 1999. 'Teleology in Spinoza and Early Modern Rationalism', in *New Essays on the Rationalists*, Rocco, Gennaro and Huenemann, Charles (eds): 310–335. Oxford: Oxford University Press.

Hajer, M. 1995. *The Politics of Environmental Discourse: Ecological Modernization and the Policy Process*. New York: Oxford University Press.

Hopwood, B., Mellor, M. and O'Brien, G. 2005. 'Sustainable Development: Mapping Different Approaches', in *Sustainable Development* 13: 38–52.

Idalovichi, I. 1992. 'Life and Teleology', in *Journal for General Philosophy of Science* 23(1): 85–103.

Johns-Putra, A. 2013. 'Environmental Care Ethics: Notes Toward a New Materialist Critique', in *Symploke* 21(1–2): 125–135.

Jordan, A.J. 2008. 'The Governance of Sustainable Development: Taking Stock and Looking Forwards', in *Environment and Planning* 26(1): 17–33.

Keller, D.R. 2008. 'Deep Ecology', in *Encyclopedia of Environmental Ethics and Philosophy*, Callicot, J. Baird and Frodeman, R. (eds): 206–210. Detroit, MI: Gale.

Foltz, B.V. 1995. *Inhabiting the Earth: Heidegger, Environmental Ethics and the Metaphysics of Nature*. New York: Humanity Books.

Latour, B. 2010. 'An Attempt at a "Compositionist Manifesto"', in *New Literary History* 41: 471–490.

Mathews, F. 1991. *The Ecological Self*. London: Routledge.

Melamed, Y. 2013. 'Charitable Interpretations and the Political Domestication of Spinoza, or, Benedict in the Land of the Secular Imagination', in *Philosophy and Its History*, Laerke, M., Smith, J. and Schliesser, E. (eds): 258–277. Oxford: Oxford University Press.

Morrow, K. 2011. 'Perspectives on Environmental Law and the Law Relating to Sustainability', in *Law and Ecology: New Environmental Foundations*, Philippopoulos-Mihalopoulos, Andreas (ed.): 126–147. Abingdon, UK: Routledge.

Nadler, S. 1999. *Spinoza: A Life*. Cambridge: Cambridge University Press.

Naess, A. 1973. 'The Shallow and the Deep, Long-range Ecology Movement. A Summary', in *Inquiry* 16(1): 95–100.

Naess, A. 1977. 'Spinoza and Ecology', in *Philosophia* 7(1): 45–54.

Naess, A. 2007. 'The Future Way of Thinking', in *Dagbladet*, 22 January. www.dagbladet.no/kultur/2007/01/22/489562.html, accessed 14 December, 2014.

Najam, A. 2005. 'Developing Countries and Global Environmental Governance: From Contestation to Participation to Engagement', in *International Environmental Agreements* 5: 303–321.

Peet, J. and Bossel, H. 2000. 'An Ethics-Based System Approach to Indicators of Sustainable Development', in *International Journal of Sustainable Development*, 3(3): 221–238.

Redgwell, Catherine. 2010. 'International Environmental Law', in *International Law*, Evans, Malcolm D. (ed.): 687–717. Oxford: Oxford University Press.

Ross, W.D. (ed.) 1928. *The Works of Aristotle Translated into English. Vol. VIII: Metaphysica* (2nd edn). Oxford: Clarendon Press.

Sands, P. 2003. *Principles of International Environmental Law* (2nd edn). Cambridge: Cambridge University Press.

Smuts, J.C. 1927. *Holism and Evolution*. London: MacMillan and Co.
Tahko, T.E. 2008. 'The Aristotelian Method and Aristotelian Metaphysics', in *An Anthology of Philosophical Studies*, Hanna, P. (ed.): 53–63. Athens: ATINER.
United Nations Convention on Biologial Diversity (UNCBD). 1992. UNTS, vol. 1760, No. 79.
United Nations Framework Convention on Climate Change (UNFCCC). 1992. UNTS, vol. 1771, No. 107.
Voigt, C. 2009. *Sustainable Development as a Principle of International Law: Resolving Conflicts between Climate Measures and WTO Law*. Leiden: Martinus Nijhoff Publishers.

2 Spinoza's metaphysics

Substance monism, naturalism and psychological egoism

In this chapter I will give a brief, and admittedly sketchy, presentation of Spinoza's metaphysical structure leading up to his main ethical conclusions and claims. I will focus on those aspects of Spinoza's metaphysical structure that – based on the review of the Reports in the previous chapter – seem to resonate with and provide further clarifications of their expressed claims for building an alternative to the anthropocentric metaphysical platform to which human kind so far has adhered. This and the following three chapters are necessary for considering the claims within the Reports in so far as these claims are understood as effects of a current trend of turning to Spinoza's philosophy for assistance in combating the Anthropocene. To this end, the present and coming three chapters' treatment of Spinoza's philosophy serve the double purpose of a) making sense of some of the dense claims that can be found within the Reports about a new metaphysics, while simultaneously b) preparing for the main objective of this book, which is to evaluate the feasibility of understanding these claims as implicitly relying on Spinozism of a particular kind. I will start with Spinoza's metaphysical starting point: the establishment of substance monism and some of its ontological premises. Then, I will look at how this starting point leads to a rather curious epistemological framework. Finally, I will show how the path delineated by Spinoza from a changed ontological perspective to a new way of understanding and evaluating knowledge must also mean a redefinition of ethical virtue and the human highest good.

Anyone familiar with Spinoza's metaphysics knows that he builds his entire explanation of the world and being on the idea of one single, self-causing, ever acting and all-encompassing substance (*E*1p1–14 see especially *E*1p14c1). In order to explain the complex nature of this substance – a nature that encompasses physical as well as ideal things without letting one be reducible to the other (*E*1p14c2 and *E*1p10 together with *E*2p7s); a nature that is eternal, infinite, necessary and indivisible (*E*1p11 and 13) – Spinoza refers to it as God *or* Nature (*Deus sive Natura*) (*E*4 preface, G II/206). Spinoza clearly is a substance monist par excellence in that for him everything in nature is always and everywhere united and the same, not only in terms of ontology and causation but also in terms of epistemology and explanation (cf. *E*3 preface). Moreover, Spinoza transports this ontological relation of immanence or univocality between the whole and its parts to the realm of understanding by a doctrine which is usually referred to as his commitment to philosophical naturalism (cf. Della Rocca, 2008, 5; Melamed, 2013, 110; Lord, 2014, 60; Hübner, 2014, 125). In what follows, I will demonstrate how Spinoza's substance monism and naturalism lead to a number of radical ethical upshots. Before I begin that demonstration, however, let me settle a preliminary question concerning the nature of Spinoza's philosophy.

It is widely known that Spinoza was well versed in Cartesian philosophy and that he often uses this philosophy as a point of departure for his own philosophical deliberations. Spinoza, for instance, indubitably affirms many of the basic presumptions posited by Descartes about how to gain access to knowledge about non-familiar aspects of the world, nature and human existence (cf. *Med.* 2, AT 7:30–31; Nadler, 1999, 152). To adhere to rationalism can of course mean many things. However, following Spinoza scholar Jonathan Bennett, if we narrow down these meanings to a few common denominators we see that Spinoza belongs to the rationalist tradition. It is probably safe to say, Bennett argues, that being a rationalist at least involves a resistance to giving in to *a posteriori* explanations of things and phenomena (1984, 29). So, when we talk about either Spinoza's or Descartes' methodological convictions we talk about a thinking which relies on the idea that reality has a rational structure all aspects of which, in principle, can be grasped through mathematical and logical principles (ibid.). The explanation of a thing or phenomenon through experience is, as it were, acceptable to neither Descartes nor Spinoza. This is to say that they are both committed to the proposition that all observable things and phenomena are intelligible and can be explained through a set of previously established and self-evident principles and rules (ibid.).

However, Spinoza seems to have taken these rational presumptions of thought further than Descartes or any other in the rationalist tradition had ever done (Melamed, 2013, 34, n. 98). In fact, it is one of the presumptions that he shares with Descartes – the principle of everything's explicability – that Spinoza will come to lean against when criticizing Cartesian philosophy for developing propositions that are inconsistent, self-contradictory and even absurd. Spinoza, as it were, turns rationalism and the rational argument against what is commonly regarded as its own father.

Substance monism – an ontological relation of immanence

In Part One of his principal work, *Ethics Demonstrated in Geometrical Order and Divided into Five Parts* (*Ethics*), Spinoza begins by listing the definitions and axioms upon which his following argumentation, which ends with a conceptualization of God as the sole substance, must rely.[1] He defines substance as 'that which is in itself and is conceived through itself, i.e. that whose concept does not require the concept of another thing, from which it must be formed' (*E*1d3). This definition shows what I have just hinted at: how close Spinoza's point of departure is to that of Descartes even though he is often portrayed as his principal philosophical opponent (as for instance by the Reports; see Rep. II, para.20 and

Chapter 1). Just like Descartes, Spinoza perceives substance as something that has properties but does not, in itself, constitute a property of something else. It is that thing which is complete in itself and completely *within* itself. And just like Descartes, Spinoza holds that it follows from this definition that 'substance' refers to a thing that is conceptually independent. This means that one does not have to conceive of anything else in order to conceive of – in order to understand – substance. Every other thing, on the other hand, needs substance in order to be conceived of (Descartes, *Principles* I, 51–52; *E*I def.3).

Spinoza thus establishes at the outset of the *Ethics* that the world can have only one kind of building block. He then lets his rational axioms work on this premise (between propositions 1 and 14) until it is clear that there is, in fact, only one 'thing' that fits with the definition of substance in *E*I def.3, and that, therefore, everything that exists must be regarded as either being or inhering in this single substance (*E*Ip14d by *E*Id6, *E*Ip11 and *E*Ip5 together with *E*Ia1 and *E*Ia2).

Let me explain: in proposition 14 of Part One, Spinoza establishes that '[e] xcept God, no substance can be or be conceived'. Proposition 14 is thus where Spinoza gives substance a name. We may recall that in the definition of substance we saw that it is the thing that needs the concept of no other thing in order to be conceived of. This goes to show that the definition of substance in *E*Id3, together with the classification of God as its only corresponding object, makes God stand out as an indivisible totality and not as a subject or object of any kind. For Spinoza, God is not an anthropomorphic being; God is absolute totality in so far as the totality is an indivisible and inclusive substance which both embodies and encompasses all single things – known and unknown – in the world.

Spinoza's argumentation leading up to the denomination of God as the *sole* substance in *E*Ip14 has been analysed extensively in Spinoza studies and the general conclusions of these studies may be summarized as follows. No other substance besides God can exist in so far as God is *a* substance – a thing which inheres in nothing and can be conceived of without the help of the concepts of other things (*E*Id3) – *and* in so far as God as substance is understood to have an infinite number of ways to express its essence (*E*Idef.6). If there were another substance in this scenario, it would have to share at least one of God's ways to express itself (since we saw that God was a substance with infinite ways of expression) and *that* would mean that the explanation of God could involve the concept of another thing, which would be absurd according to the definition of substance just laid down (*E*Ip7 and 11, cf. Bennett, 1984, 72–73).

This, then, is the necessary establishment of substance monism on Spinoza's rational account. On its own, the affirmation of substance monism marks a decisive difference between Spinoza's and Descartes' philosophical systems. It is also, however, what motivates Spinoza's critique of Descartes' metaphysics from an epistemological perspective. While Descartes admits that the definition of substance points, semantically, only to God, he reserves the right of other things to be called substances too:

> There is only one substance which can be understood to depend on no other thing whatsoever, namely God. In the case of all other substances, we perceive that they can exist only with the help of God's concurrence. Hence, the term 'substance' does not apply ***univocally***, as they say in the Schools, to God and to other things: that is, there is no distinctly intelligible meaning of the term which is common to God and his creatures.
>
> (*Principles* I, 51, my emphasis)

Because respecting rationalism for Spinoza means never allowing for brute facts[2] when it comes to explaining things and phenomena around us, one of the first consequences of the definition of substance is precisely the univocality which, in the passage above, Descartes denounces. In effect, Spinoza's adherence to the explanatory force of rationalism means that *if* a concept is adequately explained – voiced – in one setting, then this explanation – voice – must be respected in all other settings in which the concept may be applied. In other words, since God, in the case at hand, is the only thing that qualifies as substance according to the definition of that term, then substance cannot be applied to any other thing in the world around us. For Spinoza, adhering to rationalism means, in short, respecting the univocality of the terms and principles used for explaining and conceiving of aspects of reality.

Arguably, Descartes' definition of substance as derivable can be seen as a concession to political forces. To this end, it could be explained as a compromise between his commitment to everything's explainability on rational principles and the idea of God's benevolence, and, by extension, an independent providential deity (cf. Descartes, *Med.* 4; Della Rocca, 2008, 79; Ragland, 2005). Regardless of whether this concession was made consciously or not, it seems safe to say that the definition of derived substance clearly leaves open an opportunity to preserve the idea of a transcendent divinity which interacts *with* the worldly world, although the basic premise of rationalism seems to exclude this. For Spinoza, a consistent application of the ontological axioms for metaphysical queries leads, on the contrary, to the establishment of God's effects (or finite things) being not only law-bound but also completely causally determined and necessary (*E*1p16, p29 and p33).

For Spinoza, rationalism means that *if* the definition of substance allows for only one specific kind of ontological description of God (an impersonal and natural God, as it were), then this specificity with respect to the concept's *ideata* must be respected in *all* contexts, including the context of morality. As will become evident later on in this review, for Spinoza, the question of virtue and the question of epistemological truth are ultimately to be methodologically treated in the same way. If it is correct to hold that there is no external authority to turn to when it comes to determining questions of nature, then there is no external authority with exclusive access to an absolute morality which can be turned to when it comes to determining questions of good and evil (cf. Huenemann, 2014, 8).

As evident from this, the difference between Spinoza's and Descartes' respective take on rationalism leaves marks all the way through their philosophical systems, from metaphysics to morality. However, it would be hasty of me to direct our attention to the normative upshots of Spinoza's metaphysics at this early stage of the review, so let us now turn back to the basic variables of Spinoza's metaphysical structure. In order to clarify the implications of Spinoza's conception of substance I will now describe the relationship set up by Spinoza between God *qua* substance and singular finite things like human beings. This is a relationship that hinges on the concepts of attributes and modes. In the end of the next section, we will see that on the basis of his account of substance, attributes and modes Spinoza creates a radical explanation of the act of subjectification or individuation, by which I mean the process of answering the question of how finite things take their independent form in what we have just seen is defined as a more or less formless totality.

Attributes: thought and extension

In the *Ethics* Spinoza defines an attribute as 'what the intellect perceives of a substance, as constituting its essence' (*E*1d4). In other words, attributes are what explain substance to us intellectually. There are according to Spinoza infinitely many ways to explain God since God is 'a substance consisting of an infinity of attributes, of which each one expresses an eternal and infinite essence' (*E*1d6). Now, the key for understanding attribute according to Spinoza's explanation lies in appreciating the last part of this definition: that each of the infinitely many attributes that expresses God's essence does so fully: that is to say, in a complete manner on its own. In the tenth proposition of Part One of the *Ethics*, we get a glimpse at why this is so. Since attribute is what intellectually explains a substance (*E*1d4) and since substance is what 'is conceived through itself' (*E*1d3), each attribute of an infinite substance must on its own explain its essence (*E*1p10 and *E*1p10s). One way to grasp all this is by translating being, that is, essence, to reality (*E*1p9) which, in turn, can be understood as activity since what is real is always something positive. Then, we see how every attribute can be regarded as different kinds of acting out one and the same content (cf. *E*1p11d, G II/53/30–35). One important upshot of Spinoza's conception of the attributes as different ways of demonstrating the same thing, taken together with the univocality of substance, is shown itself later on in the *Ethics* in the form of the famous doctrine of parallelism (*E*2p7 and *E*2p7s). This doctrine, in turn, constitutes the basis for Spinoza's nonsubstantial explanation of the human being and, as such, for his naturalistic conception of moral value and ethical normativity.

Although there are infinitely many attributes, human beings are able to pick up on only two: thought and extension (*E*2p1 and *E*2p2). The common demonstration to these two propositions explains first of all that since we – human beings – evidently think (form ideas) and move physical matter, these ideas and movements of ours must be in God because everything that is, 'is either in itself or in another' (*E*1a1) and because 'except God no substance can be or be conceived' (*E*1p14). Now, since *E*1p15 makes it clear that whatever 'is in God, and nothing can be or be conceived without God', it follows that our ideas and movements inhere in

God. The attributes, in short, are what function as the means by which substance communicates its being. And, since we are limited to being instantiations of two of these means, from our perspective, the attributes of thought and extension are the means by which we perceive (corporally and intellectually) of substance.

In order to grasp the complexity of this idea, it may help to take a concrete example. Think of the attributes of thought and extension in terms of two different art forms (dance and visual art, for instance), each expressing one and the same artistic *thing* (their common substance) – for example García Lorca's *The House of Bernarda* – yet in two individual and completely separate forms. Both the dance performance and the painting will thus be expressing the same substance; that is, the object for both art forms will be the *House of Bernarda*. Each representation, however, will be irreducibly distinct from the other. The dancers will not move differently by the painter's strokes of a pen and the painting will not be manipulated into a new shape by the choreographer's alterations of the dancers' bodies. It is the same with Spinoza's attributes: there is no causal relationship between thought and extension. Ideas are caused by other ideas and movements by other moving bodies although both movement and thought represent the same substance, the same thing-ness.

Modes of substance

Continuing with the example set above, we may narrow down on the other major metaphysical building block for Spinoza, modes, in the following way. Neither the individual bodies which participate in the dance performance of *Bernarda's House* nor the artist's hand or the pen or paper that he or she uses when painting Lorca's work can be regarded as attributes in themselves. This is because none of them fully expresses the entire substance of the work, although they are all necessary for its articulation in the certain and determinate way that make it constitute precisely *that* literary work and not another. According to the illustration of Spinoza's substance as *Bernarda's House* it is thus possible to understand them all (the dancers' bodies and the artist's hand, pen and paper) as modes. In the *Ethics*, modes are defined as 'affections of substance, or that which is in another through which it is also conceived' (*E*1d6). Translated into the terminology of our illustration we see how the form, or concept of dance, is necessary in order to understand the dancers' individual movements but that the dancer's individual bodies or movements are not necessary in order to conceive of dance as a form of movement. The dancers can be regarded as instantiating something which *is* something regardless of the dancers' particular existence and which must be added to the image of them in order to explain their activity intellectually.

In Spinoza's words, we should begin by postulating that 'whatever is, is either in itself or in another' (*E*1a1). Since only substance is in itself (*E*1d3) and because only God classifies as substance (*E*1p14), all other *things* (attributes are not things strictly speaking as they are ways in which substance expresses itself) must consequently be conceived of as being *in* God (*E*1p18d). This means, first of all, that every single thing which we usually regard as a finite thing (like a body or a pen) is a mode which needs substance's attributes in order to be conceived (*E*1d6). Particular things are, later on in the work, precisely specified as 'affections of God's attributes, or modes by which God's attributes are expressed in a *certain and determinate* way' (*E*1p25c, my emphasis).

Because attributes are the (infinite) different ways by which God expresses its being – it is reasonable to conclude that the attributes amount to the 'another' in which modes inhere and through which they are conceived according to the definition of modes (*E*1d6). A particular body is *in* the attribute of extension in so far as it is necessary to conceive of extension in order to understand the particular body. In other words, any particular thing (you, me, climate change, the chair I am sitting on in this moment etc.) constitutes something that embodies both being an effect and product, as well as an aspect and instantiation *of* God's necessary and completely law-bound activity such as we perceive these effects, aspects and instantiations through either of the attributes.

The most important thing to take notice of with respect to the notion 'mode' is that even though modes will take on different shapes depending on what attribute we are paying attention to, they will always *be* the self-same thing: that is, substance taking on a particular form. A particular mode of thought, M, is substantially the *same* affection of the substance as its mode pair in extension: the only difference is that we perceive mode M as M(T) in thought and as M(E) in extension.

This gives us the following schematic relationship between the concepts of substance, attribute and mode. In so far as attributes are *general ways* (just as dance is a *form* of art) by which substance expresses itself, modes are *the* particular expressions of these general ways. Simple as this relationship may seem, the understanding of Spinoza's metaphysical structure is complicated by the split on the level of substance's expressions, which he introduces between so-called infinite and finite modes (*E*1p22–24). Modes by which substance's attributes express themselves can be either infinite (i.e. without any spatio-temporal specificity, see *E*1p22) or finite (as in single, particular concrete things, see *E*1p24). This complicates understanding, as the line between some of substance's effects or expressions (the infinite mode) and the more general *way* by which substance expresses itself (attribute) becomes blurred.

Following Michael Della Rocca's suggestion, it is possible to close in on the ontological status of modes (infinite as well as finite) if we consider modes neither as effects nor aspects but as states of substance (2008, 62). Extended modes, on this reading, are simply God *qua* extension and ideas are states of God as a particular thinking thing (ibid., 64). According to this understanding, infinite modes represent something like the tendencies by which a finite mode can be explained depending on the attribute (language or form) it is being expressed through (cf. *E*1p23). Again, each tendency will *be* the same regardless of whether we speak of extended or thinking modes since they are expressions of the same thing, but the tendencies will be perceivable exclusively from their own form of communication (*E*2p7). Infinite extended modes could be understood then as the tendencies by which extended matter moves in space according to a given pattern, and infinite modes of thought could be understood as the tendencies by which ideas are produced in thought according to a given pattern. Accordingly, singular particular things are the effects of a production process which is implied by substance's basic ways of expression (its attributes) *together* with the fact that substance's essence amounts to existence, which means production of effects according to a certain pattern (*E*1p20 and *E*4 preface, G II/209).[3]

When approaching modes this way, as 'states of being' of God, one of the more significant implications of substance monism for the conception of the human being becomes visible. God is substance (the only one) and given that, all that exists is either substance or modes inhering in substance (*E*1p4d). Human beings, since we are neither self-explainable nor self-caused, must consequently be conceived of as pertaining to the latter category of things: as modifications of God. Now, given what I have just explained with respect to the inherence relationship between modes and substance, the effect of us being modes of God is that we do not just participate in God's work as products of an omnipresent causal power; we – together with all other finite things – literally *are* God (cf. Della Rocca, 2008, 86–87).

In order to better grasp the radicalism of it all, it may be useful to turn back to the difference between Spinoza's ontological scheme and that proposed by Descartes. Because Descartes' definition of substance allows for derived substance, although the definition itself points towards univocality (as evident from the passage quoted initially in this chapter), he has at the outset introduced the possibility to turn to exceptions or special laws for the explanation of the world and reality. It is this that allows him to treat man as a special case in relation to God's other creatures. He places the human being in an intermediate position between animal instinct and God's perfect knowledge (*Discourse on the Method*, 141, AT VI/59).

The difference appears even more radical once we consider that Spinoza builds his entire argumentation upon, and carefully respects, Descartes' basic definitions and ontological axioms. There is nothing 'new' in Spinoza's conception of attributes and modes. To this end, Descartes too defines modes as conceptually dependent on the concept of the thing which expresses the essence of a substance (the attribute, of course) (*Principles* I, 53). The difference is introduced in the subsequent movement, according to Spinoza, when Descartes reserves the right of certain finite things to be something more than mere modes *of* God's attributes. Certain finite things – which strictly speaking must be classified as modes and therefore cannot be treated as *the* principal substance, he argues, as that would place them on the same ontological level as God – seem anyway to correspond to something substantially different to a simple mode, like, say, a colour constituting an aspect of a given thing. So, in order to differentiate ontologically between finite things of a more mundane character and more complex things, Descartes introduces the concept of substantially independent things (more substance than mode, less substance than God). It is in these substantially independent things (and not God) that modes, which are conceptually dependent, inhere. In order to establish this scheme, Descartes must stipulate that there is a *special* ontological rule (special in relation to the definition of a mode) governing the relations of the things that seemingly demonstrate more substantial independence than modes (see the quote from *Principles* I above). So, Descartes introduces the idea of finite substance for things which, just like modes, depend conceptually on attributes but, in contrast to modes, do not appear to inhere in attributes. These finite substances, like the primary substance, are conceived through God's attributes of thought and extension, but, he concludes, they do not themselves constitute simple accidents or states of God expressing himself as thought or extension (*Principles* I, 53). Rather they are finite, thinking and extended substances in which modes are produced.

As a result of this line of thought we get the following scheme: first, there is God, who is the conceptual condition and ultimate cause *of* all finite and infinite things in the world. Then there are two God-derived substances: extension and thought. Each of these is expressed by an attribute – a way of expressing itself: in the case of extension, movement and rest; in the case of thought, thinking. The human mind is a finite mind-substance, and all material bodies are finite corporeal substances. Last in this metaphysical scheme come modes, which are accidents or properties produced by finite substances. God has no modes, as it were, and modes do not inhere in God, they are produced by God but inhere in derived/finite substance. Thus, 'the shape, position, local motion and so on' are modes of a body as a finite substance (*The Geometrical Demonstration of Meditations on First Philosophy in The Second Set of Replies to Objections and Replies to the Meditations*, 1984, 114, AT VII/162–162 and *Principles* I, 53). Finite substance, for Descartes, is something which, on its own, constitutes the material substance, the *thing*-ness, in relation to the states in which it exists (modes). It depends ultimately, however, on God. The causal relation between God and human beings, according to Cartesian metaphysics, is a transcendental relation of cause and effect, whereas Spinoza's rejection of a derivation between substance and finite substance turns this causal relation into an immanent relation of effect within cause – the effects reside, ontologically, on the same level as their cause.

As is evident, Descartes manages to constitute the human being as a combination of two separate finite substances: thought and extension. The fact that the human being has both a body and a mind is for Descartes evidence of the fact that there is one omnipresent and all-powerful substance which embodies all of the finite substances. Body and mind, understood as finite substances, are (as mentioned) ultimately caused by God and need the concept of God in order to be conceived, but they do not inhere in God since they are in themselves substances and need no other concept than their own to be explained. Instead, each finite substance is what holds inhering modes, such as a specific human soul and a specific human body. For Spinoza, in contrast, and due to his strictly flat ontological structure in which everything expresses one and the same thing – substance monism (*E*1p15d) – and happens necessarily (*E*1p29), the particular human mind is the same *thing* as the human body. Each of them is God acting in a particular and by other finite things circumscribed way (*E*2p7s to *E*1p10).[4] To this end, the series of propositions of Part Two about the human being start to make sense only when keeping in mind that the human mind and the body, in fact, are one and the same thing. *E*2p11 states that 'the first thing that constitutes the actual being of a human Mind is nothing but the idea of a singular thing which actually exists'. Then, *E*2p13 states that 'the object of the idea constituting the human Mind is the Body, or a certain mode of Extension which actually exists and nothing else'.

It is not only the image of the human being that comes out differently in Descartes and Spinoza's respective schemes, however. Perhaps more importantly than the difference with respect to the conception of the human being is the difference with respect to the image of substance: that is, God. In introducing a derivation of primary substance which cannot be explained, neither by its own definition nor any of the metaphysics' basic axioms, Descartes, in effect, personalizes and introduces intention to the image of God. Spinoza says explicitly in the appendix to Part One of the *Ethics* that the definitions and axioms which he (along with, as we have seen, Descartes) deems self-explanatory and thus adequate to start off from, cannot lead to any other conception of God than one of a completely naturalized, non-teleological and mechanistic being but that this will be, due to common prejudices caused by insufficient knowledge, hard to accept for many (G II/77–78). The Cartesian insistence that substance should not solely be equated with such a being is important because it allows for a certain degree of mystery attached to the image of God. If it does not suffice to analyse and deconstruct nature in order to understand divine causality, then there might be acts of God which we cannot readily, not without guidance from special authority that is, decode and understand.

Naturalism – from ontological immanence to epistemological univocality

As evident from of our review thus far, it is impossible to close in on Spinoza and his philosophical system without discussing Descartes. In the previous section, I have tried to show how Spinoza's 'radical' faithfulness to rationalism expresses itself with respect to the basic building blocks of his metaphysical explanation. In this section, I will discuss how this faithfulness affects his epistemology. After a general outline of Spinoza's take on epistemology, I will discuss more specifically some of the conditions which that epistemology posits with respect to our human ability to know and understand ourselves and things around us.

For Spinoza, the commitment to rationalism means that all things and phenomena should be taken to follow identical laws. By extension, every single thing should be explained according to one and the same set of principles. This is what scholars usually refer to as the commitment to philosophical naturalism in Spinoza's rational system of thought (Bennett, 1984, 36; Della Rocca, 1996, 192; Garrett, 1996, 270). The doctrine of naturalism is most clearly expressed in the preface to Part Three of the *Ethics*, where the conditions for a new understanding of human psychology are introduced (*E*3 preface, G II/138; see also *E*l appendix, G II/78 and G II/79 where the erroneous understanding of the human being is described in terms of being non-naturalistic). For Spinoza, the commitment to rationalism presupposes a commitment to philosophical naturalism: to commit oneself to the intelligibility of all things is simply to commit to the idea that identical rules should be applied in the explanation of everything.

> nature is always the same, and its virtue and power of acting are everywhere the same, i.e. the laws and rules of nature, according to which all things happen, and change from one form to another, are always and everywhere the same. So the way of understanding the nature of anything, of whatever kind, must also be the same, *viz.* through the universal laws and rules of nature.
>
> (*E*3 preface, G II/138/13–18)

As evident, naturalism for Spinoza means that where a definition communicates a univocal meaning, anything which does not fit this definition is excluded from the possibility of being classified as the defined thing, even if the thing in our sensory experience of it appears to be identical to the defined meaning. So, as stated in the quoted passage, the commitment to naturalism leads Spinoza to disqualify the existence of special laws in relation to the explanation of things. The conception of a thing is simply not complete, he argues, if it involves special laws or *a posteriori* sensations. For Spinoza, this is because turning to *special* laws when explaining things amounts to explaining them on the basis of something that was not available before the thing to be explained: special laws give priority to particular effects not to general causes, as it were. Turning to special laws for the metaphysical explanation of things is to explain an effect by turning to another effect, not its cause. To this end, there is no difference, according to Spinoza, between special laws and experience. Like experience, special laws amount to unacceptable brute facts in the light of Spinoza's take on rationalism (cf. Della Rocca, 2008, 6–7).

Knowing what is not satisfactory in relation to a given explanation does not automatically, however, provide us with an understanding of what it does take, according to Spinoza, to really explain a thing. Spinoza's epistemological account is largely to be found in Part Two of the *Ethics*, but the centrality of this theme for his entire philosophical project is foreboded in his earlier and unfinished work *Treatise on the Emendation of the Intellect* (*TdIE*). [5] In the *TdIE*, however, truth or certainty is explained in slightly different terms than those used in the *Ethics*. In the *TdIE* certainty (i.e. truth) seems to be related to the idea itself and not to its object (*ideatum*), while the *Ethics*' axiom about truth reads: 'A true idea must agree with its object' (*E*1a6).

One way of reconciling the slight shift in these two positions in Spinoza's thought is to read both of them in light of the ontological premise of parallelism (*E*1p10 and *E*2p7). In order to respect parallelism and the separation of the attributes, the notion of a true idea must refer to something that is internal to the attribute of thought (just as stated in the *TdIE*) and not the correspondence between ideas and *ideata* which usually points to the attribute of extension (as in the axiom of Part One of the *Ethics*).[6] If Spinoza's statement about truth in *E*1a6 is read in this light, it is possible to regard it as describing not so much the qualities of a true idea as one of the extrinsic effects of such an idea. In so far as truth is understood as one of the extrinsic effects of an idea being of a particular character, the fact that an idea of this character always correctly represents an object does not reveal what this particular character is. It is possible, I would argue, to achieve this reconciliation by treating Spinoza's different statements about certainty and truth according to the following scheme: In the *TdIE*, without having launched the terminology he will later have recourse to in the *Ethics*, Spinoza explains the relationship between the qualities of an idea and its representational force in terms of certainty and truth. He writes that certainty 'is nothing but the objective essence itself, i.e., the *mode by which we are aware* of the formal essence is certainty itself' (*TdIE* [35], G II/15/7–8, my emphasis). Complex as it may look; this is actually a quite straightforward claim: certainty refers to the idea, nothing more. Given that a thing's (e.g. an idea's) formal essence – according to the Cartesian tradition from which Spinoza clearly draws when it comes to scientific method – refers to its actuality or existence, and its objective essence to its representational character (cf. Smith, 2017), what Spinoza posits in this paragraph is that it is the *way* by which we conceive of a thing (i.e. our idea of it), and not the correspondence between the idea and its object, that is decisive for the idea's truthfulness (certainty). This is clarified a little further on, but in a passage in which the word of choice is truth instead of certainty.

> Since truth, therefore, requires no sign, but it suffices, in order to remove all doubt, to have the objective essence of things, or what is the same, ideas, it follows that the true Method is not to seek a sign of truth, *after the acquisition of ideas*, but the true Method is the way that truth itself, or the objective essence of things, or the ideas (all those signify the same) should be sought in the proper order.
>
> (*TdIE* [36], G II/15/15–20, my emphasis)

In the *Ethics*, Spinoza posits truth as a necessary condition of correspondence between idea and object (*E*1a6). However, a statement very similar to that just cited from the earlier treatise can be found later on in the fourth definition of the opening section of Part Two. Unlike the terminology opted for in the *TdIE*, though, Spinoza here introduces a separate term to describe the intrinsic quality of a true or certain idea: adequacy. That there is no contradiction between this account (and thus the previous ones made in the *TdIE*) and *E*1a6 is clear once we consider this definition carefully.

> D4: By an adequate idea I understand an idea which, insofar as it is considered in itself, without relation to an object, has all the properties, *or* intrinsic denominations of a true idea.
>
> Exp.: *I say intrinsic to exclude what it is extrinsic, viz. the agreement of the idea with its object.*
>
> (*E*2d4, emphasis in original)

In so far, then, as the correspondence spoken of in *E*1a6 is regarded as the extrinsic effect of an adequate idea (which the explanation attached to the just cited definition clearly indicates) and not as a characteristic aspect *of* such an idea in itself, the following relationship between truth and adequacy can be delineated. An effect of adequate ideas is that they are true representations of their objects but the determination of whether they are adequate or not, however, cannot be made based on the criteria of truth. Rather, as Margret Wilson puts it, central to Spinoza's conception of adequacy is 'an appropriate rational ordering' of the ideas leading up to the idea in question (1996, 95). This way, we have clarified the reference to intrinsic denominations which is found in *E*2d4. It is not only of exegetical importance to note the shift in meaning between truth and adequacy in Spinoza's mature thought. As we will see shortly, it is precisely the process of securing certainty – the ability to form adequate ideas – that will come to play a central role in Spinoza's outlining of the ethical consequences of his metaphysics. The concept of adequacy thus effectively ties epistemology to ethics and turns the act of knowing into an act of ethical significance. In order to get full disclosure of the implications of this position, let us now proceed to Spinoza's epistemological doctrines in Part Three of the *Ethics*.

Epistemological upshots of naturalism: rejecting exceptionalism and flattening out the mind's ability to know

If Spinoza's commitment to naturalism should be understood as an effect of rationalism and this philosophical perspective's general take on truth and intelligibility, then what about the purpose of naturalism? In other words, is there an end to which naturalism correspond as a general epistemological principle? Based on the unusual autobiographical introduction to what is presumed to be one of his earliest works, I am tempted to suggest that the answer to this question is closely related to the end of Spinoza's philosophical project as a whole. In the famous opening paragraphs of the *Treatise on the Emendation of the Intellect* Spinoza writes, in a style very unlike the one we will encounter in the *Ethics*, about what led him to philosophical inquiry:

> After experience had taught me that all the things which regularly occur in ordinary life are empty and futile, and I saw that all the things which were the cause or object of my fear had nothing of good or bad in themselves, except insofar as [my] mind was moved by them, I resolved at last to try to find out whether there was anything which would be the true good, capable of communicating itself, and which was something which, once found and acquired, would continuously give me the greatest joy, to eternity.
>
> (*TdIE* 1, G II/5)

As is evident from this passage, after having found that those things that normally were despised or desired had nothing good or bad in themselves, Spinoza set out to find the true good: good that cannot perish. He continues the introduction to the treatise by stating that he soon also found out that finding this true good – if it indeed existed – required the giving up of the 'conduct and plan of life which [he] shared with other men' because this conduct and plan hinged happiness upon the requirement of one of three categories: wealth, honour and sensual pleasure (ibid., G II/6). Although he doubts at first, the nature of the true good as he will come to understand it is such that it makes up for giving up the aspiration of a normal plan of life involving the acquisition of wealth, honour and sensory pleasure. The key for Spinoza to finding out what is truly good lies in understanding that *all* negative emotions and every reason for a person's misery are connected to loving and being emotionally attached to finite things that can perish:

> Furthermore, these evils seemed to have arisen from the fact that all happiness and unhappiness was placed in the quality of the object to which we cling with love. For strife will never arise on account of what is not loved, nor will there be sadness if it perishes, nor envy if it is possessed by another, nor fear, nor hatred – in a word, no disturbances of the mind. Indeed, all these happen only in the love of those things that can perish, as all the things we have just spoken of can do.
>
> (*TdIE* 9, G II/7/16–24).

Despite this bleak image, Spinoza concludes that there is a love which feeds the mind with a joy that is entirely exempt from sadness. This is the love directed towards the only eternal and infinite thing in the world (ibid. 10, G II/7/25). Having established this, Spinoza reveals the aim of his ethics: it is to acquire a nature that allows for him to attain maximum wellbeing and sustainable happiness (ibid. 13–14, G II/8/20–30). Because true and sustainable wellbeing is connected to the love of an infinite and eternal thing, this is where philosophical inquiry and the importance of rational understanding come into the picture. He writes:

> [B]efore anything else we must devise a way of healing the intellect, and purifying it, as much as we can in the beginning, so that it understands things successfully, without error and as well as possible. Everyone will now be able to see that I wish to direct all the sciences toward one end and goal, viz. that we should achieve, as we have said, the highest human perfection.
>
> (*TdIE* 16, G II/9/10–15).

With this description in place, it seems possible to return to the question with which I began this section. Being part of a philosophical inquiry aiming at accounting for the human highest good and at guiding us humans towards this good, naturalism as a general epistemological principle functions as a corrective means with which we may approach the pitfalls of our common conceptions of things around us, ourselves and the relationship between our experience of the good and the true good.

Exceptionalism

One of the principal pitfalls when it comes to our understanding of ourselves and what is truly good for us is expressed in the very same preface wherein we find the commitment to naturalism first being expressed in the *Ethics* (*E*3 preface). There, Spinoza accuses, without immediately specifying whom, that 'those who have written about the Affects, and men's way of living' have done so while treating these things 'not of natural things, which follows from the common laws of nature, but of things which are outside of nature' (G II/137). A little further on, however, it is indeed revealed that one of the thinkers Spinoza has in mind in this section is, not surprisingly, Descartes (G II/137/25). What Descartes (and arguably others) are responsible for, according to Spinoza, is to 'conceive of man in nature as a *dominion within a dominion*. For they believe that man disturbs, rather than follows, the order of nature, that he has absolute power over his actions, and that he is determined only himself' (G II/137/10–15, my emphasis). This critique can easily be linked to Spinoza's rejection of substance dualism and the split between God as the primary substance and finite things as derived substances. The only way that the human being can be regarded this way – as in full power over her own actions; as determined by herself; as a reflection of God as it were – is to regard her as a derived, finite substance, exempted from the main rules and principles of rational metaphysics.

So much for the causes of this position which Spinoza famously terms dominion within a dominion. But, what about its consequences? Its main consequence, according to Spinoza, spells lack of power to moderate emotions. Spinoza writes vibrantly:

> And they attribute the cause of human impotence, not to the common power of nature, but to I know not what vice of human nature, which they therefore bewail, or laugh at, or disdain, or (as usually happens) curse. And he who knows how to censure more eloquently and cunning the weakness of the human mind is held to be Godly.
>
> (*E*3 preface, G II/137/15–20)

Spinoza points to something interesting here. In the attempt to secure a way to make us more powerful than the rest of nature by separating ourselves from other natural things, we actually make ourselves less powerful with respect to our own shortcomings. It is precisely the fact that we tend to portray ourselves as substantially more powerful than other things and beings in nature that renders it impossible to blame our faults and shortcomings on nature. This is because blaming nature would contradict the entire scheme with us as beyond and above nature. The deception must be carried on in order not to render fragile the entire metaphysical construction upon which this image of the human being rests. The effect of all this, however, is according to Spinoza that human beings are denied a true and honest method for actually dealing with the problem of wellbeing and happiness.

Thus, in the face of this situation, where human weaknesses are not seriously addressed because this would imply a questioning of a carefully built up metaphysical structure, Spinoza connects his own metaphysics to the goal of remedying precisely this ethical deficit as it appears in previous accounts of human nature. So, after having stated the familiar commitment to naturalism, Spinoza concludes the preface by stipulating that:

> [t]he affects, therefore, of hate, anger, envy, etc., considered in themselves, follow from the same necessity and force of nature as the other singular things. And therefore they acknowledge certain causes, through which they are understood, and have certain properties, *as worthy of our knowledge as the properties of any other thing*, by the mere contemplation of which we are pleased. Therefore, I shall treat the nature and powers of the Affects, and the power of the Mind over them, by the same Method by which, in the preceding parts, I treated God and the Mind, and I shall consider human actions and appetites just as if it were a Question of lines, planes and bodies.
>
> (*E*3 preface, G II/138/19–30, my emphasis)

Part Three of the *Ethics* is thus introduced as a remedy to a false conception of the human mind's ability and emotions.

The human mind: abilities and challenges

According to the standard contemporary conception of Spinoza's account of the human mind and its functions, all thoughts are for him representational (Della Rocca, 2008, 118; Nadler 2008, 155–157; LeBuffe, 2010, 16).[7] This means that Spinoza believes that there is no substantial difference between representational thoughts containing ideas *of* something and seemingly non-representational thoughts, such as the so-called affects or emotions (fear, love, hope, despair, etc.) (*E*2a3; *E*2p11d). I will now discuss how this representational understanding of the mind's function affects Spinoza's conception of the human ability to achieve wellbeing.

We know that owing to his commitment to the strict rationalism implied by naturalism, Spinoza must explain what thoughts are about with the same general laws and principles which he believes govern everything else in the world. This means that all individual thoughts – modes of the attribute of thought – must be explained in the same way in relation to their attribute as the attribute of thought is explained in relation to substance. Since the attribute of thought is the substance's way of expressing itself through ideas, individual particular and finite thoughts must be conceived of as the attribute's particular *ways* of expressing the substance. This account enables Spinoza to explain the human mind as the idea corresponding to a particular extended body (*E*2p7 together with *E*2p7s).

The essence of the mind is defined solely by its ability to produce ideas and affirm through these ideas one or another quality/feature to the object they represent (*E*2p49 and *E*2p49c). Ideas function to represent things (ideal as well as extended) and since a mind is nothing but a compilation of ideas together representing the extended components that constitute a given body, there is no additional or essential objective attached to the mind. This naturalization of the mind follows from the metaphysical premises which Spinoza in the earlier parts of the *Ethics* declares his commitment to generally. He simply applies the prohibition of special rules of explanation in relation to nature and its laws to the study of the human nature. For the same reason he is forced to reject the familiar idea of a twofold function of the mind: one passive and one active. The passive function would be the ability to perceive images and form intellectual ideas. The active function would involve producing non-representational thoughts to empower the individual thinking them to act or abstain from acting on the ideas formed. Spinoza famously rejects this division because it cannot be consistently explained by reference to the basic laws of nature which, as we know, are to be applied generally and without exception to all events and phenomena around us.

For Descartes, who has already allowed for bifurcation in the basic ontological rules (there can be two substances), a second bifurcation of the mind's function is necessary for separating human beings from other beings in nature. Descartes allows for the separation of 'the will' from the more passive or perceptive intellect because it is what permits him to preserve the existence of a transcendental force (presumably God) invested especially in the human being. It is the free will that separates the human being from animals and 'unanimated' things which clearly do not appear to act according to higher-order, or special rationality. Descartes develops this idea in the Fourth Meditation while contemplating the possibility of the imperfection of God given that our human constitution – which involves error – is to be considered as God's reflections.

> What I think is very noteworthy is that there is nothing else in me that is so perfect and so great [as the will] that I cannot think of it as being even greater still or more perfect. If, for example, I consider my faculty of understanding, I recognize immediately that it is very limited and finite and, at the same time, I form the idea of another similar faculty which is much greater – in fact, the greatest possible, and infinite – and from the mere fact that I can form this idea I perceive that it belongs to the nature of God. [...] I experience the will alone, or freedom of choice, as being so extensive in my own case that I conceive the idea of none greater, so that it is principally because of this faculty that I understand myself as being in some sense the image and likeness of God.
>
> (AT VII/57)

In these remarks we see how Descartes separates the human will from human understanding, arguing that whereas we have access to a will as great as God's, our understanding is limited and finite. According to Della Rocca, Descartes arguably creates, by doing this, an escape clause for a divine teleology within an otherwise rational and mechanical explanation of the world (2008, 125). This is because God's unlimited and infinite will appears, on this account, as an ultimate plan of sorts, in relation to which our human and limited understanding functions (ibid.).

The problem with this account for Spinoza is both that it turns an unexplained faculty (the will) into a key notion for our self-knowledge, and that it turns God into a reflection of man. In *E*2p49s, G II/132/23–135/32, Spinoza rejects the idea that human will is greater – and thus closer to God – than the intellect. His answer is formulated along the lines that what we perceive as infinite in relation to our intellect is merely the result of the fact that we hold many inadequate ideas of things. Thus, if by 'intellect' we mean only those ideas which represent that which we actually know with certainty, then, yes, the intellect is indeed more limited than the will. However, if by 'intellect' we mean the faculty of thinking, then, no, that faculty is not more limited than the will. To the claim that there are 'infinitely many things which we cannot perceive', his reply is 'that we cannot reach them by any thought, and consequently not by any faculty of willing' either (*E*2p49s [IIIB (i)]).

In the appendix to Part One of the *Ethics* Spinoza bluntly asks those who promote the idea of a will separated from the intellect and the connected idea of a 'willing' God: why would God have a free will separated from his ability to understand? That would seem to make God into a being who acts with a purpose in a way that appears to conflict considerably with the definition of God as substance and with rationalism. In other words, on this account God would act like a finite mode rather than the indifferent, always active being that substance must be (*E*1 appendix, G II/78 and 79). By contrast, human error, according to Spinoza, can be understood only in relation to a human standard of understanding, not God's. So, whereas Spinoza agrees with Descartes that God understands everything he, unlike Descartes, concludes from this position that error is therefore something entirely human, something that cannot be measured in relation to God's superior understanding. Error is not something willed by God in relation to us because God's will is, like his understanding, unlimited, and therefore never negative. God's existence is the same as is his essence, which means that his essence is all of reality. Therefore, everything God produces, including understanding and will, is perfect as it is.

In order to prove the human hubris built into Descartes' metaphysical system, Spinoza emphasizes that what Descartes takes as a special feature of the human mind is nothing over and above what the intellect – any intellect – does each and every time it forms an idea (*E*2p49). The will is not a separate faculty of the mind; it is the intellectual affirmation of the particular nature of an *ideatum* which the formation of an idea necessarily involves. As such, the will is involved in the formation of each and every thought we hold. This way, Spinoza manages to demystify the will so that it no longer appears to be a feature making the human being stand outside the realm of nature and the univocal explanation of substance.

The fact is that for Spinoza, there can only be gradual and never substantial differences between finite modes. Otherwise, the metaphysical premises of rational explanation and naturalism would not be respected. In so far as things are extended modes, parallelism dictates (*E*2p7) that they must have a corresponding idea because everything that is *is* substance and only appears different to the extent that it is expressed in different ways. The intuitively stronger appearance of an 'independent' will in the case of humans in comparison with animals or tables is not a difference in kind. It is, according to Spinoza, a difference in degree. We appear to have an independent will and the power to control the outcomes of causal chains which involve our participation because we have a relatively greater ability to produce ideas on our own – that is, with less impact from external things. This appearance is not an adequate reflection of our natures however and what it reflects is ultimately a difference in physical composition, as our mind (still a mere collection of ideas) is a representation of a more complex body than the body of an animal or a table. The more complex an individual's physical activity is, the more complex ideas it can form, because its ideas will reflect the complexity of the body. However, this does not remove the fact that there is no special mental capacity (will) in some beings which is able to control their actions. The idea of an independent and free will and that the succession of events may be controlled by the force of this will is no less inadequate and false in the case of the human than it is in the case of an animal. No one is able to act or refrain from acting upon a given idea because of a separate faculty of the will that affirms this idea and not another; all things act because one particular idea and its affirmative power happens to be stronger than the affirmative power of other, simultaneous ideas. The difference between us and a cat is not that we can will what to affirm or not but that we are relatively more aware of the affirmative powers inherent in ideas.

Thus, for Spinoza 'the will' does not step in to determine whether an idea is true or false after the intellect has performed its task of forming it. Rather, we come to hold an idea to be false only to the extent that our mind picks up on a new object and forms another, more powerful, idea that affirms the content opposite to that of the first idea. We do not negatively reject an idea by denying its positive content; we form a new idea with a new, positive content which is stronger and opposite to the first. Thus, error is not something positive within a given (false) idea: it is rather the lack of a stronger, competing idea. Spinoza states:

> I deny that a man affirms nothing in so far as he perceives. For what is perceiving a winged horse other than affirming wings of the horse? For if the mind perceived nothing else except the winged horse, it would regard it as present to itself, and would not have any cause of doubting its existence, or any faculty of dissenting, unless either the imagination of the winged horse were joined to an idea which excluded the existence of the same horse, or the mind perceived that its idea of a winged horse was inadequate. And then either it will necessarily deny the horse's existence, or it will necessarily doubt it.
>
> (*E*2p49s)

We see in this passage precisely how Spinoza describes the mind and its function one-dimensionally. There is no special mental force governing what to do with the mind's product; the mind simply *is* the power to form ideas. A mind which understands everything, like God's infinite mind, affirms also that which is detrimental for a particular mode at a particular time. In so far as error is just a lack of knowledge about the whole picture, then, what to one finite thing appears as detrimental appears on the whole as natural and all good. This is the position, then, from which Spinoza questions that which Descartes perceives as a separate faculty of the mind – the faculty of willing. Instead of being a faculty of its own it is just the way by which we (humans) perceive the effects of the attribute of thought (*E*1, appendix, G II/80/10–14). Now, facing Spinoza's identification of the mind's ability to understand with its will, it seems reasonable to ask how this flat understanding of the human mind affects the concepts which seem to be premised on the ideas of free will and contingency; such as the concepts involved in normative judgements and determination of value. For Spinoza, the concepts used in those instances are coupled entirely with affects, which is the term he uses when denoting what is normally understood as emotions: that is, changes in the thinking being's state of being. This is why Spinoza moves from the constitution of the mind as a collection of ideas into a theory of the affects. This theory is central to Spinoza's normative ethics as it not only constitutes part of the attempt to correct a misguiding representation of epistemology and the question of how to attain and evaluate knowledge but also, in doing so, coincides with the means for achieving the highest possible human wellbeing. I will return to the specific upshots of Spinoza's reconfiguration of the idea of free will in relation to the human ability to make moral and legal judgements in the next chapter. Here, we will instead focus on how this reconfiguration leads to a different theorization of emotions and moral evaluation in general.

Understanding emotions as increases and decreases in the mind's power

As evidenced by the final words of the preface to Part Three of the *Ethics*, Spinoza defines emotions as affects (G II/138, in fine). Faithful to his commitment to philosophical naturalism, he defines affects, in turn, as ideas 'by which the mind affirms of its body, or some part of it, a greater or lesser force of existing than before' (*E*3d3 and *E*3'General Definitions of the Affects', G II/203/29–32). In short, emotions are nothing but ideas that as objects of affirmation have not external objects as most other ideas do but changes in the body's force of existing (*E*3d3).

Now, if the change in power is caused by the body acting on its own – the body's own movements alone causing new movements – then the corresponding idea will also, due to parallelism, be caused by an idea whose cause stems from within the mind itself (*E*3d2). According to Part Three's first definition, these causes are considered adequate since their 'effect[s] can be clearly and distinctly perceived through it'. This means that when the mind adequately causes its own ideas – that is, when the mind infers these from previously self-caused ideas – then, it acts. To form adequate ideas means, in short, for the mind to be active. In contrast with this, Spinoza calls the intellectual reflection of a change in the body's state of being which is provoked by external bodies, and which thus proceeds by ideas provoked by external ideas, a *passion* (*E*3p3).

Even though all externally induced changes in the body's state of being lead necessarily to a passive reflection in so far as the mind is worked upon by external ideas, these changes may still vary between causing a greater and lesser force of existing. In the case of a passive change in state of being which increases one's power of acting, Spinoza calls the intellectual reflection of it a joyful passion, or joy. In the case of a passive change of a body's state of being which decreases its power of acting, the mind's reflection of the change is called a sad passion, or sadness (*E*3def.3). However, changes in a body's power to act which are caused by the body itself and thus reflected by a self-produced – active – idea can only give rise to joy. The idea (emotion) representing such a change is called an active affection by Spinoza.

The explanation of why activity for Spinoza always gives rise to a joyful affection is related to Spinoza's definition of the concept of essence in relation to finite things and the impossibility of self-negation which pertains to this essence. It is important to pass through this conception as the key for understanding Spinoza's normative ethics lies in a considered understanding of the identification between activity, joy and adequate ideas.

In Part Three of the *Ethics*, Spinoza explains that 'the striving by which each thing strives to persevere in its being is nothing but the actual essence of the thing' (*E*3p7). In contrast with essence as it is described in relation to substance, the essence of finite things does not include a reference to existence (cf. *E*1d1 and *E*3p7). This implies that substance exists necessarily whereas existence is not essential to modal nature. This follows simply from the fact that to be a finite thing – a mode of substance – means *not* being identical with substance. Because substance's existence is infinite and unlimited, the existence of modes (finite as they are) must consequently be limited. Now, since being a mode implies being a particular expression of substance's being and existence, its essence involves striving to persevere in that being for as long and as much as it can. Hence, since the definition of a finite thing cannot involve existence, it consists merely in an indefinite striving to continue to be the kind of particular and durational expression of substance that it is (*E*1p24 and *E*3p6–8).

To the proposition that the striving to persevere in its being amounts to a mode's essence, we should add that *E*3p4 states that '[n]o thing can be destroyed except through an external cause'. The self-explanatory character of this proposition lies, according to the subsequent demonstration, in the fact that a thing's definition (i.e. explanation) can only affirm, never deny its nature (*E*3p4d). In other words, a thing's essence must be understood as something positive in itself. To judge by these propositions we have found Spinoza's explanation as to why adequate ideas necessarily give rise to a sensation of joy. Since these ideas constitute the mind's essence in so far as the mind's essence considered in itself implies producing ideas and adequate ideas is Spinoza's denomination of self-produced ideas, they can never be detrimental for the perseverance of the mind. Hence, the mental reflection of the change in the individual's state of being caused by an adequate idea must always amount to an increase in power, which amounts, as we have seen, to a joyful affection, or sensation. To this end, an adequate idea increases not only the individual's understanding but also his or her wellbeing for Spinoza.

It is important to point out here that this conclusion does not amount to a grounding of Spinoza's ethics in a stoic account of joy since the increase in the mind's power necessarily will be reflected in the body's increase in perseverance in being because of parallelism (*E*2p7). Thus, there is no separate sensory rewarding experience to be expected *as a result* of an increase in understanding. Understanding amounts, to this end, to both the means and end of wellbeing.

Very well, we have in place now a brief explanation of what for Spinoza amounts to ethical wellbeing, in relation to humans, and the close connection between this wellbeing and one of the means available for humans in their striving towards it. But what about the question of how to go about finding this means and not turning towards another in striving towards wellbeing: what are the major obstacles in the human ethical quest? This query constitutes the centre of concern for Spinoza's argumentation in the *Ethics* once the general ontological and metaphysical premises for a correct conception of the world, Being, existence and human nature have been clarified in Parts One, Two and Three. Crucial for Spinoza's answer is, unsurprisingly, cognition. In fact, his entire explanation of ethical impoverishment – once the close affinity between adequate ideas and wellbeing has been established – revolves around sadness as an effect of epistemological error and the removal of error as a means to remove sadness. In order to understand this approach, we must first briefly look at how Spinoza conceives of error and the relationship between epistemological error and sadness.

Association and anticipation: explanation of the relationship between inadequate ideas and sadness

Let us begin by recapitulating the core of Spinoza's theory of knowledge: ideas are reflections of objects (cf. *E*d3 together with *E*2d4exp and *E*2p8c).[8] The human mind is a reflection of the human body (*E*2p13). Because the human body is a collection of composite parts, so too is the human mind a collection of composite parts: ideas (*E*2p15d). Everything that happens in the body is, due to parallelism, reflected by an idea in the mind (*E*2p12 with *E*2p7s).

To this account we should add that since the *ideatum* of the idea which constitutes the human mind is the human body (a particular human body), external bodies that interfere with that human body will be reflected by the marks they leave on the body; by the change caused in its state of being, or power of persevering, by the interaction between itself and the external affecting body (*E*2p16c2). Strictly speaking, the mind's representation of external bodies will always be more about their effects on the body of which the mind is a reflection, not the external bodies as such.

Moreover, if, at some point, one external body which previously has affected a given body together with a group of other bodies affects that body again, the idea of the external body will carry with it the recollection of the other bodies involved in the first encounter as well (*E*2p18). The ideas of the single external body and the group of which it previously composed a part will be associated, in the perceiving mind, by their original common trace on the mind's body. In general terms, the human mind takes in external objects by the traces they leave upon the body which constitutes its primary *ideatum*, and if two or more separate bodies create a common mark, the mind's representation of them as independent singular bodies will be associated also in future encounters with either of them (*E*2p18d). This is what for Spinoza constitutes the associative function of the mind which often comes to confuse our ability to trace things' real and natural causes.

Now, let us take this associative function of the mind and put it together with the explanation of emotions as reflections of changes in one's own state of being, or, what amounts to the same (since the essence of finite things is to strive to persevere): one's power of perseverance. The result is yet another associative function in the mind. When the mind thinks of a thing that is present as the cause of more than one simultaneous emotional effect (affect), it will always associate that thing with either of these affects whenever any of them occur again even when the thing is not present in these new scenarios (*E*3p14). Thus, because of the associative function of the mind's ideas, humans will always 'be affected with the image of the thing in the same way as if the thing itself were present' (*E*3p18s1).

One effect of this associative function of ideas, according to Spinoza, is the sensation which we usually recognize as anticipation. Explaining anticipation as a result of the associative function of the mind enables Spinoza to provide rational and naturalistic explanations of emotions such as hope and fear. In the second scholium of *E*3p18, Spinoza clarifies his take on what these two emotional states amount to. They are affects (i.e. the mind's reflection of a change in the body's state of being) caused by the impact of an external object which is lacking. Thus, per definition, hope and fear reflect changes to one's state and being that are associated with one or many external things. They are, therefore, representations which do not stem entirely from the mind itself but rely on the ideas of external things to be produced. In other words, by *passively* representing changes of one's state of being, as something that is effectuated by other things, they are inadequate representations (ideas) of both the change effectuated and the thing actualizing it. The difference between them is that hope is a passive joyful affect as the idea of the missing object is connected to an increase in power to persevere, whereas fear is a passive saddening affect as the idea of the missing object is connected to a decrease in power (*E*3p18s2). The affects of hope and fear are immediate, they are not related to the actual occurrence of the things hoped for or feared. This is because of the purely representational character of ideas and parallelism. When one is hopeful one rejoices, not because it is possible to anticipate the increase in power that is the object of one's hope but because the idea of an increase in power is already present as the idea of an object which has previously increased our power, and which is now being projected into the future. So, hope as an anticipation of joy is in itself a state of joy, a state of increase, because in the act of anticipating one is, in fact, associating – representing – an event which has once affected one with joy.

From all of the above, it is clear how closely related the mind's production of ideas is to individual wellbeing. Part Three of the *Ethics* is structured so as to demonstrate the correlation between epistemological error and sadness as a lack of power and essential activity, with respect to the human being. So, let us move on now to what I said above constitute Spinoza's account of the best means towards a successful striving for perseverance and ethical wellbeing. We have seen in this section how removing epistemological error is essential for this striving, but let us now look closer at how, according to Spinoza, we should go about doing so.

In what follows I will therefore turn to the ethics of the *Ethics* and the means by which Spinoza suggests the possibility of successfully combating negative affects, that is, decreases in power to persevere in being (or wellbeing). In order to understand this question, it is absolutely essential that we keep in mind the just discussed notions of hope, fear and anticipation. This is so, not only because Spinoza's unconventional representation of hope and fear constitutes a key to understanding his ethical project in general, but also because my response to the Reports' suggestion to turn to an alternative metaphysics – understood as Spinoza's metaphysics – as a basis for a new normative ethics, wholly depends on a considered discussion of this aspect of Spinoza's ethics. This, in turn, is because international environmental law and the normative structure within which the Reports are naturally incorporated to a large degree presume a real and positive content of the notions of hope, fear and anticipation in relation to the question of an effective implementation of regulations for the protection of the natural environment.

Ethical upshots of naturalism: curing passions by knowledge

From what I have discussed so far about Spinoza's philosophical project, it should come as no surprise that Spinoza, in delineating an ethical guide, does so consistently with naturalism. Because the commitment to naturalism requires that everything is explained according to the same set of rules and definitions, Spinoza is limited to explaining 'ought' based on the same premises as are used for explaining the descriptive aspects of existence. At the outset we can say, then, that Spinoza is completely blocked from deriving ethical prescriptions from his study of human nature according to any kind of external moral standard. This is because such a standard, in virtue of being external, does not meet the basic rational requirement of philosophical naturalism. The only ethical prescriptions which can be justified in light of Spinoza's commitment to naturalism are prescripts in conformity with the natural order in which particular human beings find themselves. It is an order that includes mapping out the concrete living circumstances of a particular individual taken together with the psychological and cognitive conditions governing that particular individual at the moment and place of the evaluation. These factors; the individual's constitution together with its place in the causal order of other finite modes are, as we have seen, what determine the existence of single finite modes (see *E*p19).

Unable to define joy as an external effect of a given behaviour, Spinoza must instead explain it in relation to wellbeing understood as the immanent effect of an increase in power to exist. This is hinted at in his definition of virtue as power (*E*4d8). I said before that power (as an increase in one's present state of being) is represented as wellbeing (joy) by the mind when it has succeeded in causing its own change or when an encounter with an external object has affected its power to persevere in a positive direction. This means, then, that the mind's representation of its body's achievement of virtue amounts to the production of adequate ideas of the body's increase in power to persevere in its present state of being. In parallel, virtue in terms of the body amounts to achieving this increase in power to persevere on its own account; that is, independently of other bodies' impulses. It is impossible to give priority to either activity (physical or mental), however, with respect to ethical wellbeing since there is an absolute rule of univocality at play and parallelism that dictates the expression of substance monism. To think rationally – understanding by way of adequate ideas – simply means that the body is becoming more independent from other bodies in its actions and vice versa.

So, how ought one to go about trying to become more independent (intellectually and by parallel physically) of external things? This, for Spinoza, is the key question for normative ethics. So far, in this first part of my review of Spinoza's ethics I have argued that, according to Spinoza, there can be no prior, abstract ethical code which, if followed, will be rewarded with a subsequent sense of happiness. Because of the rational commitment to naturalism, happiness cannot be defined as a proximate result of a specific kind of virtuous activity. Happiness is adequately explained, I said, as the nature of virtue understood as power. Power, therefore, is perceived by humans as wellbeing, or happiness. However, this understanding of power is not compatible with an explanation of power as a mere increase in physical strength as that would constitute an arbitrary priority given to one of the attributes. Instead, according to the definition of the actual essence of finite things, power must be understood as all those movements (physical as well as intellectual) which make the finite mode in question (a given mind or body) close in on its own natural sense of being: thinking and moving. Keeping this qualification of power in mind, I think it is possible to go on and conclude that the transformation of Spinoza's conception of virtue into a concrete normative ethics must hinge upon the concrete and particular determination in each singular case of what increases a mode's power and what is detrimental to the same.

Perspectival evaluation of good and bad

The immediate effect of Spinoza's reconceptualization of virtue as power is a formal moral theory which does not define good and bad in terms of anything beyond our natural striving to persevere in being. Thus, the evaluation of what is good and evil can be universally and naturally explained according to each thing's particular constitution in conjunction with its essence as striving to persevere. It is not that there is one abstract universal definition of what is morally good, but there is indeed one universal way according to which all individual determinations of value proceed. So, Spinoza radically exclaims that 'we neither strive for, nor will, neither want, nor desire anything because we judge it to be good; on the contrary, we judge something to be good because we strive for it, will it, want it, and desire it' (*E*3p9s). Based on this, Spinoza's aim in Part Four of the *Ethics* can be read as to emphasize that goodness is not a standard that descends to us from a higher source, it is simply a measurement for whether we are closing in on or distance ourselves from our essential activity – and, by extension, wellbeing. Doubtlessly, he believes that the term as such does perform an important psychological function for humans, but if we are to stay consistent with the commitment to naturalism (which stipulates that everything is explained by the same laws of nature) we must understand that a human being's intellectual evaluation of other beings, always and inevitably, is conditioned by its inner driving force – the striving to persevere in its own being (*E*4 preface G II/208/8–15) and that this process is the only universal aspect there is with regard to morality.

In accordance with Spinoza's epistemological theory, when an individual sets out to determine the value of a given thing s/he cannot do so based on the nature of the evaluated thing since we are, as finite modes, ontologically speaking, prevented from taking that perspective. Rather, s/he must do so based on the mark this thing has left on her or his own body. This is because, epistemologically speaking, it is the mark on the body that is the way in which one comes to perceive and know things (*E*4 preface G II 208/10). In short, since human knowledge about external things is conditioned by the concrete impact made on the perceiving individual by the external thing in question, so too is a human evaluation of external things' value conditioned by the concrete impact of the encounter. Because this evaluative scheme is a consequence of Spinoza's general epistemology, it applies not only with respect to human beings but also when it comes to all evaluations from a modal perspective, independent of what kind of mode or being we are speaking about. To see how perspective on moral value is the only possible one for Spinoza, let us make a small digression into the metaphysical meaning of the concept of perfection.

From the perspective of the totality, things can be in no other way than they are. Substance is, for Spinoza, as I have said throughout the discussion of this chapter, the same as God understood as the whole of nature. As such, God *or* nature (*Deus sive Natura*) are Spinoza's two different ways of denominating the same thing: a single, unique, all-inclusive, active and omnipresent substance that may be called nature: (*E*4 preface, G II/206/20–25). Understood this way, substance can be conceptualized in two additional ways: as *Natura Naturans* (nurturing nature) and as *Natura Naturata* (nurtured nature). The first concept refers to when substance is regarded as a thing of its own (indeed the only thing there is) and the second concept refers to when substance is regarded as the sum total of all its concrete instantiations, or modes (*E*1p29s). Now, from the perspective of nature or substance as *Natura Naturans*, there is no room for improvement of anything, as its essence (its being or nature) amounts to its existence; its reality matches its essence (*E*1p7). Thus, it pertains to its essence to exist in precisely the way (instantiation) that it does. And because reality amounts to perfection according to *E*2d6, it follows that substance as *Natura Naturans* is perfect by way of its mere being since its essence is nothing but existence. It is also against this background we must understand the proposition that modes essentially strive towards perfection; they strive towards more reality (*E*4 preface G II 206/20–25 and *E*4 preface G II 207/20–25).

In sum, from the perspective of *Natura Naturans* (or substance as a thing), everything in it is perfect. To better understand why this conclusion is inevitable we need to consider the following. If it was possible to evaluate a given event in nature from the perspective of the whole, then there would have to be a purpose which was not yet fulfilled in relation to the existence of nature-as-a-whole. It would mean that the totality could move towards or away from a better and more ultimate state of being. That, in turn, would imply that nature-as-a-whole (substance or the totality) lacked something, at least at the moment of the evaluation, and this, in the last step, would imply the existence of a second substance. Because its perfection could not exist in a vacuum, it would have to collect its standard from somewhere. As we know, Spinoza rejects this possibility almost from the outset of his metaphysics.

Returning now to the question of moral evaluations from a modal perspective, the next thing Spinoza does in handling what he feels is a false use of the notion of good – and the first thing which we should note with respect to his construction of a normative ethics – is to say that *if* we are interested in finding out what in fact is good absolutely speaking (that is, according to the perspective of the totality or substance/nature/God), then we should look for the proper standard of measurement *within the thing in itself* and not in any of the potential responses to it (*E*3p39s, also *E*l appendix G II 83/25). This is to say that the increase or decrease in power to persevere of each and every single thing as aspects of *Natura Naturata* (i.e. as single effects or states of beings inhering in *Natura Naturans*) is the only objective variable for determining the content of the terms 'good' and 'evil'. In relation to nature as *Natura Naturans*, nothing can ever be more perfect because nature's essence amounts to a reality that is complete, lacking nothing. But, in relation to nature as *Natura Naturata*, the finite existence of every mode can of course, always be increased as its essence does not involve existence.

Spinoza emphasizes that in so far as a formal moral theory is concerned, such can never be found in the position of a being external to the acting being/thing itself. This is so because the objective standard of the good is one that varies with nature's actual and concrete activity and instantiations. Spinoza's answer to the moral problem, therefore, is a continuation of the metaphysical study's findings of what, in fact, increases an individual mode's power of persevering. To this end, Spinoza turns the good – or a thing's value – into something intrinsic. But what is intrinsic in value evaluations is not an abstract definition of the good but a measurement of power that is concrete and contextual. In doing this, he manages to simultaneously confirm that virtue can be measured objectively and reject the existence of an abstract and external variable as its standard of measurement. There is no external abstract standard which can be appealed to in advance in order to reveal what action or thing is good for oneself in a given situation; in each situation what one does will determine whether it was good or bad. Good will be whatever increases one's power. The naturalistic aspect of Spinoza's moral theory reveals that, unless we are familiar enough with our own bodies and minds to understand their relation entirely through the laws and functions of nature – the determination of right will only function as *a posteriori* affair (*E*2p44).

Spinoza's formal moral theory – that the good is whatever increases one's power – serves to prepare us for the corrective aspect of Spinoza's ethics. Relying on his version of an objective standard for value evaluations, we are in a position where we can explain how this standard can be turned into an ethical tool. What Spinoza tells us in his admittedly curious formulation of intrinsic value is that it is entirely in accordance with our nature as human beings to take our own perspectives in evaluating things in so far as taking this perspective may enhance our power. Another being's given action – which is objectively good if it increases *its own* power – *should* be understood as bad from the human perspective in so far as it diminishes the power of the human being. I say should as the human being would otherwise be acting against its own essence and, by extension, not virtuously at all – from the perspective of the objective standard of virtue.

The remaining problem in closing in on Spinoza's normative ethics is to understand what Spinoza considers to be the best way for us to find out what is *really* good – empowering – to us. Could it be, as suggested by the Reports and by the eco-ethical reading of Spinoza, that what is really useful to me is the conservation and enhancement of other beings' endeavour to persevere their beings as far as they can? In order to deal with this problem, I will now turn back to the previously established connection between the notions of power and rational understanding and I will add to the upshots of that discussion a consideration of Spinoza's definition of freedom and wellbeing.

Power, understanding, freedom

We know by now that in the specific case of the human being more power coincides with the acquisition of more knowledge, that is, a greater number of adequate ideas. To remind ourselves of what is at stake here, let us break down this argument one last time: it lies in the nature of all bodies to seek more ability to act without the impulse from external things; therefore bodies strive to seek more power to act from their own abilities. Intellectually, this process will be paralleled by a striving in the mind for more ideas stemming from within the mind itself. In light of this, we see that an increase in the mind's power requires ideas of things around the mind's body that do not depend on these things' effects one's own body. One idea is more adequate than another if it is produced by ideas already present in the mind. Paradoxical as it may sound, this way it will explain the thing it reflects not by the effects it produces on the thinking mind's body but by its causes in the laws of nature (*E*2d4, p11c). The resolution of the paradox lies in the fact that because it is ideas of our own bodies that reside naturally within our minds originally (*E*2p13), and because our bodies function in precisely the same way and according to the same natural laws as any other thing in nature, it is upon the ideas of our own body that we must rely when we try to explain external things. Reliance on these ideas for constructions of explanations of more and more things will make the explanation of external things active (as in, produced by the acting thing itself), unlike an explanation that relies on the images produced in the body by the impact of the things in question (*E*4p26–27). Passive affects are, as we know, reflections of the body's state of being that are always, regardless of producing joy or sadness, inadequate. Internally produced ideas, on the other hand, are always active and therefore always producing joy. The only certain path towards ethical wellbeing – that is, increase in power – coincides therefore with relying less on passive representations of things: representations of things that are based on their effect on us.

It becomes clear from this argument that the function of power, as the standard by which to evaluate a thing's goodness and rightness in relation to the thing itself, corresponds to the process by which we determine whether or not an idea is adequate. To be powerful, in the Spinozistic sense, is to have a mind that is fully the cause of its thoughts – which is the same as saying that the mind has adequate knowledge of things (*E*2p34, 4p26d). Later, in my evaluation of the Reports' call for a new metaphysics as a means to a new kind of normativity, I shall have reason to revisit this metaphysical premise. For now, let us focus on how the notion of power not only coincides with adequate knowledge on Spinoza's account but also takes us all the way back to the notion of freedom defined in Part One of the *Ethics*:

> That thing is called free which exists from the necessity of its nature alone, and is determined to act by itself alone. But a thing is called necessary, or rather compelled, which is determined by another to exist and to produce an effect in a certain and determinate manner.
>
> (*E*1d7)

This definition shows that according to Spinoza the idea of freedom as a state where a thing (an idea or a physical thing) is undetermined by previous causes is nonsensical and absurd. Where there is existence there is a cause. I agree with Bennett in that it follows from this that, in so far as substance understood as nature is an existing thing, it has been caused and that its actions follow laws even though these happen to be self-determined (Bennett, 1984, 315–316). Consequently, freedom instead of being synonymous with contingency is for Spinoza the measurement of events or things in accordance with their level of self-determination. Only substance (or nature) as the only completely self-caused and self-explained thing is, according to this definition, absolutely free. This does not mean that it is undetermined, as in following no causal laws. Thus, we see that as far as freedom is understood as the *ability to cause* one's own ideas or actions, power has been turned into freedom.

The human being is always, as a finite mode, subject to the limitations of other finite modes (*E*1d7). Human beings – as finite modes of substance – can therefore be free only in the same *sense*, but never to the same degree, as nature is completely free. The difference in degree between our freedom and that of nature can be explained furthermore in term of intelligibility.[9] Nature is a completely self-caused thing because it is, following from its definition in Part One, completely self-explained (rendered intelligible only by way of its own concept). We need no human being to explain nature. But, in order to understand the human being we do need to turn to the concept of nature and some of its other modes. A thing that needs another in order to be rendered intelligible cannot be called self-caused in so far as an effect is that which is *understood* through its cause (*E*1a4).

Now, what is important in this account with respect to ethics is that the relationship just described between power and freedom is a reflection of the relationship between freedom and wellbeing, or the good. An action is less good – leads less consistently to wellbeing – when it causes a decrease in an individual's power to persevere in being (to move for the body / think for the mind). A decrease in power understood this way means, in turn, that the individual mode has become less free to determine its own actions, not in so far as it is less free to choose actions (since this sense of freedom is illusory) but in so far as it holds less adequate understanding of why it must act as it does. It is at this point, as Spinoza picks up the notion of freedom as defined in Part One and lets it encounter the description of the human being in Part Three, that he finally establishes the normative ethics with an idea that, I would argue, constitutes the most radical aspect of his entire philosophy.

The notion of freedom in relation to the human mind, Spinoza cautions, should not be conceived of as a neutral freedom of choice (in relation to the affirmation of ideas) where the mind evaluates two ideas and, like a judge, chooses which one it likes best (*E*2p35s, G II/117/10–22). The only notion of freedom at play, in nature and therefore so too in ethics, is, as we have seen, a notion of freedom which defines it as the power to be the cause of one's own effects (see *E*1d7 and *E*2p48). The importance of this re-definition of freedom becomes visible once we consider (which we shall do shortly) its role in his works on political philosophy. In the *Political Treatise* (*TP*), for instance, Spinoza articulates that it is the ability to *understand* and affirm our particular existence (including its delimitation and determination) by adequate ideas that amounts to freedom in the case of the human being. This is indeed a bold claim: it is an affirmation that choice, as we normally would have it, in fact, has nothing to do with freedom, not even political freedom. Spinoza writes:

> a man can't be called free on the grounds that he can *not* exist, or that he can *not* use reason; only insofar as he has the power to exist and have effects, according to the laws of human nature, can he be called free. So the more we consider a man to be free, the less can we say that he can fail to use reason and choose evils in preference to goods.
>
> That's why God, who exists, understands, and has effects, all with absolute freedom, also exists, understands, and has effects necessarily, i.e., from the necessity of his own nature.
>
> (*TP*, 2 [7–8], G III/279/4–11, emphasis in original)

From the perspective of a normative ethics, the passage above is especially interesting. It indicates that from Spinoza's naturalistic perspective, an action which is bad – that is,. weakening – is less fully the acting agent's (free) action and more fully an action in which the acting agent is indebted to others. If we were to take this perspective as a guideline for the law, responsibility for an action would have to be treated merely as a function of how good an action is for the acting individual. If an action increases the acting individual's power, it is good, and in this case, we can say that the acting individual may be responsible for it (as long as she caused it). If an action decreases the individual's power, it is bad, but in this case, it cannot be attributed to the acting individual – alone, at any rate – since one is only able to increase one's own power, not to cause its decrease (*E*3p29s together with *E*3p48).

Now, all this may help us, I believe, to close in on the normative upshots of Spinoza's ethics: to see what human beings *ought* to do in order to maximize their freedom and, by extension, power or wellbeing. From this starting point two things follow: first, that there is no object of understanding that in itself causes more joy than another – that is, there is no physical nature or emotional state of being which on its own is better than another. It is the act of understanding that, in itself, gives rise to and constitutes joy. The extreme upshot of this is that understanding misery adequately is more conducive to a persistent sense of joy than is sensory pleasure accompanied by the inadequate idea of the external thing causing the sensation. Second, in the case of another being hurting me, the way to recuperate from the decrease of power inflicted on me is connected with an adequate understanding of the causes of the hurting action, not with removing the other being. Instead of blaming the acting agent for the hurt it has inflicted on me in an attempt to recuperate from my decrease in power – which involves staying passive, as the decrease in power is externalized – I should set out to understand adequately (that is, by ideas from within my power) the causes of my reduced power. Only this kind of *re*action to my being saddened by a passive affect (externally induced change in my state of being) can restore my level of activity and perhaps even increase it. This is so, because the increase in understanding corresponds, as we have seen, to an increase in my own activity – my own power. In a way, what Spinoza appears to be arguing in the end is that the more we can curb the spontaneous reactions of hate and blame that we feel tempted to direct towards external individuals performing actions that affect us with sadness, and the more we can come to understand how these agents came to be in the position where affecting us is necessitated in order to persevere in their own striving, the more we will experience, instead of suffering, an increase in power and a sense of freedom (cf. Della Rocca, 2008, 190). It is ideas which explain things inducing changes to our power inadequately (as something happening *to* us) rather than adequately (as the ultimate effect of a necessary chain of causes) that make us passive and reactive, not the changes or their causes as such.

Spinoza's own account of the main consequences of his conceptualization of power, understanding and freedom is presented in the fifth and final part of the *Ethics*. There, he explains that adequate understanding is a key of sorts for breaking loose from a reactive and passive existence which blocks us from becoming free and from achieving the highest possible level of wellbeing. At the beginning of Part Five, Spinoza couples the epistemological notion of adequate understanding as an increase in ethical power with the basic axiom that *everything* is the same *thing*. From this, it is evident that the most perfect state for an individual (i.e. the highest form of happiness/joy) is thus when the mind creates an understanding of its own and its object's nature and their causes from the self-explanatory principles and eternal truths of nature. This is to say that when one truly comes to understand one's own union with nature, one will find a true state of rejoicing (*E*5p3, 4 and 15).

Spinoza calls the state of joy resulting from (or rather, simultaneously to) a complete understanding of oneself as an integrated aspect of nature *amor dei* (love of God) (*E*5p36c). As such, this amounts to the human highest good. It is towards the achievement of this state that each and every piece of ethical advice in Spinoza's work is directed (cf. LeBuffe, 2010, 28–29). One possible interpretation of Part Five's representation of the perfect human being is as an individual for whom the misuse or abuse of anything external to him/herself is unthinkable as that would be, precisely, to misuse and abuse one's own body and mind. This then, is where it indeed is possible to see the virtues of arguments and calls such as those made by the Reports to turn to a philosophical order like Spinoza's as it provides us with hopes for how combating environmental destruction may be connected with establishing a new understanding of ourselves.

However, there is a problem attached to the practical execution of this idea once we understand it as an ethical imperative. The problem with identifying a collectively applicable norm with the individual ethical advice of the *Ethics* can be described as follows. Suppose, for the sake of argument that the ultimate sense of joy arising from a complete ability to cause one's own ideas is indeed attainable, not only in rare cases but for an entire collective. Only inadequate knowledge – reflections of changes in one's states of being that rely on ideas of external things – may lead to a decrease in being (i.e. sadness). Hence, a person who knows everything adequately experiences only increases in her or his own state of being. Such a person, therefore, has no conception of evil, as Spinoza also explicates (*E*4p64c). So, since good and evil are comparative and linked terms, there is no function left for the remaining concept of good once its counterpart has been taken away. Thus, in the case of the successful creation of a completely rational human being and the subsequent successful dissemination of this being's features there remains no knowledge either of good or of bad. Spinoza says as much in Part Five of the *Ethics* (*E*4p68 with 4p64). How could the collective, in this case, uphold laws created for the protection of things? Can a distinction between useful and not-useful things, in this scenario, even be upheld at all?

The same problem can be formulated as an outcome of another of Spinoza's basic ontological claims. In so far as nature includes everything (*E*1d6), how can looking at ourselves and other things from nature's perspective lead to an active protection of things? From nurturing nature's perspective, everything is equally worthy of protection; there is no difference between the artefact and the natural (*E*1p15d). The striving of carbon dioxide is as valuable as the striving of chlorophyll because perfection amounts – from this perspective – to reality. Or, to use one of Spinoza's own examples, from the perspective of *Natura Naturans* there is no evil in the storm fulfilling its striving to persevere in existence by blowing harder and harder winds and destroying more and more settlements and crops. From the perspective of nature as substance, the storm (like a nuclear explosion, or the fall of acid rain) is part of nature's reality and is – as such – necessarily perfect (*E*1 appendix G II/79/20; *E*1d7 and *E*2d7). This means that in so far as we are looking for practical advice on how to organize ourselves collectively in accordance with Spinoza's conception of virtue, it seems problematic to rely on the imperatives that can be drawn directly from Spinoza's metaphysical doctrines in the *Ethics*.

Even if we take the perspective of a single finite – necessarily passive – human being, instead of the perspective of the perfectly active nature or God, we will have difficulty in finding the basis for a normative imperative to protect other beings than ourselves in nature. Of all the normative implications noted here, it is perhaps Spinoza's conception of freedom that gives us most cause to stop and think in face of the problem of conservation and protection of non-human beings.

To properly incorporate Spinoza's conception of freedom in a normative theory one must first posit that nature (understood as substance) is free only in the sense that it understands perfectly the laws by which its effects follow. From this, it follows that humanity – as it is a finite expression of substance – does not have the power to control and steer things in nature in any direction, since this control does not pertain to substance in the first place. We may try to do so, but because all things which we perceive as unnatural interferences caused by us in relation to nature's natural systems are things that nature embraces with its complete power to understand all things, it appears mistaken to think of nature's determined freedom to act and understand as something for which humanity can take responsibility. In the following three chapters I will map out how Spinoza himself deals with this problem and how he portrays the meaning and function of political philosophy in general and the notions of law, state and international in particular.

Notes

1 Definitions 1–8 establish the meaning of the concepts of cause; finite in kind; substance; attribute; mode; God; free; and eternity. The thereupon following axioms (1–7) treat inherence/existence; conceptual dependence; causal relationship; knowledge of effects; communality among things; the relation between idea and object; and finally, the relationship between essence and existence.

2 Spinoza understands brute facts as facts without explanation. Since rationalism dictates that everything can be explained in terms of its causes, brute facts stand for facts that have not been provided with any cause and are considered to *be* just because they *are* (Bennett, 1984, 29. See also Della Rocca, 2008, 7).

3 In the preface to Part Four reality is identified with 'the essence of each thing insofar as it exists and produces an effect', see G II/209.

4 *E*2p7s referring back to Part One states:

> Before we proceed further, we must recall here what we showed [NS: in the First Part], viz. that whatever can be perceived by an infinite intellect as constituting an essence of substance pertains to one substance only, and consequently that the thinking substance and extended substance are one and the same substance, which is now comprehended under this attribute, now under that. So also a mode of extension and the idea of that mode are one and the same thing, but expressed in two ways.
>
> (G II/90, insertion in original)

5 The treatise constitutes, as Margaret Wilson points out, Spinoza's other major work on epistemology which was written before its more elaborated counterpart in the *Ethics* (Part Two). It has been considered notoriously difficult to interpret, lacking, as it does, the metaphysical structure of the later work (see Wilson, 1996, 91). However, when it comes to delineating Spinoza's understanding of truth and certainty it makes for a good starting point as it is especially concerned with 'work[ing] out a method of altering the intellect and of purifying it, as far as is feasible at the outset, so that it may succeed in understanding things without error and as well as possible' (*TdIE* 16, G II/9/10–15).

6 I say usually refers to the attribute of extension as there are ideas which arguably represent other ideas. Ideas of ideas are those that make self-consciousness possible, for instance. However, when one says the object of an idea one usually thinks of a concrete physical, that is, extended object.

7 In LeBuffe's account of Spinoza's metaphysics the representational idea of thought can be derived from his emphasis on the equivalence in Spinoza between moral error and cognitive error. It is by a different kind of representation of the thing that we find truth; equally it is by a different representation of our affects that we cure our passions. All this will be clearer shortly.

8 Curley explicates in his glossary index to vol. 1 of *The Collected Works of Spinoza* that Spinoza, following the 'Cartesian (ultimately scholastic) usage' contrasts formal reality with objective reality. Curley clarifies that according to this usage '[a]ll ideas have the same formal reality insofar as they are modes of a thinking thing. They differ in their objective reality insofar as they represent things which differ in their formal reality' (Spinoza, 1985, 648 under entry: objectively). This passage supports my definition of an idea as being of a representational character as it allows us to conclude that in so far as the nature of ideas is concerned it seems to consist in two separate aspects: being produced by, or in, the attribute of thought and being a representation of a given object.

9 In my description of the identification of self-causation with self-explanation, I rely on Della Rocca's account of Spinoza's use of the Principle of Sufficient Reason (PSR), see Della Rocca, 2008.

References

Bennett, J. 1984. *A Study of Spinoza's Ethics.* Indianapolis, IN: Hackett Publishing Company.

Della Rocca, M. 1996. 'Spinoza's Metaphysical Psychology', in *The Cambridge Companion to Spinoza*, Garrett, D. (ed.): 192–266. Cambridge: Cambridge University Press.

Della Rocca, M. 2008. *Spinoza.* New York: Routledge.

Descartes, R. 1984 and 1985. *Meditations on First Philosophy; Principles of Philosophy* and *Discourse on the Method.* Cotingham, J., Stoothoff, R. and Murdoch, D. (trans.), *The Philosophical Writings of Descartes.* 2 vols. Cambridge: Cambridge University Press.

Garrett, D. 1996. 'Spinoza's Ethical Theory', in *The Cambridge Companion to Spinoza*, Garrett, D. (ed.): 267–314. Cambridge: Cambridge University Press.

Hübner, K. 2014. 'Spinoza on Being Human and Human Perfection', in *Essays on Spinoza's Ethical Theory*, Kisner, Matthew J. and Youpa, Andrew (eds): 124–142. Oxford: Oxford University Press.

Huenemann, C. 2014. *Spinoza's Radical Theology: The Metaphysics of the Infinite.* Durham, UK: Acumen Publishing.

LeBuffe, M. 2010. *From Bondage to Freedom: Spinoza on Human Excellence.* Oxford: Oxford University Press.

Lord, B. 2014. 'Spinoza, Equality, and Hierarchy', in *History of Philosophy Quarterly* 31(1): 59–77.

Melamed, Y. 2013. *Spinoza's Metaphysics: Substance and Thought*. Oxford: Oxford University Press.

Nadler, S. 1999. *Spinoza: A Life*. Cambridge: Cambridge University Press.

Nadler, S. 2008. 'Spinoza and Consciousness', in *Mind*, New Series, 117(467): 575–601.

Newman, Lex. 2016. 'Descartes' Epistemology', in *The Stanford Encyclopedia of Philosophy* (Winter), Zalta, Edward N. (ed.). https://plato.stanford.edu/archives/win2016/entries/descartes-epistemology/, accessed on 13 February 2018.

Ragland, C.P. 2005. 'Descartes on Divine Providence and Human Freedom', in *Archive für Geschichte der Philosophie* 87(2): 159–188.

Smith, Kurt. 2017. 'Descartes' Theory of Ideas', in *The Stanford Encyclopedia of Philosophy* (Summer), Zalta, Edward N. (ed.). https://plato.stanford.edu/archives/sum2017/entries/descartes-ideas/, accessed 25 June 2018.

Spinoza, B. 1985. *Ethics; Treatise on the Emendation of the Intellect (TdIE) and Letters (Ep.):1–28.* Curley, E. (ed. and trans.), *The Collected Works of Spinoza*, vol. I. Princeton, NJ: Princeton University Press.

Spinoza, B. 2007. *Theological-Political Treatise (TTP)*. Israel, J. (ed.). Cambridge: Cambridge University Press.

Spinoza, B. 2002. *Political Treatise (TP)*. Shirley, S. (trans.). Indianapolis, IN: Hackett Publishing.

Spinoza, B. 1995. *Spinoza: the Letters (Ep)*. Shirley, S. (trans.). Indianapolis, IN: Hackett Publishing.

Wilson, M. 1996. 'Spinoza's Theory of Knowledge', in *The Cambridge Companion to Spinoza*, Garrett, D. (ed.): 89–141, New York: Cambridge University Press.

3 Spinoza and law

Preliminary question: how to narrow down Spinoza's normative ideas

In recent Spinoza studies, there is a visible tendency to approach the question of normative upshots of Spinoza's metaphysics from a wider perspective than one focusing merely on the propositions explicitly concerned with law and the state[1] (cf. Melamed and Rosenthal, 2010, introduction, 3; Steinberg, 2009, 35). While a considered discussion of any aspect of Spinoza's political philosophy obviously must centre on its explicit normative ideas, the systematicity of his philosophy as a whole supports this broadening of perspectives, so that the normative ideas are read in light of the metaphysical foundation on which they are supposed to be grounded.

Further support for taking into account the metaphysics when approaching Spinoza's normative propositions can be found within the *Ethics*. In a short passage which is situated just before the introduction of the concept of organized society, Spinoza provides support for an integrated approach to the reading of his normative ideas. The passage in question, which concludes the first two-thirds of the work's metaphysical exposition, ends with the words: '[i]n addition to this, I have also shown what the foundations of the state are' (*E*4p37s1). According to Edwin Curley, editor of the *Collected Works of Spinoza* (vols I and II), this sentence has caused confusion ever since the first translations of the *Ethics* because in it Spinoza refers in the past tense to a concept which is yet to be introduced in the subsequent proposition. He claims, even though the concept of the state is yet to be introduced, that its basis has already been established. Curley proposes that this reference means that Spinoza considers all normative ideas and concepts to be based in accounts of nature and human nature. Curley writes to this end that 'the *foundations* of [Spinoza's political] philosophy in human nature have already been laid in the various propositions [which are then subsequently] cited in Scholium 2 [of the next proposition]' (Curley, 1985, 566, fn. 20). It is not a coincidence, then, that all of the propositions cited in the scholium to *E*4p38 belong to the *Ethics*' first part which is entirely dedicated to metaphysics. In effect, Curley's argument can be understood as saying that it makes sense to read Spinoza's normative doctrines as closely related and conditioned by his metaphysical exposition of nature and human nature.

For these reasons, I will in this chapter approach Spinoza's conceptualization of law (and in the next, the concept of the state) as something that is inseparable from his metaphysics, psychology, moral theory and ethics (cf. LeBuffe, 2010, 3). The present chapter focuses on how Spinoza through the concept of law, on the one hand, ties the function of civil society with nature, and, on the other hand, ties the achievement of ethical wellbeing and virtue with an external measurement of morality. To this end, the discussion of law that I will present in this chapter functions to enable considered discussions of both Spinoza's conceptualization of the state and that of international law in the chapters to come. The overall problem which I aim to circle in on here is the fact that Spinoza's metaphysical foundation, due to its main components necessitarianism, radical naturalism and strict determinism (cf. *E*1p33 and its scholia; *E*3 preface; *E*1p25c and *E*1p29), heavily restricts the idea of a practical deliberation in a contingent context which seems to be a principal condition for any kind of normative thought (cf. Miller, 2014, 103).

Law

The *TTP* is the only of Spinoza's works which deals with the meaning and function of the concept of law explicitly and extensively (Rutherford, 2010, 166). In the *TP*, Spinoza merely reiterates what is already stated about the law in the earlier political treatise. A considered understanding of Spinoza's conceptualization of law and, by extension, his conceptualization of normativity is not only complicated by the above-mentioned conflict between contingency and determinism but also by the fact that the *TTP*'s analysis makes use of more than one definition of the term law (cf. James, 2012, 87–90).

Even though a full disclosure of Spinoza's reasons for defining law in a less than straightforward way may never be possible to recreate, the tension which is caused by Spinoza's seemingly inconsistent use of the term law can to some extent be resolved by reference to the treatise's double purpose. The first part is primarily concerned with a critique of traditional theological method whereas the second part is an argument for certain political freedoms (to philosophize primarily) and the separation of powers (*TTP* preface [8], G III/7). Thus, it seems natural to assume that the concept of law is put to work by Spinoza with slightly varying accentuations in each of these parts.

In relation to the first part's critique, the notion of law is used to demonstrate the errors of traditional interpretation of Scripture by highlighting the natural limits of human cognition (Rutherford, 2010, 166).[2] In the second part, the concept of law helps explain and motivate the divisions between the society, its sovereign authority, its subjects and citizens, and religious authority (ibid.). It may thus be tempting to think that it is the second part and its use of the concept of law that is principally relevant for a study such as the present. As mentioned, however, there are reasons for questioning this strict division and the critique it may open up with respect to the question of consistency between Spinoza's different uses of the concept of law (cf. James, 2012, 85–87). Going through

Spinoza's different conceptions of law as these appear (mainly) in the *TTP* will show that the notion of human-made, civil law (the conception that dominates the second part of the *TTP* and the *TP* in its entirety) is entirely consistent with Spinoza's very curious conceptions of divine and natural law (the conceptions of which dominate the first part of the *TTP*).

Descriptive and prescriptive definition of law

Spinoza introduces the term law [*legis*] in Chapter 4 of the *TTP*. Thus, he introduces law in the part of that work that is dedicated not to inter-human coexistence but to questions related to faith, religion and interpretation of Scripture. In this first instance, Spinoza begins by explaining the sense of the term in its most general and unqualified meaning. Understood this way, the word law accordingly means '*that* according to which each individual, or all or some members of the same species, act in one and the same fixed and determinate way' (*TTP* 4 [1], G III/57/23–25, emphasis added). There are quite a few questions that could be posed in light of this passage.[3]

What does seem to stand as reasonably clear from the passage, however, is that the definition highlights two important aspects of Spinoza's most general definition of law. First, the fact that law determines actions in a way that make these actions regular and, hence, predictable. Second, the fact that there is nothing in the general definition that points to a distinction between laws describing and those that prescribe behaviour (cf. Rutherford, 2010, 144). As a matter of fact, such a distinction is indeed inserted further on in the same chapter. It is important to remember, however, that the distinction between prescriptions and descriptions does not pertain to the definition of law as such. Continuing the same passage as the one just cited, Spinoza writes that '[t]his [law] depends either on a necessity of nature or on a *human decision*' (*TTP* 4 [1], G III/57/25–26, emphasis added).

In light of Spinoza's metaphysical commitments, this clarification seems problematic, as it highlights the necessity of reconciling prescriptive laws with the metaphysical commitments to substance monism: determinism and naturalism. Jon Miller recently pointed out in a study on Spinoza's take on the normative aspects of the ethical striving towards virtue, that Spinoza is committed to the following two propositions:

1 '[W]e are active when something' follows from our nature alone (*E*3d2).
2 '[W]e do not endeavour, will, seek after or desire because we judge a thing to be good. On the contrary, we judge a thing to be good because we endeavour, will, seek after and desire it' (*E*3p9).

(Miller, 2014, 103)

These two descriptive accounts of aspects of human nature go to illustrate, Miller argues, that the possibility of practical deliberation is at best heavily circumscribed in Spinoza's metaphysical system. How, then, is it possible to state as Spinoza does in the *TTP* that there are two *kinds* of law: one that follows from nature and is consistent with his metaphysical account and one that seems to contradict this very account?

Susan James (2012) deals with this question in her work on Spinoza's political philosophy. She notes that Spinoza differentiates between law as prescriptions issued by humans and law understood as an inert pattern of action manifesting itself naturally from the way that things behave (89). The lack of prescription in the latter category makes this kind of law appear, strictly speaking, less law-like than its human counterpart, at least in so far as the common usage of the term is concerned. James reflects that 'when philosophers or jurists describe the patterns of action they find in nature as law, they are using the term in what Spinoza characterizes as a figurative sense' (ibid.).

The most basic feature of the law, then, is not so much that of being a prescript but rather that of being *the cause of* actions. Actions which, once the laws become known become predictable and follow a predetermined pattern. According to James, the distinction drawn between descriptive and prescriptive law underscores the fact that Spinoza allows for an independent author as the cause of a given regular and determined action (someone who prescribes it) *only* in the case of human-made laws. There is textual support for this view in the section of the *TTP* concerned with the general and unqualified definition of law. In Chapter 4, Spinoza writes:

> [a] law which depends on a necessity of nature is one which follows necessarily from the very nature *or* definition of a thing. One which depends on a human decision, and which is more properly called legislation [*lex*], is one which men prescribe for themselves and others, for the sake of living more safely and conveniently, or for some other reason.
>
> (*TTP* 4 [1], G III/57/26–30)

In the case of laws described by Spinoza as those that 'follow necessarily from the very nature or definition of a thing', the cause of the externally detectable regularity and determination of the following action is something entirely internal to the action or acting thing itself. In this case, law involves no author independent of the action described. The laws described here, then, are nothing but the regularities according to which all things in nature behave. According to James' reading, what makes them laws for Spinoza are the ways by which they appear to us according to *our* limited ability to understand their real and complete causes (*TTP* 16 [53], fn. 21, Adn 34, G III/264; James, 2012, 88).

This clarification qualifies the understanding of descriptive laws as a category of law. Only if nature's laws are regarded in the light of how they *appear* to human beings suffering from limited cognitive capacities can they be said to be laws. Since descriptive laws strictly speaking are nothing but reflections produced by a human epistemological debility, they can be understood as representations of given experiences – like the notions of good and evil – rather than as carrying a positive meaning themselves. This way, at least some of the critique of Spinoza's inconsistent use of the term of law may be refuted. Descriptive laws are not laws, strictly speaking: they only appear as laws to us. If or when the causes behind that which we regard as an event determined by a descriptive law have fully been mapped out, it will seem unnatural for us to regard the event as an effect of a law and natural to start seeing it as a necessary and eternal truth. This is rendered explicit by Spinoza as he continues the quoted passage from Chapter 4 of the *TTP* with the statement that 'we've shown that the divine laws *seem to us to be* laws, *or* things instituted, just as long as we do not know their cause. But when this is known, they thereby cease to be laws, and we embrace them not as laws, but as eternal truths' (*TTP* 4 [1], emphasis added).

Resolving this tension, however, does not remove the problem of contradiction between practical deliberation and metaphysical determinism. In order to get a clearer understanding of this problem, we need to look at how Spinoza discusses prescriptive laws in his political philosophy.

Prescriptive law

As already mentioned, Spinoza barely writes about the concept of law in the *Ethics*: neither its descriptive nor its prescriptive sense. There is one striking exception to this silence, however, and it is the long and rich second scholium of the thirty-seventh proposition of Part Four (G II/237/15–239). In this scholium, Spinoza introduces the foundation of civil society and the law grounding the state. Spinoza makes this introduction by way of connecting the formation of a society with a deliberate decision and prescriptive laws. More precisely, he ties the notion of civil society to a specific kind of prescriptive human-made law.

In the scholium, civil society is presented as a product of a human deliberate decision giving rise to something that appears to be Spinoza's version of the social contract. He writes that 'it is necessary for them [humans] *to give up* their natural right and to make one another confident that they will do nothing which could harm others' (G II/238, my emphasis). Right after this explanation of deliberate choice as the ground for our human contract to cooperate, the law grounding the state is portrayed as a product of natural causes; as a mere effect of human nature being such as to always depend on the assistance of other beings for its striving towards virtue (i.e. perseverance in being) (ibid.). Spinoza's qualification of the deliberative power grounding the social contract continues with an enumeration of two entirely natural causes of the human tendency to seek mutual assistance with respect to the striving towards virtue. These are a) the fact that an affect (either passively induced or actively caused) cannot be restrained other than by a stronger affect (*E*4p7) and b) the fact that everyone always will choose the lesser of two harms and the greatest of two joys (E3p39). In short, Spinoza argues that the law grounding society can be consistently regarded as an effect of both human deliberate decision *and* strictly determined tendencies pertaining to human nature. In light of this, then, it seems warranted to ask which of these two causes of laws Spinoza refers to when he declares that '[b]y *this law*, therefore, Society can be maintained' (G II/238/10).

The same ambiguity with regards the notion of prescriptive law can be detected early on in the *TTP*'s discussion of society. In Chapter 16 ('On the Foundations of the Republic'), Spinoza first clarifies that in an unorganized state of being (state of nature) everyone's right is determined solely by one's own power. There is no external standard of right and wrong, whatever one can do one has the right to do because everything follows from nature's fully determined and active existence (*TTP* 16 [1–9]).

It is only once society has been established that it makes sense to talk about prescripts by which to evaluate behaviour in terms of right and wrong / just and unjust. Anticipating *E*4p37s2, it is stated in *TTP* 16 [5] that everyone '*had to make* a very firm *resolution and contract* to direct everything only according to the dictate of reason' (G III/191, emphasis added). To judge by this formulation, the agreement to start living according to a set of common principles (dictates of reason) seems to emerge from a *human* ability to alter the development of events. However, a little further on in the following paragraph Spinoza writes:

> And now we cannot fail to see how they had to enter into this contract, to make it valid and lasting. For it's a *universal law of human nature* that no one neglects to pursue what he judges to be good, unless he hopes for a greater good, or fears a greater harm. Nor does anyone submit to any evil, except to avoid a greater one, or because he hopes for a greater good.
>
> (*TTP* 16 [5], G III/191 in fine, emphasis added)

Here, just as we saw he did in *E*4p38s2, Spinoza qualifies the reference made to an active agency in relation to human law-making: every human being is so constituted as to always choose a constructed order over the natural order of things since everyone is naturally inclined to choose the least evil of two options available. Why? Because it is a *universal law of human nature*; that is, it is a descriptive principle of (human) nature that everyone will opt for the least of two evils and the best of two goods. This descriptive law (or fact) alone seems only apt for explaining cases where the individual holds rational knowledge about what amounts to good and bad, however. What about those cases where the decision of what is the best thing to do is being blurred by inadequate ideas of what is good and what is bad for one's own ability to persevere in the current state of being?

From the *Ethics*' discussion of affects and adequate ideas we know that what human beings perceive as deliberate decisions with respect to good and bad are, in fact, not deliberate at all. To see why we should recall Spinoza's proposition that 'we do not endeavour, will, seek after or desire because we judge a thing to be good. On the contrary, we judge a thing to be good because we endeavour, will, seek after and desire it' (*E*3p9s). It is clear from this that the determination of what amounts to good in each particular instance is far from being a deliberate decision in so far as deliberate means being free, as in an undetermined activity of the mind. Evaluations of a thing's quality are rather to be regarded as the mapping out of the effects on us humans of different natural causes. In fact, just as I hinted at in the previous chapter, Spinoza regards mental decisions as nothing but appetites or desires portrayed intellectually as deliberations (cf. *E*3p2s; Miller, 2014, 103).

Keeping all this in mind, it is evident that the tension between the idea of a deliberate foundation of the state and the metaphysical reality of necessitarianism and determinism is not lost on Spinoza. The quoted passages from *TTP* 16 [5] and *E*4p37s2 illustrate that to the extent that Spinoza grounds the origin of the state on a notion of a deliberate human contract, he does so well aware of the metaphysical restrictions on the idea of such a contract.

Now, Spinoza's resolution of this problem has much wider implications than merely those related to our understanding of the concept of law. Indeed, to judge by his self-referential and somewhat tentative presentation of the scope of the philosophical endeavour as a whole, which we can find in the early *Treatise on the Emendation of the Intellect*, all of what I have been discussing so far applies not only to law but to ethics generally (cf. Kisner, 2011, Ch. 9; Miller, 2014, 111–117). This is so at least in so far as we understand the tension that I have just outlined between deliberate choice and determinism as a tension between Spinoza's metaphysical conceptualization of the notion of freedom (and especially the free will) and a conception necessary for accommodating this notion to the context of its moral and normative use.[4] If this understanding of the problem is correct then it is important to carefully study Spinoza's explanation of freedom and the free will, not only for developing a considered understanding of his treatment of human prescriptive law but also for the development of a considered understanding of his normative philosophy in general.

In a recent essay, Yitzhak Melamed (2017) suggests that we regard Spinoza's position with respect to the idea of free will as one holding that it pertains to human nature to affirm a version of that idea that identifies freedom with uncaused deliberation, even though we are capable of learning that this, in fact, is an absurdity metaphysically speaking. Melamed argues that Spinoza considers the human idea of free (uncaused) will to be a consequence of an erroneous representation of the human mind and its functions (see the discussion above in Chapter 2). However, this does not stop him from positing, according to Melamed, that this erroneous idea plays an essential part in the human experience of life and that it is necessary for a successful human striving towards virtue.

In brief, Melamed's line of argument goes as follows. First (2017, 123), he clarifies that Spinoza's commitment to strict determinism (*E*1p28) together with absolute necessitarianism (*E*1p16) render impossible a traditional conceptualization of the notion of free will. Melamed points out that Spinoza at the beginning of the *Ethics* defines the concept of freedom as an action or thing that exists by the necessity of *its own nature alone* (*E*1d7). Thus, no single thing, not even nature (*or* God) understood as the most complete thing of all – as substance – can be considered free in the sense of being in control over what actions it will or will not undertake. According to Spinoza's metaphysical definition of freedom nature as a whole is free to the extent that its activities follow from its nature alone, not to the extent that it chooses what activities to do. Because it pertains to the essence of finite things to be effects of external causal powers and to be affected by things around them, they are literally blocked from ever achieving the same *degree* of freedom as nature or God (i.e. substance). In fact, finite things are finite precisely because of their ontological status as unfree; their own power to cause is necessarily limited by the power of other finite things all through which substance expresses itself.

So, first Spinoza rejects the definition of freedom as being an activity unaffected by previous causes (*E*1d7). Then, he restricts the application of this already qualified definition of freedom with respect to delimited finite things like the human mind (*E*1p32d). The immediate upshot of this metaphysical manoeuvre with respect to human psychology and cognition shows itself in the above-mentioned *E*3p2s and *E*3p9s. The human will, understood as a faculty to make undetermined deliberate mental decisions to affirm or to act upon something is nothing but an illusion. It is an inversed representation of the true relationship between desire and deliberation because every single idea that a finite mind produces – including its desires – is always and necessarily conditioned by ideas of things external to itself. Because finite things are conditioned by causes external to themselves to exist, to continue in existence and to cease to exist, they will always be principally unfree even according to Spinoza's qualified understanding of that term. In sum, the mind's determination whether something is good or evil is not a deliberate mental act but always, at least, partially, constrained.

The human mind will determine what is good based on what it desires and it will desire whatever it associates with a positive impact on its own state of being, regardless of whether this impact comes from within or, which is most common, from an external context. To see even more clearly why this is so it may be fruitful to look at Part Two of the *Ethics* in which Spinoza discusses the ontological status of the human mind and its faculties. In *E*2p49s Spinoza postulates that the mind is nothing but a specific representation which as such involves *an affirmation* of a specific object. In other words, Spinoza argues that to think is to will. Not in the undetermined sense of choosing freely what one will think, but in the sense of necessarily producing ideas that affirm the existence and nature of any given object or piece of reality. Now, this natural affirmative capacity of the mind is not free in so far as freedom is taken to mean being uncaused. Mental affirmations will always be completely determined and law-bound. But, to be determined is for Spinoza not opposed to being free, this much should be clear by now (*E*1d7). To the extent that a singular finite mind forms ideas (affirming certain objects) by virtue of the descriptive laws (which indeed could be called eternal truths) that determine the mind's nature and not by virtue of effects caused by external things, this mind will be relatively more free and it will experience a higher sense of self-causation than other minds. This experience, as is familiar by now, amounts to well-being for Spinoza.

The first instance in which Spinoza mentions the erroneous idea of the free will as a natural effect of human nature is in the appendix to Part One of the *Ethics*. The erroneous conception of the free will, he states, is a consequence of two ontological premises: a) the premise that the cognitive ability of finite things is conditioned by their ontologically limited position and b) the premise that finite things are naturally inclined to seek their own advantage (i.e., the so-called *conatus* doctrine) (G II/78/12–21). Spinoza writes that because humans are born, and mostly remain, ignorant of things' and events' entire causal chains, yet at the same time are determined by the universal law of nature to always seek their own advantage, human experience of actions whose causes one does not fully understand will be that these are free in the sense of being contingent and caused by the will which affirms its existence (ibid).

Melamed makes an eloquent representation of Spinoza's thoughts on this theme when he writes that '[t]he data we have about why we act, or desire a certain action, is almost always incomplete, in the sense that we do not see the known causes as *necessitating* the specific course of action or desire' (2017, 129). According to Melamed, Spinoza consequently explains the human false idea of the free will as a phenomenological experience following from our ontological conditions of existence (ibid.).[5] When a human being experiences the explanatory gap between what s/he knows about the causes constraining her or his specific actions and these actions real causes, s/he experiences them as contingent and not as necessary. Melamed turns to *E*2p35s and to Spinoza's correspondence in order to demonstrate how Spinoza construes this explanation. In the scholium, Spinoza emphasizes that the 'experience of free volitions accompanies us in every single moment in our lives, and thus the belief in free will is constantly reinforced to a degree that it can hardly be shaken' (ibid., 130). Then, in a letter to Schüller, Spinoza introduces another, even stronger, claim: the belief in free will is not solely something that is constantly reinforced but indeed innate in all humans (*Ep.* 58, G IV/266/25–26).

Now, unless we are willing to jeopardize Spinoza's entire metaphysical groundwork, this claim must be qualified. The term innate cannot be understood as referring to the will as a connatural, independent part *of* the mind (like a separate faculty) as this is inconsistent with Spinoza's insistence on both philosophical naturalism and parallelism. Spinoza's reference in the letter to the idea of free will as being innate must rather be understood as an explanation of the will as a natural consequence of certain cognitive, *necessary* conditions pertaining to human nature. Indeed, Melamed suggests this understanding when he concludes his essay:

> Spinoza seems to be asserting here that it is a *universal human condition* that we are born as beings who are striving (i.e., have volitions) [*conatus* doctrine], conscious of our striving, and ignorant of the causes of our striving. In other words, we are born into a condition that *necessarily* excites the mechanism generating the belief in free will.
>
> (2017, 133, emphasis in original)

Melamed's analysis of Spinoza's treatment of the idea of free will can help us wrap up our discussion about human-made law and how maintaining the idea of such law is possible despite a commitment to a strict version of determinism as well as necessitarianism. In Chapter 4 of the *TTP*, which opens with the already mentioned general and absolute definition of law, Spinoza himself admits the apparent tension between his definition of prescriptive of law and determinism. He explains why the notion of human prescriptive orders is worth retaining despite this tension. The paragraphs in question read:

> [3] Though I grant, without reservation, that *everything is determined by the universal laws of nature to exist and produce effects in a fixed and determined way*, nevertheless I have two reasons for saying that laws of this second kind depend on a decision of men. First,
>
> because insofar as man is a part of nature, he constitutes part of the power of nature. So the things which follow from the necessity of human nature – i. e., from nature itself insofar as we conceive it to be determinate through human nature – still follow, even though by necessity, from human power.
>
> That's why we can say quite properly that the enactment of those laws depends on a decision of men: it depends mainly on the power of the human mind, but in such a way that the human mind, insofar as it perceives things as either true or false, can be conceived quite clearly without these laws [that depend on human decision], although it cannot be conceived without a necessary law, as we have just defined it.
>
> [4] Second, I have also said that these laws depend on a human decision
>
> because we ought to define and explain things through their proximate causes. That universal considerations concerning fate and the connection of causes cannot help us to form and order our thoughts concerning particular things.
>
> Furthermore, we are completely ignorant of the order and connection of things itself, i.e., of how things are really ordered and connected. So for practical purposes, it is better, indeed *necessary*, to consider things as possible. These remarks will suffice concerning law, taken without qualifications.
>
> (*TTP* 4 [3–4], G II/58/7–28, emphasis added, insertion in original)

The first thing to note in relation to this passage is that both of the reasons given for conserving the idea of human 'made' laws, despite the ontological impossibility surrounding the existence of those laws, are reasons directed towards *representation*. First, Spinoza qualifies the notion of human decision by way of emphasizing that human power (to agree upon a law, for instance) forms part of nature's power. He writes that when something happens involving the determined nature of human beings it can, in a sense, be regarded as following from human power as human power is an integral part of nature's power. In other words, being one of the ways in which nature expresses itself, human power partakes of nature's power expression as much as anything else. To denominate certain laws as human is just another way of stating the ontological fact that there is no substantial difference between what we *perceive* as human power and nature's power.

Second, Spinoza argues that it is practical, '*indeed necessary*' for human beings to consider certain laws as caused by human deliberate decision. This is because humans are 'completely ignorant of the order and connection of things itself'. On my reading, it is possible to understand this second reason as being tightly connected to Spinoza's defence in the letter to Schüller (*Ep.* 58, G IV/266/25–26) of the fact that the idea of free will is inherent to human nature. Both arguments go to show, I believe, that Spinoza considers the idea of human-made laws as holding a distinctive and positive, pragmatic function although its ontological nature, *qua* idea, is indeed inadequate.

In being inadequate, the idea of human-made laws is not conducive to the true understanding of the object represented. Nevertheless, the pragmatic importance which Spinoza attributes to the idea of human-made law seems to indicate that he does consider this idea as an essential means to ethical virtue, which, in turn, amounts to nothing but an adequate understanding of 'the mind's union with all of nature' (*TdIE* 1 [14], G II/8/25–30; see also *TTP* 4 [4], G III/60). To judge by this twist, the false idea of the free will ends up playing an important role in the quest for adequate ideas about human nature, including the mind and the will. Consequently, human-made laws can be regarded as similar psychological facts. They are products of humans' necessarily limited cognition of the world. Even though human-made laws are inadequate ideas, they are nevertheless essential for the achievement of a less inadequate understanding of the world that corresponds to the human highest good.

Spinoza's emphasis on the practical necessity of *a belief* in an ability to create normative prescripts hints at a perspective from which it is impossible to deny the importance of the *experience* of contingency with respect to the human condition. Such a perspective can be reconciled with Spinoza's metaphysics if it is regarded in the light of Melamed's conclusion about the innate yet false idea of the free will.

All this goes to show that the idea of freedom as contingency is not only a side effect of human nature being limited. Quite independently, the idea as such is responsible for the production of a general belief in a human ability to prescribe behaviour which has a practical and normative function in so far as it phenomenologically orders human experience and provides life with a certain logic. The question that remains to be investigated is how this production relates to Spinoza's wider ethical project aimed at becoming independent of inadequate notions in understanding oneself and nature. In order to answer this question, I will now turn to discuss Spinoza's classification of prescriptive human laws according to different kinds.

Human-made laws: means to human happiness or a sovereign's decrees

Having clarified how Spinoza understands prescriptive laws generally as products of an epistemological error made by human beings, it is time to discuss the different functions which Spinoza envisions with respect to these laws. Spinoza divides the category of prescriptive laws into two further subcategories: human-made prescriptions of living for a given end, and prescriptions authored by a sovereign authority powerful enough to enforce its prescripts by the threat of punishments and rewards. As already mentioned, Spinoza initiates the discussion of law in the *TTP* by stating that humans cannot, ontologically speaking, be regarded as authors of any laws as human existence is fully determined (*TTP* 4, G III/58). As mentioned, Spinoza anticipates the strict determinism that will be expressed in the *Ethics* when he in the *TTP* writes that everything 'is determined by the universal laws of nature to exist and produce an effect in a certain and determinate way' (*TTP* 4, G III/58).

Despite the blunt rejection of human agency, Spinoza is quick to add that there are two compelling reasons for upholding the division between (human-made) prescriptive laws and (natural) descriptive laws. These are the reasons that I discussed at the end of the previous section. With these reasons in place, Spinoza has reached a position from where it is possible to elaborate on the different functions which may be performed by the phenomenological experience giving rise to the idea of humans as authors of law. Human-made laws are either laws that are prescribed (or so we think at least) by a human being or group of humans with 'the end of living safely *or some other* end', or laws that are prescribed by a sovereign ruler with the end of making people comply with its will (*TTP* 4 [3]). For the same reason that we practically benefit from regarding our actions as being guided by principles of living designed by ourselves – even though we are never, strictly speaking, the sole cause of anything in nature – so we ethically benefit from thinking that we can hand over the task of designing these principles to a third party and from letting that same third party attach a 'new purpose very different from the one which necessarily follows from the nature of laws' to them (*TTP* 4 [2]).

Just as the law grounding society, both of these subcategories of human-made law are underpinned by the supreme law of nature 'that each thing strives to persist in its state, as far as it can by its own power, and does this, not on account of anything else, but only of itself' (*TTP* 16 [4], G III/189). As is evident, *TTP* 16 [4] anticipates the *conatus* doctrine which will be given a central position in the *Ethics* (*E*3p6). I have already discussed how this natural law, or rather eternal truth, is what ultimately motivates and explains humans' misconception of themselves as legislators in so far as maintaining this belief helps preserve human beings in their current state of being. Let us now look at how, according to the same logic, this law may also explain the idea and experience of handing over one's natural right to a third party.

Basically, it is by believing that there is an individual possibility to prescribe one's own actions that humans end up establishing the state as a safeguard against a life with a constant fear of the power of others (*TTP* 4 and 16). It is imperative for Spinoza to explain the rights of the third power – the sovereign – by way of turning to a descriptive law of (human) nature because the natural right of those who better see what kind of life (life in a state) is truly conducive to ethical wellbeing is of course no greater than the right of those who do not see this (*TTP* 16 [2]).

Again, anticipating an argument we recognize from the *Ethics* (*E*4p37s2), Spinoza writes in Chapter 16 of the *TTP* that:

> among men who are considered as living only under the rule of nature, one who does not know reason, or does not yet have a habit of virtue, has a supreme right to live according to the laws of appetite alone – just as much as one who guides his life according to the laws of reason. I.e., just as the wise man has the supreme right to do everything which reason dictates, *or* to live according to the laws of reason so also the ignorant and weak-minded have the supreme right to do everything appetite urges, *or* to live according to the laws of the appetite.
>
> (G III/190/3–10)

We see in this passage how, even though shaped only in the minds of human beings, the state seems to take on a real form and perform a real function with respect to the ethical striving towards wellbeing. After the sovereign body has been (from a phenomenological perspective) installed, laws become synonymous with the rules decreed by this body. The function of laws in this context is till psychological in the sense that they are firmly attached to a promise to 'those who support the law what people most love and a threat to those who would break the law with what they most fear' (*TTP* 4 [6–7], G III/59/5–10). The notion of law, then, as it ends up being framed within the context of civil society is but a means of control, much like 'you might rein in a horse', and should be conceptualized in this context as a 'principle of living prescribed to men by the command of others' (*TTP* 4 [6–7], G III/59/5–10).

Natural laws

In both the *TTP* and the *Ethics*, Spinoza emphasizes that the difference between right in the state of nature and right in civil society is that whereas the term in the state of nature denotes an entirely descriptive aspect of life (right amounts to what one *can* do), it means in the civil state whatever is *prescribed* by the sovereign authority (cf. *TTP* 16 [1–4] and *E*4p37s2). Because the concept of human natural right coincides with whatever action an individual human being naturally does, it is evident that Spinoza couples this notion to his first non-normative definition of descriptive laws in Chapter 4 of the *TTP* (cf. *TTP* 16 [2]).

As is familiar, Spinoza conceives of nature as God or substance; as an all-inclusive and always active being which 'has no principle or end of existing' or 'acting' (*E*4 preface, G II/206/207). According to this conception, there is no basis for thinking about natural rights as rights handed down to us from a law-making power above nature. Rather, Spinoza's conceptualization of nature as an omnipresent, fully determined being that understands and affirms everything and lacks nothing, makes it impossible to think of laws produced by this being as laws only in so far as they are regarded from a human perspective: they are human description of given determined patterns of behaviour which in themselves carry no normativity. To this end, there can be no consequence or natural punishment following from not complying with one of nature's laws other than a diminished degree of one's natural capacity to act. Nature determines human actions by way of being the ultimate cause of the inner action-producing force of all finite things: the *conatus* (cf. *E*3p7 and *E*4p18s, G II/222/25–30). In the state of nature, as indicated by the *TTP*'s first descriptive definition of law in Chapter 4, humans are no more bound by an external order of conduct than are lions, rocks or carbon dioxide (cf. *TTP* 16 [2–3]). Indeed, entering into society is nothing but pretending to create such an external order of conduct and subsuming one's own power to it. The only thing that constrains human actions in a state of nature is the individual human being's ability to perform his or her particular natural functions and inclinations. This is precisely what Spinoza emphasizes in a letter to his friend Oldenburgh:

> 'But', you urge, 'if men sin from the necessity of their nature, they are therefore excusable.' You do not explain what conclusion you wish to draw from this. Is it that God cannot be angry with them, or is it that they are worthy of blessedness, that is, the knowledge and love of God? If you say the former, I entirely agree that God is not angry and that all things happen in accordance with his will; but I deny that on that account all men ought to be blessed; for men may be excusable but nevertheless be without blessedness and afflicted in many ways. A horse is excusable, for being a horse and not a man; but, nevertheless, he must be a horse and not a man. He who goes mad from the bite of a dog is indeed to be excused, yet he is rightly suffocated. Finally, he who cannot control his desires, and keeps them in check through fear of the laws, he is also to be excused for his weakness, nevertheless cannot enjoy the tranquility of mind and the knowledge and love of God, but of necessity, he is lost.
>
> (*Ep.* 78)

So, if our self-imposed constraints on behaviour (such as sovereign decrees or a common moral standard) are removed, what remains is not an absolute (divine) judgement of right and wrong. Rather, what remains are more or less successful attempts to live in a way that is conducive to one's own individual wellbeing. Thus, for Spinoza, the notion of adjudicative right is clearly part and parcel of the concept of civil society and the state. In nature there is nothing or no one that can be trusted or has the agency, to formulate, enact and supervise the implementation of prescriptive laws.

According to Spinoza, there are no *natural* means for the normative evaluation of an action's merit and this is because the notions of perfection and of good and evil have no positive meaning in themselves (*E*4 preface together with *E*1 appendix). All this we know from the review of Spinoza's metaphysics in the previous chapter. Spinoza's commitment to strong necessitarianism as well as philosophical naturalism blocks the possibility of evaluating things in nature in terms of perfection from nature's perspective. Nature, by virtue of its ontological status and constitution, must necessarily affirm *every single* modification of its attributes (*E*1p29 and *E*3 preface). For Spinoza, an adequate idea of a thing's perfect state of being amounts to nothing more than a true representation of the thing as it is, in every single moment of its instantiation. Because nature as a whole always and completely understands itself as it is, nature is always perfect. Or rather: it makes no sense to talk about perfection with respect to nature as a whole (*E*1 appendix). Humans, however, with a flawed cognitive ability and a limited perspective that confuses perception, tend to apply a fixed and external standard of perfection on themselves as well as other things in nature (*E*1 appendix). This external standard, understood in line with the definition of prescriptive laws as discussed in the two preceding sections of this chapter, appears to be nothing but a psychological mechanism (*E*4 preface, G II/205/209). Nature's laws with respect to human behaviour contain no such standard or ideals.

Divine law: prescriptive, descriptive or both?

By now, it should be reasonably clear that Spinoza makes various terminological distinctions and qualifications as he discusses the meaning of law. So far, I have tried to demonstrate how Spinoza initially divides laws into one category consisting of principles *describing* ways and natures of living and one consisting of principles *prescribing* ways of living. He then divides the latter of these two categories into the following two subcategories: principles aimed at directing behaviour without having an apparatus of obedience attached to their operation (*TTP* 4 [9], G III/59/25) and principles decreed by a supreme power having an apparatus of obedience at its service. In the previous section, my main focus was on the second of these two subcategories. In what follows, I will turn to discuss the first subcategory of prescriptive laws and explain why, paradoxical as it may seem, Spinoza sometimes refers to the laws of this category as 'divine' laws, indicating their proximity to nature's descriptive laws even though they are clearly human-made.

For the contemporary reader, Spinoza's discussion of divine law may, at first sight, seem outdated and irrelevant for our needs and concerns. However, at a closer look, it would seem that it contains elements radical enough to unsettle even the most secular and un-suspicious participants of today's post-modern and critical discourse. Not only does Spinoza's conception of divine law distance him from a large part of the Judeo-Christian theological tradition with which he contends during the first part of the *TTP*, [6] he also demonstrates that the existence of anything non-human (like God, or a general morality, or nature) acting according to an anthropomorphic scheme of prescripts and evaluations, is an unsustainable idea. What is more, he demonstrates this from a perspective internal to the Christian logic of the seventeenth century as well as from the perspective of objective reason and philosophical inquiry (cf. Melamed, 2010, 133). When Spinoza emphasizes the identity between God and nature he not only presents rational motives for rejecting an anthropocentric image of God (cf. *TTP* 6, G III/60) but erases also every possibility of differentiating between artefacts and naturally produced entities (cf. Melamed, 2010, 133–137). And this has much wider consequences for moral and political philosophy than the act of secularizing moral theory. Because everything *is in* nature (or God) and because nature's (or God's) entire existence is identical with its essence, nature (or God) is in every single aspect and expression perfect. Every singular thing – even those that do not exist in temporality – are perfect from nature's perspective, because every singular thing forms part of nature's necessary and perfect existence. This applies even to ideas of non-existing things as well as the physical causes for the non-existence of the corresponding objects to those ideas (*E*2p45s). Thus, Spinoza's discussion of divine law, as will become evident shortly, is radical even by contemporary standards of moral theory. It becomes impossible, for instance, to talk about a neutral or natural evaluation of things and events like pollution, hazardous waste and sustainability in so far as there is no natural authority of justice other than nature's constant patterns of action.

So we might feel tempted to ask, then, why Spinoza conserves the term divine law. One possible answer to this question, I think, is that it enables him to situate his own image of God as nature within a context totally dominated by the anthropomorphic terminology of traditional theology. Spinoza must take recourse to the distinction between prescriptive and descriptive laws which he has introduced and he must classify those descriptive laws that concern human wellbeing as pertaining to the first category in so far as our human perception of them is concerned. So, on the one hand, the term divine law refers to the entire spectra of principles that merely describe things' determined pattern of actions and on the other hand, he uses the term to refer to a more limited group of human-made prescriptive laws: those concerned with wellbeing directly as it were.

Spinoza's first and most general definition of law includes a distinction between rules of living issued by someone, and, rationally grounded conclusions about patterns of actions which can be called laws only figuratively speaking as they have no author. In making this division he is in good company with one of the most influential theorists in the history of political philosophy: Thomas Hobbes. According to Susan James, both philosophers argue that whereas a philosophical examination of human nature may lead to correct conclusions about the nature of the human highest good, something more is needed for this conclusion to become law in a literal sense (2012, 96).

Hobbes, presumably backing away from unwanted controversy with religious authorities, argues that the transformation of the truth about the human highest good from rational precepts to laws goes through God, who, literally speaking, decrees principles of living to us (ibid.). According to Hobbes (1998), laws of nature 'are very properly called by the name of laws; for Holy Scripture is the utterance of God, who issues commands in all things by the highest right' (66–67. See also Hobbes, 1996, 111). It is apparent that this solution is not available for Spinoza: Spinoza's God can never express itself as a subject with an independent will:[7] as a law-maker and judge. Spinoza's God expresses itself only through necessary and fully determined patterns of action which indeed are caused by God alone but not chosen in any free or deliberate sense. So for Spinoza, James argues, the only way in which the precepts to 'know and love God' can become law in the prescriptive, literal sense of the term is if some human agent prescribes:

> a way of life designed to realize them, and there are at least two ways in which this can be done. Nothing rules out the possibility that a political legislator or some other public authority may impose rules and conventions aimed at the highest good. In addition, rational individuals and communities can set themselves to realize this goal by devoting themselves to knowing and loving God.
>
> (James, 2012, 96)

As evident from this passage, James takes notice of the second division between human civil law and other human-made laws which is made subsequent to the first separation of descriptive laws from their prescriptive counterparts. Unlike Hobbes, Spinoza cannot admit that Scripture is a literal transcription of God's laws because he does not recognize God as a lawmaker. So, God's laws are simply regular patterns of action (i.e. nature's law or eternal truths, see *TTP* 4 [18], G III/61/20). He argues in the *TTP* that one can think of nature's patterns of action as decrees issued by God *in so far as* one recognizes that God is identical with nature *and* in so far as one recognizes that God understands everything that happens (James, 2012, 84–85). It is when these patterns of action slowly are being decoded by humans that they appear as divine laws, divine in relation to the human perspective.

Understanding the concept of divine laws this way – as nature's patterns of acting decoded and translated by human beings – implies of course that the act of decoding them can be done by anyone and anywhere. Because God is identical with nature, it suffices to get to know nature in order to understand God and to understand nature does not require either faith or connection to a higher authority (ibid.). From this it is clear that there is an immediate relationship between the two different kinds of divine law sketched out by Spinoza: between human-divine laws as interpretations of natural laws with respect to the human highest good and these, latter, natural (divine) laws themselves.

Now, the difference between human *civil prescriptive* laws and those laws that Spinoza calls human-divine laws is that while the first group is directed towards the preservation of the society formed by humans in order to live in peace and security, the second is directed towards achieving the human highest good individually. The two kinds of law coincide, however, in that the security of the collective, as I shall detail shortly, is a (necessary) means to human individual wellbeing (Steinberg, 2013). What is more, and as pointed out by James in the above-quoted passage, the interpretations of human-divine law which themselves do not concern civil matters may very well be placed under the supervision of a sovereign body politic. This way, this category of law is converted into a political matter and its ends become automatically means for protecting and enhancing the power of the state. In contrast, natural divine law (or nature's law), which amounts to the substantial content the perception of which is the end of human-divine law, can never be made the subject of the sovereign body's power to punish and reward compliance with laws. The 'only' effect of transgressing natural laws is the experience of becoming more distanced from the ethical state of wellbeing. So, Spinoza states that '[t]he highest reward of the divine law is the law itself viz. to know God and to love him from true freedom and with a whole and constant heart' (*TTP* 4, G III/62).

The fact that transgressions of natural divine laws are not followed by an externally measurable punishment means that these laws can be administered and rendered into prescripts by an individual or group of individuals for their own purposes. It also means that there may be different kinds of such human law (about what leads to wellbeing according to nature or God) at work in one and the same society. This conclusion fits well with Spinoza's purpose in the *TTP* to unify the concept of nature's law with that of divine law. Since the achievement of true knowledge of nature is completely independent of formal position, training and context, so too must the corresponding achievement of virtue be an entirely personal and non-institutional matter. The conclusion also fits well with the *TTP*'s other major purpose, which is to motivate and defend the freedom to philosophize (*TTP* preface [8]). To conclude this chapter, I will explain how the freedom to philosophize relates to this aspect of Spinoza's definition of human-divine laws.

Spinoza has accomplished two things with his discussion of divine law: he has made divine law valid *qua* law in so far as it is pronounced by humans and he has added that there is room for more than one such pronouncement within one and the same society as long as that pronouncement does not interfere with questions that concern 'the security of the whole people and of the state' (*TTP* 19 [10], G III/232). The simple reason for this second accomplishment is that the end goal for which human-divine law exists – the adequate knowledge and love of God – cannot collide, ever, with the principal interest of the body politic which is to ensure a safe life and security for its inhabitants (*TTP* 19 [11]).

The human civil law cannot be concerned with the achievement of the highest good for humans because of the nature of this good. The supreme law of nature, according to Spinoza, stipulates that everything strives according to its own power to persist in being (*TTP* 4 [11–14], G III/60). As we have seen, when this law applies to humans it becomes the prescript to know and love nature or God. Due to Spinoza's understanding of God as nature, this prescript consists in nothing more than an urge for humans to get to know nature as a whole. Now, as we have seen in the discussion of human and natural divine laws, because of the equivalence between knowing God/nature and the highest human good, the highest human good is attainable through the act of philosophizing and rational contemplation only, and not through obedience to any specific ceremonies or rules of conduct. Moreover, because the means and ends of the highest good (adequate knowledge) are the same, there is no civil or religious authority that can ever properly claim jurisdiction over it (*TTP* 20 [7]). To this end, we see that even though Spinoza, to a certain degree at least, seems to defend the existence of 'divine' decrees, he is also very clear on downplaying the power, or right, of religious or other authorities to interpret these decrees.

Having laid out most of Spinoza's propositions on law, it remains for me to turn to the concept of the state and state authority before we can start in Chapter 5 to tie together everything we have seen so far and relate it to the question of international law and justice. Keeping the categories of natural (divine) law/

human law and human civil/human-divine law in mind, I will in the next chapter investigate the effects of Spinoza's metaphysics on the concept of the state.

Notes

1 Spinoza does not use the term state in his discussion of civil society. Rather, he makes use of the terms republic and imperium interchangeably when discussing the organizations of civil life. In addition, he clearly uses the Latin term *imperium* ambiguously, referring sometimes to the entity of the civil state and sometimes to the sovereign authority/right of that entity. Sometimes, as in the case of *TP* 3 [17], this dual significance appears in one and the same paragraph, see Curley, 2016, 514, fn. 35. As we will see, however, this ambiguity can be explained by Spinoza's non-formal definition of the state which allows him to actually equate the exercise of effective power with the entity of the state.

2 One of these errors is for instance that we conceive of the natural events as law bound because we see them being repeated over and over again without understanding and being able to explain the causal chain leading up to their occurrence.

3 For instance, one could ask what Spinoza means by species given his non-substantial definition of an individual in the *Ethics.*

4 The understanding of freedom (and the free will) that I argue is necessary for a discourse on moral and normative responsibility is an understanding that is able to dodge not only the determinist position that everything happens in a causal continuous chain but also the extreme opposite indeterminist position that everything, is in fact, the product of chance, see Smart, 2013, 63. For a careful review of the traditional ways to approach this problem see Dahlbeck, 2018.

5 The same conclusion can be drawn from Hassing's (1980) analysis of the use and non-use of physics in the *Ethics.*

6 For an excellent discussion of this critique and its double recipients (conservative Calvinists theologians contemporary with Spinoza on the one hand and medieval Jewish philosophers on the other) see James, 2012.

7 Indeed, as will become apparent later on in this chapter, according to Spinoza the idea of a free will turns out to also be a fiction with regard to the human being.

References

Curley, E. 1985. *The Collected Works of Spinoza*, vol. I. Princeton, NJ: Princeton University Press.

Curley, E. 2016. *The Collected Works of Spinoza*, vol. II. Princeton, NJ: Princeton University Press.

Dahlbeck, J. 2018. *Education and Free Will: Causal Determinism and Moral Formation.* Abingdon, UK: Routledge.

Hassings, R.F. 1980. 'The Use and Non-Use of Physics in Spinoza's Ethics', in *The Southwestern Journal of Philosophy* 11(2): 41–70.

Hobbes, T. 1996. *Leviathan.* Tuck, R. (ed.). Cambridge: Cambridge University Press.

Hobbes, T. 1998. *On the Citizen.* Tuck, R. and Silverthorne, M. (eds). Cambridge: Cambridge University Press.

James, S. 2012. *Spinoza on Philosophy, Religion, and Politics: The Theologico-Political Treatise.* Oxford: Oxford University Press.

Kisner, M.J. 2011. *Spinoza on Human Freedom: Reason, Autonomy and the Good Life.* Cambridge: Cambridge University Press.

LeBuffe, M. 2010. *From Bondage to Freedom: Spinoza on Human Excellence*. Oxford: Oxford University Press.

Miller, J. 2014. 'Spinoza on the Life According to Nature', in *Essays on Spinoza's Ethical Theory*, Kisner, M.J. and Youpa, A. (eds): 102–123. Oxford: Oxford University Press.

Melamed, Y. 2010. 'The Metaphysics of the Theological-Political Treatise', in *Spinoza's 'Theological-Political Treatise': A Critical Guide*, Melamed, Y. and Rosenthal, M.A. (eds): 128–142. Cambridge: Cambridge University Press.

Melamed, Y. 2017. 'The Causes of Our Belief in Free Will: Spinoza on Necessary, "Innate," yet False Cognition', in *Spinoza's Ethics: A Critical Guide*, Melamed, Y. (ed.): 121–141. Cambridge: Cambridge University Press.

Melamed, Y. and Rosenthal, M.A. 2010. 'Introduction', in *Spinoza's 'Theologica-Political Treatise': A Critical Guide*, Melamed, Y. and Rosenthal, M.A. (eds): 1–11. Cambridge: Cambridge University Press.

Rutherford, D. 2010. 'Spinoza's Conception of Law: Metaphysics and Ethics', in *Spinoza's 'Theological-Political Treatise': A Critical Guide*, Melamed, Y. and Rosenthal, M.A. (eds): 143–167. Cambridge: Cambridge University Press.

Smart, J.J.C. 2013. 'Free Will, Praise and Blame', in *Free Will* (2nd edn), Watson, G. (ed.): 58–71. Oxford: Oxford University Press.

Spinoza, B. 2016. *Letters (EP)*: 29–41 and 42–84. Curley, E. (ed. and trans.), *The Collected Works of Spinoza*, vol. II. Princeton, NJ: Princeton University Press.

Spinoza, B. 1985. *Ethics; Treatise on the Emendation of the Intellect (TdIE) and Letters (Ep.):1–28.* Curley, E. (ed. and trans.), *The Collected Works of Spinoza*, vol. I. Princeton, NJ: Princeton University Press.

Spinoza, B. 2007. *Theological-Political Treatise (TTP).* Israel, J. (ed.). Cambridge: Cambridge University Press.

Spinoza, B. 1995. *Spinoza: The Letters (Ep).* Shirley, S. (trans.). Indianapolis, IN: Hackett Publishing.

Steinberg, J. 2009. 'Spinoza on Civil Liberation', in *Journal of the History of Philosophy* 47 (1): 35–58.

Steinberg, J. 2013. 'Spinoza's Political Philosophy', in *The Stanford Encyclopedia of Philosophy* (Winter Edition), Zalta, E.N. (ed.). https://plato.stanford.edu/archives/win2013/entries/spinoza-political/, accessed on 19 March 2018.

4 Spinoza and the state

The first obstacle to overcome with respect to Spinoza's explanation of the state is the fact that he explains it in a way that opens up for both a contractualist and a naturalist understanding of the social contract. Drawing on the previous chapter's analysis of prescriptive laws in the light of Spinoza's commitment to strict determinism and philosophical naturalism, I will in this chapter argue that the idea of the state for Spinoza is premised on the same mechanisms that render necessary the false idea of the free will and the concept of law. In the end, my review of Spinoza's conception of the state will show that the question of *how* to organize civil society is secondary to the question of the idea's pragmatic *function* in relation to our human experience of the ethical striving towards wellbeing (cf. Steinberg, 2008).

One of the most contended issues in the contemporary reception of Spinoza's political philosophy is whether he sustains a social contract or not. Most discussions about his political philosophy revolve around the question whether Spinoza affirms that the state is a natural consequence of human nature, or whether it emerges as a result of human deliberate decision to break free from nature (Wernham, 1958; Matheron, 1990; Balibar, 1997; Barbone and Rice, 2000). The fact that this issue has not yet been satisfactorily settled indicates that the debate is related to an ambiguity inherent to the arguments used by Spinoza for detailing his version of the foundation of civil society. Revealingly, there are statements in his works which seem to support a theory of the state based on a social, conscious contract among human beings (*TTP*, G III/58; G III/198 and E4p37s2).[1] Simultaneously, however, there are other statements (mainly in the *TP*) which seem to describe the state as an individual finite mode, like any other in nature (cf. Steinberg, 2008, 249). For instance, in *TP* 1 [7], Spinoza claims that 'we must seek the causes and natural foundations of the state, not from the teachings of reason, but from the common nature, *or* condition, of men' (G III/276, emphasis in original).

As delineated in the previous chapter, the same problem of ambiguity seems to be present in Spinoza's account of the notions of law and right. Do individuals deliberately give up their natural rights going into civil society or do these rights, descriptive as they are, co-exist with the state's order? Indubitably, there is textual evidence for both positions in the *Ethics* as well as the *TTP*. On the one hand,

Spinoza clearly expresses in the *TTP* (cf. 16 [2], G III/291/14–15) that no one can give up one's natural right entirely as this would mean giving up one's existence (as right in the state of nature amounts to power and existence ultimately boils down to power to act). On the other hand, Spinoza writes at various places things like:

> unless we want to be enemies of the state and act contrary to reason, which urges us to defend the state with all our powers, we're bound to carry out absolutely all the commands of the supreme power – even if it commands the greatest absurdities.

This implies that we sometimes must act contrary to our natural right to do what best preserves our states of being (*TTP* 16 [27], G III/194. See also *TP* 2 [16], G III/282/3–4).

I will suggest in this chapter that there is a way to avoid the conclusion that the two kinds of statement amount to a contradiction. In what follows, I will review Spinoza's treatment of the notions of governance and sovereignty in order to demonstrate that it is possible to formulate a solution to this apparent paradox. In the end, I will maintain that the seemingly contradictory positions expressed throughout Spinoza's work when it comes to the state can indeed be understood as forming a coherent argument in which all of the statements and their corresponding ideas are mutually reinforcing. I will first of all admit that Spinoza's metaphysical account of the state leaves no room for a deliberate human decision as the basis of the social contract. However, I will also emphasize that this does not mean that the references made to such deliberate decisions in Spinoza's discussions of the state (like those we find in his discussions of law in the *TTP*) should be rejected as mistaken. The idea of the state (just like that of law) understood as a human product seem to play a decisive role in Spinoza's philosophy, as it forms part of a phenomenological explanation of normativity which is necessary for a successful human striving towards virtue and wellbeing.

Governance, power and self-knowledge

In *TP* 2 [10] Spinoza defines what it means to have another being in one's power. He does so in a way that makes it clear that for him governance covers a much broader spectrum of activities than merely those involving physical or psychological forms of coercion. It is also evident from this paragraph that Spinozistic governance does not require a formal or substantial transference of rights or titles. *TP* 2 [10] reads:

> One person has another in his power [a] if he has him tied up, or [b] if he has taken away his arms and means of defending himself or escaping, or [c] if he has instilled fear in him, or [d] if he has so bound him to himself by a benefit that the other person would rather conduct himself according to his benefactor's wishes than according to his own, and wants to live according to his

> benefactor's opinion, not according to his own. Someone who has another person in his power in the first or second of these ways possesses only his Body, not his Mind. If he has him in his power in the third or fourth way, then he has made both his Mind and his Body subject to his control – but only while the fear or hope lasts. When either of these is taken away, the other person remains his own master.
>
> (G III/280/7–10)

The way by which Spinoza in this passage places the emphasis on the connection between psychological dependence and losing one's self-mastering ability is truly remarkable. It is so in so far as singling out the second and third means of governance from those connected to physical coercion has the double effect of emphasizing the importance of the notions of hope and fear with respect to governance, and of disconnecting the question of self-control from the question of physical dependence. In other words, it appears as if Spinoza in this passage rejects the existence of a contradiction between being physically completely limited by another being and being in complete self-control. This rejection is troublesome for a coherent understanding of his political philosophy because it seems to indicate that there is indeed a substantial difference between mind and body (physical coercion being less intrusive on 'the self' than mental coercion) at work here, in the normative writings, which is not present in the metaphysical system. How is it possible to understand this passage, then, given Spinoza's clear commitment to philosophical naturalism and the doctrine of parallelism? One way, I think, is to focus on what Spinoza means, metaphysically speaking, by control and self-control.

Taking this focus will lead us to *TP* 2 [15] where Spinoza accentuates that 'as long as the human natural right is determined by each person's power, and belongs to that person [i.e. in the state of nature], *there is no human natural right.* It consists more in opinion than in fact, since there's no secure way to maintain it' (G III/281/15–20, emphasis added). This statement clearly indicates a correlation between the existence of a formal apparatus of governance and right. Without the act of formally handing over one's own power (right) to someone else, there can be no right more than in a nominal sense, because right understood as power requires a certain level of effective order to be extinguished immediately. Understanding power and natural right this way appears to create another contradiction however: a contradiction between this nullification of right in a state of nature and the emphasis (in both the *TTP* and Part Four of the *Ethics*) on the naturalness by which there is a transformation of the notion of right when people move from a state of nature to that of civilized society. As far as I can tell, the emphasis on a natural transformation from the state of nature to the civil state implies that there are rights before the conclusion of a social contract. If I am correct in this, then the passage in *TP* 2 [15] seems to also contradict what Spinoza writes in the previously quoted passage from *TP* 2 about governance being a question of both psychological and physical power.

It is in the context of making sense of these apparently conflicting statements about governance that it seems reasonable to proceed with a careful reading of

Spinoza's conception of self-control, or *sui iuris*, which is term of choice for Spinoza when he speaks of this in relation to the context of the metaphysical aspects of rights.[2] Justin Steinberg (2008) makes some very valuable points with respect to decoding Spinoza's understanding of *sui iuris* and its relationship to the concept of governance (239–249). In brief, Steinberg's argument is that one must turn to Spinoza's twofold metaphysical definition of power in order to fully appreciate the political significance of *sui iuris* as a mark of good governance (ibid.). I would add to this reflection, perhaps, that a careful study of power and *sui iuris* also can help us comprehend the ambiguity communicated by the various meanings attached to the term governance in Spinoza's political philosophy.

Like so many other notions, Spinoza works with a multifaceted conception of power. First, he defines power in terms of metaphysics and then he recalls the concept's traditional normative meaning and points out the difference between the two conceptualizations. Spinoza does not reject but retains the meaning attributed to power in traditional normative contexts (just as he does when he discusses the concepts of good and evil). He does so, however, in a way that is compatible with his metaphysical understanding of the concept although the two seem to be mutually exclusive. It is Spinoza's commitment to respect the metaphysical definition of the concept of power *within* the realm of normativity where an alternative conception simultaneously must be entertained that renders his work on governance unique. As evident from the passage quoted above (*TP* 2 [10]), Spinoza clearly affirms a 'relational' political conception of governance which is usually associated with traditional liberal political philosophy: to be governed is to be under someone else's control or authority (Steinberg, 2008, 244). However, as I have already pointed out, 2 [10] also extends this conception so as to include all kinds of dependence, not merely physical and psychological coercion. What is more, this extension is effectuated by an invocation of precisely the metaphysical sense of power as a kind of self-determination, or self-mastering, which does not produce any empirically measurable effects.

Steinberg argues that in fusing the two conceptions of power Spinoza inserts a more fundamental – metaphysical – non-relational definition of power into his own political theory. The metaphysical definition inserted is arguably non-relational in so far as power for Spinoza (metaphysically) means activity and activity, in turn, is the same as being the sole cause of whatever effects are produced. In the case of the human being, the ultimate expression of power understood this way is a mind able to cause all of its ideas on its own (Steinberg, 2008, 247). Continuing Steinberg's line of thought, we can say that Spinoza argues that to be under the physical governance of another being does not automatically amount to rendering a person more dependent, or constrained, at least not in terms of metaphysical independence. And conversely, one ought to be able to have another completely under one's control without this control having any empirically detectable repercussions. In other words, all cases of being governed by another in the sense that one's thoughts and actions are determined by this other are not empirically detectable and measurable.

However, this only brings us back to the problem with which I began this discussion: the fact that Spinoza states that even though there are no formal restrictions on one's expressions of power in the state of nature, any power expression in this state of being is in practice of an illusory character, because human beings have no ability to express or safeguard that power without the formal apparatus of the state. The problem, now, is to reconcile this idea with the idea that physical and psychological expressions of power are *not* sufficient to cover the concept of power, not even in the civil state. In other words, the problem is that *if* there is a sense of power pertaining to the state of nature that can be conserved and expressed in the civil state but that collects its original meaning only in a state of nature, then, how can the expression of this sense be exclusive to the civil state?

Spinoza uses the terms *potestas* and *potentia* interchangeably to denote aspects of power. It is possible to juxtapose Spinoza's use of these two terms with Steinberg's discussion of *sui iuris* and the difference between a metaphysical and a normative understanding of power. Doing so renders visible that the split between *potestas* and *potentia* enables Spinoza to express his political theory in a way that fits with both the classic libertarian equation of individual freedom with a political right to participation (*TTP* 5, G III/95 and *TTP* 16, G III/137), and, with a less instrumental and more functional definition of governance as something that impacts positively the individual ability to think independently and understand the nature of things (Steinberg, 2008, 243–248). Power as *potestas* can be read as pointing to the phenomenological experience of giving up one's right to decide over one's own activities when the real causes for these activities are not clear to oneself. *Potentia*, on the other hand, seems to refer more to the underlying natural power to strive to persevere in one's present state of being and to the power which determines every action one makes, including the action to obey a law or someone else's order. Spinoza seems to give primacy to this metaphysical definition of power.

Accordingly, perhaps the solution to the apparent paradox between the following kinds of statement lies in Spinoza's metaphysical explanation of human power (cf. *E*3p7d):

> it follows that obedience has no place in a social order where sovereignty is in the hands of everyone and laws are enacted by common consent, and that whether the laws in such a social order are increased or diminished, the people nevertheless remains equally free, *because it does not act from the authority of someone else, but by its own consent.*
>
> (*TTP* 5 [25], G III/74/21–27, my emphasis)

> insofar as one is made to obey the law from *any motive whatsoever*, one stands under the right of the commonwealth and thereby is not *sui iuris* [i.e. in control of one's own power].
>
> (*TP* 3 [5], my emphasis)

When the last passage ends, the following paragraph states that 'sound reason cannot dictate that everyone should remain *sui iuris*' (*TP* 3 [6]). This, to me, implies a slight conceptual primacy given to *potentia*. Let me explain. *TP* 3 [6] may be a good place to start when looking for a solution to the paradox described above. The conceptual primacy is established in so far as 'sound reason' in *TP* 3 [6] is read as making reference to the metaphysical meaning of power (power as self-production of acts and ideas, as *potentia*)[3] while the concept of '*sui iuris*' here is read as making reference to power as the cause of empirically noticeable effects (power perceived as physical and psychological coercion, as *potestas*). Reading the statement this way allows for the following interpretation: metaphysical *power*, that is, self-determination as in an individual, internal and ethical experience of independence, will lead to appreciating the fact that causal control over physical events is not possible, let alone desirable.

This conclusion explains how the question of maximization of one's independence ethically speaking (*potentia*) can be administered only while we conceive of the will and desire as something that can be handed over to someone else, as something that indeed *can* be mastered by someone else. The fact is of course that since a human being never can be completely in causal control over her own production of ideas (natural right is illusory in the state of nature), her will and her desire are not really hers to give away. However, and here is the twist, this fact amounts to parts of the content of the knowledge required for achieving ethical wellbeing. The twist, then, is that the knowledge required for ethical wellbeing amounts to the determined and necessitarian nature of things whereas the successful achievement of this knowledge is facilitated by the opposite representation of things. Going back to the paradoxical statements which we have detected in the *TP*'s discussion of governance and *sui iuris*, I suggest that we read the reference in *TP* 3 [5] about all kinds of handing over of rights amounting to a loss of one's freedom as referring to a loss of power only in the sense of *potestas*, of the empirically measurable effects of being in a position of physical and psychological disadvantage.

This suggestion is indeed supported by further propositions of the *TP*. *TP* 3 [7], for instance, reads:

> just as in the state of nature the man who is guided by reason is most powerful [*maxime potens*] and most fully *sui iuris* (by Section 11 of the previous Chapter), so also the commonwealth which is based on and directed by reason will be the most powerful [*maxime potens*] and most fully *sui iuris*.
> (G III/287/4–8)

In line with the understanding of power/governance that I have been outlining here, this passage too can be read as maintaining that the ethical power to cause ideas of one's own may be enhanced by a particular organization of society. Phrased differently, a sovereign body that grounds its orders on certain principles about what will enhance individuals' ability to understand, will also be absolutely powerful in terms of *potestas*. This is so at least in so far as its subjects will have no desire to express an individual, empirically measurable power in contrast to that of the state. In short, there is a correlative between power as *potestas*, that is, as a relational force and power as *potential*, that is, as an unrelational force.

Steinberg instructs us well when he writes 'there is a sense of "right" (*ius*) that is bound up not with *potestas*, or authority, but with *potentia*, or power/strength; and there is a corresponding sense of being *sui iuris* (being of one's own right) [*potentia*] that is coextensive with being powerful [as in *potestas*]' (2008, 246). The correlation which is drawn by Steinberg between the different senses attributed by Spinoza to the notion of power is not, however, either a parallel or a symmetric relation. There are many arguments both in the *TTP* and the *TP* that demonstrate this. For instance, it is clear that an individual human being's ethical *sui iuris* (powerful *qua potentia*) does not depend to the same degree on political freedom to determine those of one's actions which have an empirical measurability (power as *potestas*) as good governance on part of the state – a governance that increases its subjects' ethical *sui iuris* as it were – depends on the state's degree of ethical *potentia*, demonstrated by rational laws and decrees.

Finally, and to underscore the relationship that I have been trying to show between *potestas* and *potentia* with respect to governance, it may be wise to go back to the question of how the state is formed in the first place. In *TP* 2 [13] Spinoza writes that if we are to satisfy our basic ends in life, of living safely and in a state of mutual respect, then it is essential that we join forces with each other. Such a joining, we know, requires that our natural right to do what we want is given up: 'putting ourselves under the authority (*sub potestate*) of the sovereign' (Steinberg, 2008, 248).[4] The same message can be found within one of the pieces of the *Ethics*' self-therapeutic advice where Spinoza writes that a person 'is more free in a state, where he lives according to a common decision, than in solitude, where he *obeys* [*potestas*] only himself' (*E*4p73, G II/264). It would seem then that the term *potestas* denotes only a partial understanding of what freedom and power are and that an adequate understanding of these concepts requires the incorporation also of the notion of *potentia*. According to Spinoza, it is *not* more beneficial for the individual human being's striving towards a maximization of her metaphysical power (*potentia*) to live in the state of nature than it is to live in a civilized community. In fact, it is the other way around. In a state, where everyone's ability to influence others' power (*potentia*) to persevere, that is, their power to rationally understand, is restrained by an external power [*potestas*] who limits and governs the external expressions of inter-human influence, the individual striving towards ethical wellbeing is always enhanced, regardless of the state's formal constitution. This is why Spinoza states in the *TP* that any kind of state is better for the expression of a human natural right, which cannot find the means for expressing itself on its own; that is, in the state of nature.

There is one particular upshot from all of the above stated that I think deserves special consideration. It may be wise to depart from this point when returning to the problem underscored by the passage from *TP* 2 [10] (cited above) concerning how to reconcile governance understood as physical and psychological coercion and the overarching metaphysical commitment to strict philosophical naturalism and determinism. The upshot is the following: it is evident from Spinoza's use of the concept of power that he considers ethical wellbeing understood as one of the ways in which power can be expressed as being not a contradiction but rather a consequence of adhering to the sovereign's demands, even in cases where these demands seem absurd and contrary to reason (cf. Steinberg, 2008, 243–248 where he calls attention to *TP* 3 [5–6] and *E*4p73, G II/264). As pointed out at various places in the *TTP*, however, this does not take away the fact that a rationally governed state is better for the individual pursuit of ethical wellbeing than is an irrationally governed one. In sum, then, we can say that although the individual striving towards wellbeing *always* benefits from being subjugated by a (any) sovereign order, certain kinds of order will be better than others in enhancing their subjects' ethical striving.

Spinoza's separation of the normative understanding of power from its metaphysical counterpart makes it possible to argue for an almost absolute right of the state without jeopardizing the individual ethical project. Relying on *TP* 3 [6] to explain the apparently problematic result of juxtaposing *TP* 2 [10] with 2 [15] makes it clear that it is more beneficial for the individual ethical project to respect the authority (*potestas*) of the state than it is to ensure that one's actions are always guided by reason independently of what the law stipulates. This is to say that it is always in one's true self-interest, that is, it is always in accordance with reason, to obey the commands of the sovereign. This is so, even to the extent that these commands are irrational or absurd. The key for decoding Spinoza's seemingly paradoxical statements with regard to governance seems to be to remember that a state's *form of governance* [5] is not of as central importance as is its actual existence, for the question of success or failure of its subjects' ethical striving (Steinberg, 2008, 249).

As already mentioned, this does not mean that the question of the form of government is irrelevant for Spinoza. Quite the contrary, Spinoza is clear on highlighting the superiority of one form of governance over all other plausible ones. This form is superior in so far as it has a greater capacity for producing the kind of self-determination of the human mind that Spinoza in the *Ethics* associates with the ethical power (*potentia*) to persevere in being. Spinoza's discussion of this particular form of governing is what I will delineate next.

Sovereignty as freedom

In the *TP*'s first chapter Spinoza defines sovereignty as the common right of men when they are led *as if* by one mind (1 [16–17]). Thus, sovereignty is attached to a substantial requisite of *absolute* power (*potestas*) over those who are affected by the power (ibid.). Now, according to a later paragraph in the same chapter, the requisite of absolute power attached to sovereignty cannot be obtained 'unless the State has laws established according to the prescription of reason' (*TP* 1 [21]). So, from paragraphs 16, 17 and 21 of *TP* 1 we can infer that a) sovereignty is accomplished to the degree that the governing body's power (*potestas*) is absolute, and, b) this can only be established through orders that are rational, that is, orders that aim at increasing the state's own *potentia* by increasing its subjects' *potentia*.

Given this first description of sovereignty, Spinoza's following declaration that 'taken strictly, injustice can be conceived only in a State' seems a little odd to say the least (ibid.). It seems odd in so far as it indicates precisely the opposite of what we have just said can be inferred from *TP* 1 [11, 17 and 21]: namely that the question of what constitutes good (just) governance can be objectively measured by way of relying on the variable of reason. If this indeed is Spinoza's position, how come he qualifies this right away by indicating (in the same paragraph 21) that there is no variable beyond the one opted for by the sovereign power itself for determining justice and righteousness?

Again, we seem to have stumbled over an apparent paradox in Spinoza's account of the state. On the one hand, Spinoza states that 'it's not improper for men who've become accustomed to live in a State to call something a sin [or unjust] if it is contrary to the dictate of reason' (*TP* 2 [21]). On the other hand, he holds that 'we ought to be mindful that we are in God's power as clay is in the power of the potter, who from the same mass makes one vessel for an honorable purpose and another for a dishonorable one' (*TP* 2 [22]). In the first statement there seems to be an absolute requisite of justice at work, in the second statement the existence of such a requisite seems to be rejected.

Let us see if this paradox too can be resolved by clarifying to whom each statement is directed. In absolute, metaphysical terms, we know that acting contrary to reason is acting contrary to what is right (or just) since right in an absolute – non-social – sense means whatever is conducive for *potentia*: that is, increase in power reflected by rational understanding. From the concrete and particular perspective of the human being as a finite mode, however, it is right – as in beneficial for *potentia* – to act in accordance with a fixed external scale of what is just and unjust. Reading *TP* 2[21] and [22] together, we end up with the following image. All expressions of power (whether *potestas* or *potentia*) are from the metaphysical perspective perfect, just or righteous. This is because all expressions amount to nature's fulfilment of its own necessary and absolutely active power. What appears as a lessened degree of someone's expression of *potentia* or *potestas* is only this to the extent that it is being superimposed by someone else's increase of the same. From the perspective of the whole, the power-expression will always be positive and complete. This ontological position brings about two immediate consequences with respect to the discussion of sovereignty of the state. First, from the individual's perspective, righteousness and justice can effectively be measured in relation to what increases the individual's (the state or one of its subjects) power understood as *potentia*: that is, the ability to form rational ideas. This means that the state, functioning like any other individual with respect to the metaphysical understanding of power, will be more powerful and thus more sovereign if it implements standards of justice and righteousness that are solely based on rational terms. *TP* 2 [21] establishes that the subjects of a state that rules this way will think of the question of righteousness in terms of rationality since this state has effectively equated the two standards. However, as is clarified by 2 [22], the fact that a sovereign state is one in which the subjects are encouraged to associate its definition of just and unjust with what is dictated by reason *does not* mean that its definition ceases to be, strictly speaking, an irrational one in so far as its dissemination and implementation are concerned. The subjects of this state are equally constrained in their expressions of power as *potestas* as are the subjects governed by a strict, physically violent and irrational state power. This amounts to the second consequence. To sum this up, Spinoza explains that:

> we ought to remember that a man can indeed do something against these decrees of God [dictates of reason] which has been inscribed as laws in our Mind, or in the Mind of the Prophets. But he can't do anything against God's eternal decree, which has been inscribed in the whole of nature and concerns the order of the whole of nature. Therefore, like sin and obedience, taken strictly, so also justice and injustice can be conceived only in a state.
>
> (*TP* 2 [22–23])

We may, first of all, infer from this passage that the state's own striving to persevere in being benefits from formulating and enacting rational dictates; dictates associating right with what certainly increases people's ability to self-preserve. We may also infer, however, that the state's practical ability to assist its subjects in their individual striving towards self-preservation (i.e. rational understanding) hinges on a capacity to formulate norms and principles which are able to affect all of its subjects. Thus, these norms must be cast in inadequate terms – even if they happen to revolve around rational precepts – in so far as their affective power must be able to reach individuals who nourish hopes of rewards and fears of punishments. This means that even though a state, in theory, could be able to achieve complete sovereignty – which we know now means that its form of government is entirely rational – its dictates must still operate on a level inherently attached to irrational and inadequate understandings. All laws emitted by the sovereign power of a body politic, indeed all human-made laws, are necessarily of an illusory character in so far as their ontological status is concerned. As we saw in the previous chapter, this is because they operate with an evaluative apparatus that presumes a fixed and absolute standard of good and evil. Such a standard is completely nonsensical from the perspective of nature as a whole and its purely descriptive principles of behaviour.

In short, in accordance with the same structure that we detected with respect to the concept of governance in the previous section, Spinoza maintains with respect to sovereignty that while there is no metaphysical basis for saying that a governing body's particular intent to become sovereign is more legitimate than any other, there is indeed a substantial standard (rationality) for measuring a state's ability to encourage its subjects to live in peace and security which, in turn, constitutes a necessary condition for its sovereignty. A state will indubitably be less successful in becoming sovereign if it only makes laws and orders by way of tapping into peoples' deepest and most primal fears and hopes. But, even a state that refrains from this method and instead allows reason to dominate public discourse will have to operate, to some degree at least, on the level of irrationality. Because it is natural for human beings to evaluate and desire according to their own limited and confused perspectives, and because an adequate idea does not necessarily hold more affective power than an inadequate one, the state must manifest its power by way of irrational ideas and images in order to get *everyone* to see the individual benefits of living under a common rule.

The fact that the issue of sovereignty impedes the state's operation on the level of irrationality does not make sovereignty, or the state, into less natural phenomena. Spinoza applies the same logic to the question of sovereignty as he does to the metaphysical explanation of natural right and the right of human beings in a state of nature:

> If men were bound by the established practice of nature to be guided by reason, everyone would necessarily be guided by reason. For the established practices of nature are the established practices of God (by paragraphs 2 and 3 [of Chapter 2 of the *TP*]). God established them with the same freedom with which he exists. So, these things follow from the necessity of the divine nature (see paragraph 7 [of Chapter 2 of the *TP*]). They're eternal and can't be violated. But men are mostly guided by appetite without reason. They don't disturb the order of nature: they necessarily follow it. So the ignorant and weak-minded are no more bound by the Law of nature to organize their lives wisely than a sick man is bound to have a sound body.
>
> (*TP* 5 [18], G III/282/20–29)

This quote highlights that there is no form of government that is *naturally* more justified than another. Just as with respect to the individual human being in the state of nature, the only standard by which sovereignty can be measured is the standard of approximation towards one's own internal maximization of power or perseverance in being. A state whose empirically measurable expressions of power (*potestas*) are completely governed by rational ideas (by what certainly is best for it) is sovereign; that is, it holds absolute power over its subjects. Such a state has an unlimited ability to fulfil its ultimate purpose: to provide a practical and concrete platform for individual striving towards wellbeing (*TP* 3 [7]). A state that manages to exercise its power (*potestas*) to control people's activities, movements and ideas in a way that steers them towards a rational expression of power (*potentia*) is unthreatened in its power (*potestas*) with respect to its subjects. This is because every single one of these subjects will be obeying the sovereign's laws, not out of fear of punishment but out of rational affirmation (love) in a way that liberates their individual *potentia* far beyond anything like a state relying on irrational ideas can do (ibid.).

Now, there are a number of ways, according to Spinoza, in which such a rational affirmation or love towards the state may be installed in its subjects. In Chapter 3 of the *TP* Spinoza discusses the limits of the sovereign power's rights. He begins by reiterating that in a state 'no citizen either does anything or has anything by right except what he can defend by the common decision of the Commonwealth' (3 [3]). From this, it is clear that the sovereign, first of all, has the prerogative to decide the limits of all of its subjects' expressions of power as *potestas*, that is, their power to empirically act out on, or possess things. Spinoza then adds something that is usually taken as a strong rejection on his part of the right to revolution:

> because the body of the state must be guided as if by one mind, and hence the will of the Commonwealth must be considered the will of all, what the Commonwealth has decided is just and good must be thought of as having been decreed by each [citizen.] So, though the subject may think the decrees of the Commonwealth unfair, he's nevertheless bound to carry them out.
> (*TP* 3 [5], G III/286/6–11)

Reading these two sections from *TP* 3 in the light of the previous chapter's review of natural law and that law's relation to power, it seems reasonable to conclude that the power 'handed over' by individual human beings to the sovereign body should be understood as power carrying with it some kind of external, measurable effect (*potestas*), rather than as an internal force to understand and affirm one's own role and position with respect to events (*potentia*). *Potentia* is never handed over; it can, however, increase by the handing over of *potestas*. In fact, if we recall the statement in *TP* 2 [22] about us being in relation to nature what clay is in the hands of the potter, the result seems to be that the act of handing over power, which Spinoza alludes to repeatedly with respect to the consolidation of the state and a sovereign power, is nothing but a psychological event.

Looking at Spinoza's (in)famous negation of a right to revolution from this perspective changes things slightly. Ontologically speaking, an individual who has successfully maximized her own power to persevere in being (*potentia*) is an individual who uses reason, and, because an individual who uses reason seeks peace 'which certainly can't be obtained unless the laws of the Commonwealth are observed without violation', 'no one, insofar as he does what he must according to the laws of the Commonwealth, acts contrary to the prescription of his own reason' (*TP* 3 [6] G III/286/20 and G III/287). The right to revolution is denied in so far as it would be contrary to the principle of ethical well-being to grant such a right. It is always better in terms of the individual chances to approach a more powerful and free state of being to keep within the irrationally governed but stable compound of the state. Even though there is nothing in the state of nature that hinders individuals from becoming as rational as their nature permits, the state of nature does not, therefore, cease to be a state of being that is insecure and therefore indubitably bad for ethical striving.

None of this means, however, that there are no limits to a state's expression of power. Spinoza writes rather cryptically that the sovereign body cannot command people to do things that no one, by no means, *can* be compelled to do (*TP* 3 [8]). He sets out to clarify this by way of turning to some practical examples: a list of categories, or ways of thinking, that presumably cannot be conceded to another being's judgement. The list includes making scientific conclusions, forming metaphysical ideas and changing already established affections towards a thing. He also exemplifies by way of adding certain actions to the list, like witnessing against oneself and self-torture. In sum, any order to perform an activity that expresses a negation of the principle of the striving for perseverance in being (*potentia*) cannot be enforced, ever, regardless of the level of pressure or violence (*potestas*) that is put on the individual by the sovereign body to do so. To judge by the list, it is evident that the events that lie beyond the scope of the sovereign are such events that all, in some way or another, are related to the exercise of one's internal and essential power (*potentia*) to persevere in one's own present state of being. In contrast, there seems to be no impossibility attached to the formulation of rules and orders that aim at limiting an individual's exercise of power understood as *potestas.*

By way of a metaphor, Spinoza illustrates that even though we can imagine a state powerful enough to enforce laws about the listed impossible things, to think of the implementation of these laws is to think of a sane human being requested to become mad (*TP* 3 [8], G III/287/30). I take this to mean that even if it may lie within a state's cohesive power (*potestas*) to legislate about anything it deems fit, some legislations will in practice lead to a dissolution of the glue that holds together the state in the first place: the idea of security. Such laws are therefore, in fact, impossible for the state to enact. While they can be imposed, their effect will be detrimental rather than beneficial for the conservation of the sovereign body. In this context, Spinoza links the concept of *sui iuris* which we became familiar with in the previous section to sovereignty. He writes that '[b]ecause the Commonwealth's Right is defined by the common power [*potentia*] of a multitude, it's certain that its power [*potentiam*] and Right are diminished to the extent that it provides many people with reasons to conspire against it' (*TP* 3[9]). Because for a state, 'like each individual citizen, *or* like a man in the state of nature, the greater the reason for fear it has, the less it is its own master [*sui iuris*]' (ibid.). In other words, enacting laws that no one can respect will lead to a lessened degree of sovereignty in so far as the effect of these laws are that people keep thinking and living according to their own accord rather than the commonly established state accord. This makes the sovereign body not only less powerful (*potestas*) with respect to its subjects but also with respect to itself (less its own master), since its identity depends on the psychological import given to it by its subjects.

TP 3 [9] has made some commentators argue that Spinoza rescues a grain of the right of revolution in so far as it can be read as postulating that states that try to assume sovereign power over certain impossible things can presumably 'not complain if they face violent resistance' (cf. Curley, 2016, 521, fn. 13). I would argue, however, that rather than establishing a right to revolution in a traditional sense, Spinoza simply explains with these statements that if the sovereign body transgresses the limits of its own natural power (*potentia*) to preserve it loses its own ability to master itself (*sui iuris*) (i.e. enact rational decrees), which, in turn, amounts to an annihilation of its cohesive power (*potestas*) over its subjects. This is because the state's natural power to persevere in being is measured by the degree to which it manages to provide its subjects with a safe and peaceful path towards rationality. Even though a state's decrease in *potentia* may not manifest itself immediately in terms of a decreased power to force people into given actions and directions (*potestas*), it will sooner or later lead to a decreased ability to provide both peace and rationality. It is at this point that the notions of *potentia* and *potestas* prove to form an inseparable unity.

State power and sovereignty as phenomenological experiences

In this chapter, I have come to the conclusion that Spinoza can motivate the experience of a third-body governance even in the light of absolute necessitarianism, causal determinism and philosophical naturalism. As we know from the previous review of Spinoza's metaphysics, human nature is not limited to being rational even though its essence considered on its own can be understood as a striving towards reason. Quite the contrary, rationality is the *ideal* form of being for a human being in so far as it is the most powerful or most human form of being human. To this end, it is also the way of being towards which all of us naturally strive since we all naturally strive towards a maximization of our ability to remain in the states of being that we are. Very rarely, however, are we conscious of this end with regard to our own striving. This is because we are constantly affected by others who impact our ability to form ideas. To use a metaphor, our view constantly gets blurred by external things passing by requiring attention. A human being does not experience herself through her own nature taken in isolation. She experiences herself through the impacts on her body and mind that external things cause on her body and mind. This means that most of the time, humans will be unable to rationally explain both themselves and external objects. The perception of both categories will simply be mixed up with each other: we can only get to know the external world through ourselves – but we cannot see ourselves clearly as we are since the external world interferes in our perception. According to Spinoza, it is the confused and blurred perception of ourselves and things around us that makes us think that it is possible to determine and evaluate things and events in an otherwise entirely determined and complete nature. This, in turn, makes for the metaphysical explanation of the conceptual conditions of the state: the state as an ability to govern and as a sovereign body.

As far as my understanding of Spinoza's political philosophy is concerned, the social organization of our human condition is metaphysically speaking a wholly unintentional outcome of a natural interplay between human affections (most of which are passive). We must regard things this way if we are not to contradict Spinoza's basic principles of determinism and necessitarianism (*E*1p28 and 33). Spinoza's normative twist lies in arguing that the determined state of things does not remove the fact that we benefit from regarding the civil state as a state of affairs constituted by a formal, binding contract set up by a formal handing over of rights and titles. We benefit by this idea to the extent that we are dealing with our striving to achieve a state of being in which we approach wellbeing, that is, a state of being in which we fully understand and rejoice over the fact that we, in fact, do not control or determine anything at all.

Notes

1 In *TTP* 4 [2] Spinoza writes: 'But [the law] that men should yield, or be compelled to yield, the right they have from nature, and *bind themselves to a fixed way of living*, depends on a human decision' (G III/58, my emphasis). In *TTP* 16 [55] he writes: 'So we must grant, without qualification, that [human] divine law began when, in an *explicit agreement*, men promised God to obey him in everything. By this they, as it were, *surrendered* their natural freedom, and *transferred* their right to God, as we've said happens in the civil state' (G III/198/26–30, my emphasis). The position which these statements portray can easily be recognized in the *Ethics*' definition of the state: 'In order, therefore, that men may be able to live harmoniously and be of assistance to one another, it is necessary for them to *give up their natural right* and to make one another confident that they will do nothing that could harm others' (G II/237 in fine–328, my emphasis).

2 *Sui iuris* can be translated into English as approximately 'in control of one's own rights'.

3 This reading can be motivated by reference to the two step description in the *Ethics* of self-determination as rationality. First it is demonstrated that being rational – living according to reason – amounts to the highest degree of freedom available for human beings. This demonstration should then be coupled to the definition of freedom as meaning, not contingency or being uncaused but rather, having control over one's own effects in the sense of adequately understanding them and their full chain of causes.

4 The way in which this subordination takes place will be discussed in more detail in the subsequent section but it is certain from what we have already said that we are dealing with a kind of psychological event rather than a handing over of a formal, or real, competence.

5 Form of governance in the sense of whether its *potestas* is upheld by irrational or by rational means, that is, means aimed at being conducive to a higher degree of individual rationality, *potentia*, by being itself rational.

References

Balibar, E. 1997. 'Spinoza: From Individuality to Transindividuality', *Mededelingen vanwege het Spinozahuis*, vol. 71, Delft: Eburon.

Barbone, S. and Rice, L. 2000. 'Introduction' and 'Notes' in Spinoza's *Political Treatise*, Shirley, S. (trans.), Indianapolis, IN: Hackett Publishers.

Curley, E. 2016. *The Collected Works of Spinoza*, vol. II. Princeton, NJ: Princeton University Press.

Matheron, A. 1990. 'Le problème de l'évolution de Spinoza du Traité théologico-politique au Traité politique', in *Spinoza: Issues and Directions*, Curley, E. and Moreau, P.F. (eds): 258–270. Leiden: Brill.

Spinoza, B. 2016. *Political Treatise (TP); Letters (EP)*: 29–41 and 42–84. Curley, E. (ed. and trans.), *The Collected Works of Spinoza*, vol. II. Princeton, NJ: Princeton University Press

Spinoza, B. 1985. *Ethics; Treatise on the Emendation of the Intellect (TdIE) and Letters (Ep.):1–28.* Curley, E. (ed. and trans.), *The Collected Works of Spinoza*, vol. I. Princeton, NJ: Princeton University Press.

Spinoza, B. 2007. *Theological-Political Treatise (TTP).* Israel, J. (ed.). Cambridge: Cambridge University Press.

Spinoza, B. 1995. *Spinoza: The Letters (Ep).* Shirley, S. (trans.). Indianapolis, IN: Hackett Publishing.

Steinberg, J. 2008. 'On Being *Sui Iuris*: Spinoza and the Republican Idea of Liberty', *History of European Ideas*, 34(3): 239–249.

Wernham, A.G. 1958. 'Notes' and 'Introduction', in Spinoza, *The Political Works.* Oxford: Clarendon Press.

5 A Spinozistic theory of international law

Previous attempts to construe a theory of international law based on the few and vague comments on international relations within Spinoza's political philosophy have met with one principal obstacle: the fact that there is very little support in that philosophy for the existence of a 'separate and independent theory of international law' (cf. Lauterpacht, 1927, 92; Walther, 2003–2004, 663). Sir Herscht Lauterpacht comes to this conclusion by relying on the following statements in *TPP* and *TP*, which constitute the core of Spinoza's few statements that explicitly deal with international relations:

> [N]o law binds the supreme power. Everyone must obey it in everything.
>
> (*TTP* 16 [26], G III/193/28–29)

> Allies are men of two states, which, to avoid the danger of war, or to gain some other advantage, contract with one another not to harm one another, but to come to one another's aid when in need, though each retains its own sovereignty. This contract will be valid just as long as its foundation, the principle of danger, *or* of advantage, is present. For no one makes a contract or is bound to stand by a contract, except out of hope for some good, or anxiety about some evil. If this foundation should be removed, the contract is removed of itself.
>
> (*TTP* 16 [43–44], G III/196/23–29, emphasis in original)

> For since (by 3 [2]) the Right of the supreme power is nothing more than the Right itself of nature, it follows that two states are related to one another as two men are in the state of nature, with one exception. A Commonwealth can take precautions against being overpowered by another Commonwealth. But a man in the state of nature – a man burdened with daily sleep, often with illness or grief, and in the end with old age – that man can't provide security for himself against being overpowered by another man. Moreover, he is liable to other disadvantages from which the Commonwealth can make itself secure.
>
> (*TP* 3 [11], G III/289/19–24)

> So, if one Commonwealth wants to make war on another, and will stop at nothing to bring it under its control, it has the Right to try this.
>
> (*TP* 3 [13], G III/290/3–5)

Taking as my point of departure the presumption that Lauterpacht is correct in concluding that it is impossible to build 'a separate and independent theory of international law' from the position taken in these statements, I will in this chapter investigate whether the lack of a robust theory of international law completely blocks us from relying on Spinoza's political philosophy in construing answers to the questions international law and legal scholarship traditionally are supposed to tackle. These are mostly questions of a practical character, but they all somehow seem to revolve around the problem of how to make international agreements, conducts, principles and rules carry legal strength and validity.

There is, for instance, a long-standing discussion within legal scholarship on international law about how to tackle the problem of deficit in legitimacy with respect to international governance, given the absence of a supra-national sovereign. Whatever theoretical perspective is opted for, studies in international law tend to affirm that in spite of lacking a formal constitution and sovereign body, international law must be grounded on *some kind of* external prescriptive system in so far as it is to be distinguished from mere politics. Most suggestions about how to construe such a prescriptive foundation point to one of the following two general approaches: explaining legality and (by extension) international law as something ultimately guided and naturally directed by a universal and abstract moral order; or, explaining legality according to a scheme where all human practices are concrete materializations of physical and mechanical laws of nature (cf. Koskenniemmi, 2010, 16–17, 210, 411 and 427–430). Despite their apparent incommensurability, these two approaches, which (roughly classified) could be labelled as an idealist and a materialist explanation of law, actually appear to stand on one and the same side when it comes to the more fundamental philosophical issue at stake.

Both can be seen, I suggest, as a product of a dialectical logic where the world and human history basically follow a natural line of progression towards a pre-established goal of liberation. While idealist accounts of international law affirm the idea of natural progression by way of attaching legality to an extrinsic and abstract force, materialist accounts affirm the very same idea by attaching legality to an internal pattern of concrete actions and phenomena (Casullo, 1996, 305–306). Both of them, however, seem to proceed from the presumption that there is a teleological order at work in the world, expressing itself in human practices like law. On this understanding, the main task for legal theory becomes to establish a) what overarching moral or natural order governs human practices and b) whether the particular configurations and expressions of law studied, respect the order settled for. The ones that do will carry a higher degree of legitimacy than the others.

If such a dialectical approach to international law is required in order for a reflection on international law to be classified as a proper theory of international law, then, clearly Spinoza's political philosophy does not reach the target. The question in this case, however, rather becomes whether there is something else in Spinoza's discussion of law and the state that can be used as a basis from where to construe a considered understanding of international law. In other words, is there a different kind of variable to be found in Spinoza's political philosophy general and objective enough to serve as a starting point for evaluations of the normative structure which we usually refer to as international law, or, does Spinoza's political philosophy make our idea of international law collapse into a completely nihilistic account of international affairs?

It is my objective in this chapter to formulate an answer to these questions that affirms the usefulness of Spinoza's political philosophy as a means for advancing a productive theorization of international law. I will argue that this political philosophy may contribute to our understanding of international law by way of instigating a critical examination of the naturalness by which attempts to understand human legal practices – practices that are usually bundled together under the concept of international law – affirm a teleological order and/or an idea of natural progression. To this end, I will argue that rather than offering a framework for an alternative or novel 'theory' of international law, Spinoza's political philosophy can facilitate a considered and productive understanding of the effects of the theorizations of international law which are already (implicitly) present within existing descriptions of international law. In my view, Spinoza's political philosophy can do so by rendering visible the ways by which studies of the *problem of legitimacy* in international law tend to use conceptualizations of sovereignty and governance that bring with them already established determinations of the law. In other words, I believe that Spinoza's political philosophy, and in particular his conception of governance and sovereignty, can help us advance a considered understanding of the cryptic statements about international relations which are cited by Lauterpacht as reasons to dismiss Spinoza's potentiality as a thinker of international law. What is more, I believe that such a considered understanding can be conducive to a productive confrontation of the problem of deficit in legitimacy. It can do so due to the way by which it destabilizes both of the two major traditions for outlining the *ideata* corresponding to the concept of international law: idealism and materialism.

Formulated this way, the approach set forth here for tackling the main problem of this chapter appears to share some traits with Spinoza's approach to the methodological challenges of practically applicable sciences, in general, and political theory, in particular. In the introduction to the *TP*, for instance, Spinoza writes that practical philosophies regularly fail in their mission to guide public affairs because they tend to take 'theory to be out of harmony with practice' (*TP* 1 [1] in fine, G III/273/20–25), as 'they conceive men not as they are, but as they want them to be' (ibid., G III/273/12). The remedy, he argues, does not lie in theorizing human behaviour from a normative perspective, but in demonstrating which normative guidelines agree best with human nature and thus practices. This is why Spinoza describes how he:

> took great pains not to laugh at human actions, or mourn them, or curse them, but only to understand them. So, I've contemplated human affects –

> like love, hate, anger, envy, love of esteem, compassion, and the other emotions – not as vices of human nature, but as properties which pertain to it in the same way heat, cold, storms, thunder, etc., pertain to the nature of the air. Though these things are inconvenient, they're still necessary and have definite causes, through which we strive to understand their nature. The mind rejoices in contemplating them truly just as much as it does knowing things pleasing to the senses.
>
> (*TP* 1 [4], G III/274/27–275)

As an echo of his well-known commitment to philosophical naturalism, expressed in the preface to Part Three of the *Ethics*, the just quoted passage (which is also followed by a direct reference to the *Ethics*) shows the close affinity among the metaphysical, physical, normative and political aspects of Spinoza's work. Keeping this in mind, we will soon look at how Spinoza's conception of sovereignty and governance qualifies his harsh repudiation of international law principally in *TP* 3 and *TTP* 16. This, in turn, will prove to be useful for dealing with Lauterpacht's critique of Spinoza's lack of theory of international law.

However, before looking at how Spinoza's conceptions of sovereignty and governance qualify what Lauterpacht takes to be a harsh repudiation of international law *qua* law, I must outline the problem of legitimacy in international law and how it has been traditionally dealt with through either a materialist or an idealist approach.

The problem of legitimacy: a brief overview

As indicated above, the dividing line for scholars concerned with anchoring international legal practices and rules in a solid normative theory cuts through the following question. Should international law be considered a legal system because a) state practice evidences a set of *a priori* universal, normative principles, or because b) state practice *a posteriori* can be systematized and reveal a set of normative principles, even though each instance of the state practices taken on its own merely appears to be, or is a product of independent contracts among sovereign states?

In *The Lotus Case* (PCIJ, 1927) the Permanent Court of International Justice (PCIJ), predecessor of the International Court of Justice (ICJ), (in)famously sided with the second position as it declared that state sovereignty was the most fundament principle of international relations. The court did so by way of stating that a state can decide upon *all* jurisdictional issues relating to its territory as long as there is no explicit prohibition against such decision in international law to which the state in question has consented. The pertinent section of the court's judgement reads:

> International law governs relations between independent States. The rules of law binding upon States therefore emanate from *their own free will* as expressed in conventions or by usages generally accepted as expressing principles of

> law and established in order to regulate the relations between these co-existing independent communities or with a view to the achievement of common aims. Restrictions upon the independence of States *cannot therefore be presumed.*
>
> (PCIJ, 1927, 18, emphasis added)

This dictum has ever since its first publication been criticized for bringing international law dangerously close to nihilism through its strong emphasis on state sovereignty as the sole source of international legal regulation (cf. Brierly, 1928, 154–155). It has been read as amounting to an unfortunate recognition of *Real politik* being the principal governing framework by which to analyse and make sense of international law (cf. Brownlie, 2003, 301).

After the settlement of *The Lotus Case*, many strategies have been launched in scholarly comments for securing international law's classification as law despite lacking the constitutional structure of domestic laws. In contrast to most domestic legal systems, international law is 'a horizontal and decentralized' structure of rules 'between various international actors [which] make the rule of law *prima facie* more difficult to respect' (Besson, 2011, 374). The various actors which Besson makes reference to here are state representatives, international organizations and other agents exercising public authority. Despite the difficulty expressed by Besson in configuring our understanding of international relations according to the rule of law, there exists a general resistance against completely stripping international law of all sense of legality. The blunt state sovereignty position expressed by the PCIJ in *The Lotus Case* has thus always been contrasted with attempts to draw from a more idealistic perspective. A perspective taking as its point of departure the position that there must be something within or beyond the law itself that binds sovereign states to international law and that provides a sense of extra- or supra-legal validity to its rules.

One contemporary scholar who affirms the more idealistically inclined perspective is Jeremy Waldron. In a recent article (2011, 324–327) he emphasizes that the rule of law, notwithstanding the abundant quantities of empirical evidence pointing to the problem highlighted by Besson, plays an important role in the conceptualization of international law. It does so, he argues, by performing the function of being a means of self-protection for states facing abuses from centralized political institutions and the internal structure of international law itself. He argues that the rule of law doctrine provides sovereign states with a predictable and secure environment (ibid.). It is difficult to evaluate the merits of Waldron's suggestion, given that he does not elaborate further on how this protection is being actualized. In an earlier essay (2006), however, he argues that it is the associative effect of the rule of law doctrine that prevents international relations from being regarded as a mere effect of politics and power expressions. He writes (15) that '[t]he phrase "the rule of law" brings to mind a particular set of values and principles associated with the idea of legality' (quotation marks in original). Continuing, Waldron claims that the set of values and principles which are brought to mind by the phrase 'the rule of law' functions to push states towards a conceptual framework fixed around the two principal goals for law making in general: to provide social good and justice to those subjected to law's authority. Thus, Waldron maintains that the rule of law and the basic values with which the doctrine is associated together constrain practitioners of international law in so far as they 'in their pursuits of these other goals [...] pursue justice and the social good through the rule of law, not around it or in spite of it' (ibid.).

The target of Waldron's critique seems to be the kind of conceptualization of international law which is being implied by the dictum of *The Lotus Case*, in so far as this conceptualization places too much emphasis on the idea of states as principal subjects of international law (cf. Brownlie, 2003, 58; Friedmann, 1964, 213; Hall, 1895, 1; Shaw, 2003: 190). On a more fundamental level, what Waldron and others seem to object to, is the idea that states, when constructed as the sole authorities of international law, become represented as autonomous individuals like those we find interacting with each other within the realm of the civil state. According to the critique of this logic, it makes the lack of a supreme power the only difference between the interaction among human and state individuals (Waldron, 2006, 23). Waldron opposes this representation of autonomy with respect to states on the assumption that it erroneously affirms that states naturally enjoy the same individual freedom and autonomy as human beings do. According to Waldron, the representation in question simplifies individuality with respect to the state, making it into a natural or material issue, when individuality in the case of statehood in actual fact is a human projection of an aspect of human nature. Waldron elaborates the critique:

> As individual humans are the subjects of domestic law, nationstates are the individual subjects of international law. And so—the argument goes—the administration and its lawyers would deserve the benefit of the same attitude toward the rule of law in the international realm as individuals and their lawyers have in relation to the law of the land. The administration should respect any law that is clearly applicable—the clear text of any treaty it has entered into, for example—but only to the extent that it is manifestly and unambiguously on point. On this theory, any lack of clarity would be resolved in favor of liberty—in favor, that is, of the freedom of action of the individual sovereign state. The state would be entitled to treat international legal restraints in a rigorously textual spirit; the restraints would have force where they clearly apply, but there would be no requirement to stretch or extend their meaning to constrain governmental freedom of action in areas that are unclear.
>
> (Ibid., 21)

Treating the state as an autonomous individual, moulded on the idea of the autonomous human subject, means for Waldron that we are responsible for making an erroneous conceptualization of the state and so too international law (ibid.). The state, for Waldron and for those who like him oppose the just described analogy, is 'quite unlike an individual when it comes to the value of its freedom of action' (ibid.). In contrasting his own position with this version of the state as a natural individual, Waldron positions himself in a tradition of thought originating in Kant's critical philosophy and furthered by legal analytical philosophy like that of Kelsen and Hart. Waldron never explicates his reasons for regarding the state's freedom of action as quite unlike that of an individual human, but it is clear that it has something to do with there being something in the nature of the state beyond its constitution as a composed individual. Drawing on both Kelsen and Hart, Waldron elaborates:

> A state's sovereignty is an artificial construct, not something whose value is to be assumed as a first principle of normative analysis. In its municipal aspect, the state is a particular tissue of legal organization: it is the upshot of organizing certain rules of public life in a particular way. Its sovereignty is something made, not assumed, and it is made for the benefit of those whose interests it protects. In its international aspect, the sovereignty and sovereign freedom of the individual state is equally an artifact of international law. *What its sovereignty is and what it amounts to is not given as a matter of the intrinsic value of its individuality, but determined by the rules of the international order.*
> (2006, 21, emphasis added)

To judge by the final sentence of this passage, the material substance of state sovereignty is evidently not fixed and outlined before the state enters into international relations. According to this view, then, sovereignty is something attributed to states *by* international law and not the other way around even though states are the main (or sole) sources of this law. This means that at least one aspect of the rule of law doctrine, which arguably is responsible for making states into the main lawmakers and subjects of international law, is being attributed to states *a priori* by something internal to the very law that the states in question are creating. As indicated by Waldron in the quoted passage: the material effects of state sovereignty cannot be explained unless the rule of law is considered as something inherent to the rules of the international order itself.

All in all, then, it is clear that the perspective represented by Waldron in this argumentation constitutes an opposition to what he considers to be the only other available option for explaining the legality of international law. To this end, the position expressed by the court in *The Lotus Case* is usually associated, as indeed is suggested by Waldron, with Thomas Hobbes' political philosophy and the materialist tradition of thought that followed from his claim that states are individuals in a state of nature just like human beings are before they deliberately agree to enter into a social contract (Waldron, 2006, 20).

As correctly pointed out by Waldron, political philosophy has ever since Kant's critique of the natural law tradition been divided between those who, in accordance with that tradition, see the state as an individual in an unregulated state of nature and those who, like Kant, see legality as something above and beyond the issue of state sovereignty. As is familiar, Kant says in his famous argument about perpetual peace that the state of nature does not apply to states as states 'already have an internal juridical condition' (1795 (1957), 18). Later, Kant's position is affirmed by Hans Kelsen who, in his seminal work on legal theory, argues that the state rather than being a natural individual is the effect of a particular way of organizing certain rules of public life (1934 (1992), 99–104). Arguably, the core of Kelsen's argument lies in an emphasis on the claim that the particularity which provides the rules of public life with an overarching and structuring form comes *with* the rules – or their normative source – and is not something provided merely by the actions or will of those applying the rules at certain moments and in certain contexts.

This kind of (idealistic) explanation of the nature of the state is precisely what is being recalled by Waldron as he claims that against the sovereignty theory expressed in *The Lotus Case* one could posit that 'any reason for a state to resist the application of international regulations must be framed in terms of legality rather than the repudiation of legality' (2006, 23). This idea, that states must argue against the application of a particular rule of law based on arguments about or from within that law itself, is not entirely easy to disentangle. Essentially, it seems to amount to saying that the law which is to be refuted to some extent exists before it has even been given a defined scope, target and subjects. In other words, the argument seems to be that legal rules of international law ultimately derive their legality from a sphere of fixed abstract ideas external to the concrete and material manifestations of the law.

Now, having laid out before us the main components of the problem of legality within international law and the two principal approaches for its solution, let us go on to discuss in what ways Spinoza differs from both of these approaches when he deals with the subject, object and scope of international law.

Sovereignty as freedom and the problem of legitimacy in international law

I will begin this section by reminding how Spinoza defines state sovereignty internally; that is, the relationship between the state and its citizens, or subjects. In the previous chapter we saw that Spinoza defines this aspect of sovereignty as the common right of a people led *as if* by one mind (*TP* 2 [16–17]). It is clear from this definition that in order to achieve sovereignty internally, the state must control not only the subjects' empirically detectable expressions of power (*potestas*), but also their ability to determine their own movements, rest and formation of ideas (*potentia*). This is because the establishment of a single mindedness in terms of reasoning, like the one required by the definition of sovereignty and which is required for a successful individual ethical striving, can only be accomplished through a certain way of living conducive to the formation of adequate ideas.

Turning to the question of what this definition of sovereignty implies in terms of inter-state relations, it may be illustrative to look at one of the sections that were highlighted by Lauterpacht, in which Spinoza discusses the phenomenon of allies:

> Allies are men of two states, which, to avoid the danger of war, or to gain some other advantage, contract with one another not to harm one another,

> but to come to one another's aid when in need, though each retains its own *sovereignty*.
>
> (*TTP* 16 [43–44], G III/196)

Spinoza's emphasis here on how inter-state relations are created without a transfer of sovereignty (power) makes it clear that even though the means for constructing alliances are similar to that of the human handing over of individual power/right to a sovereign body when forming the state, there is one principal difference.

The activity required from each individual human being in order for a state to become sovereign with respect to its subjects includes, as we have seen, the right/power to think according to one's own natural inclination. We know that to form a sovereign power in relation to a collective of human beings, everyone partaking in the formation must adhere to one common mindset (or opinion); that is, let this mindset determine and guide one's actions. Moreover, we know that in order for such a common mindset to become a reality, people need to hand over not only their power (*potestas*) to block other people's empirical expression of power but also their power (*potentia*) to create movement and form ideas (to some extent at least). In the quoted passage we see that alliances do not require giving up sovereignty in this same way. Comparing with human individuality, this means that entering into an alliance does not require giving up the part of (state) power that is connected to its self-determination: *potentia*. From all of this follows a conclusion that might seem peculiar at first glance. In relation to the individual human beings that constitute its composite parts, the state appears to be formed according to the exact same set of natural patterns of individualization: namely, those at work in explaining individuation generally. However, in relation to the potentially greater individual that a state for its own ends may partake in constituting, when some of its subjects enter into alliances with other states, the process of formation seems to be another entirely, which makes the greater body of the international community constitute an exception to the natural principles of individualization.

Thus, already at this preliminary stage we may detect how Spinoza's conceptualization of the state with respect to its inter-state relations seems to involve both a materialist and an idealist classification. Some aspects of his conception seem for instance clearly to be steeped in Hobbesian, materialist terms. Here, it could be pointed to how he explains the social contract as a continuation of the state of nature because of the mechanism of human nature to avoid greater harm, which merely is a continuation of the general principle of self-preservation (*conatus*). Other aspects, however, seem to depend for their explanation on something more or other than mere natural mechanisms. Here, the explanation of inter-state alliances serves as a good illustrative example as international alliances on his account clearly do not seem to depend on only the metaphysically established mechanical principles of individuation which govern and explain the formation of a single complex individual out of many simpler ones.

The fact that Spinoza explains allies in this way seems to underline a potentially serious problem related to consistency. It is a problem that concerns precisely the division between materialism and idealism: a problem of how a metaphysical differentiation between individuals based on distinct political categories can be upheld and defended despite a surrounding context of strict philosophical naturalism. In what follows of this section, I will deal with the question of Spinoza's conception of sovereignty in light of his discussion of freedom (maximization of power) as a sense of self-determination (or *sui iuris*). My hope is that in doing so I will also be able to find a considered response to the just pointed to problem of inconsistency emerging in his proposition about allies.

As discussed in the previous chapter, Spinoza's conception of sovereignty is connected to his accentuation of *sui iuris* as the mark of metaphysical freedom, understood as the highest degree of power/right available to humans. Studies of Spinoza's idea of the state make it clear that, based on statements especially in the *TTP* 5 and the *TP* 3, it is possible for an individual, according to Spinoza, to remain his or her own master (*sui iuris*), even if s/he is completely under the control of someone else's power as far as the empirical effects of her or his activities are concerned (cf. Steinberg, 2009). There is, then, an intricate relationship between self-determination and giving up one's right to decide for oneself in Spinoza's discussion of sovereignty.

The intrinsic relationship is outlined in *TP* 3[6] which first makes reference to *TP* 1 [5] and then elaborates by referring to *TP* 2 [15]. The paragraph in Chapter 3 reads: 'But since reason teaches nothing contrary to nature, sound reason cannot dictate that each person remain his own master, so long as men are subject to affects (by i, 5), *i.e.* (by ii,15), reason denies that it can happen'. Now, *TP* 1 [5] is a restatement of the *Ethics*' establishment of the metaphysical proposition that human beings are necessarily subject to affects, that is, changes to their power to act (in body and mind) which are either self-inflicted or caused by external inputs. This is, as the *Ethics* demonstrates, part of the human condition. It is also part of the human condition for there to be no qualitatively measurable difference between different attempts at self-mastering, whether rational or irrational, although self-mastering ultimately lies in 'exerting the most of one's power with reason, and by being mostly guided by reason' in so far as this means determining one's actions by causes which can be understood through a person's own nature alone (*TP* 2 [11], *TP* 2 [9]). According to Spinoza, it is most definitely the case that because of human beings' affective natural state of being, most attempts to become one's own master will be played out according to irrational means. As long as this is the case, the human individual search for the ultimate form of self-mastering (reason, cf. *TP* 2 [11]) will always be obstructed by the impacts of other individuals' search for the same thing.

This is precisely what Spinoza indicates by referring to *TP* 2 [15] in *TP* 3 [6]. The ultimate upshot of the natural (moral) equality between irrational and rational means for self-determination is that the human natural right to do what one can to persevere in one's present state of being must be regarded as illusory in the state of nature. Spinoza elaborates:

> Moreover, since (by §9) everyone in the state of nature is his own master just as long as he can prevent others from overpowering him, and since it's futile

> for one person alone to try to protect himself from all others, it follows that as long as human natural right is determined by each person's power and belongs to that person, there's no human natural right. *It consists more in opinion than in fact, since there's no secure way to maintain it.*
>
> (*TP* 2 [15], emphasis added)

Spinoza continues this discussion by stating that it thus may be concluded that:

> the Right of Nature which is a peculiar property of the human race can hardly be conceived except where men have common rights and are jointly able to claim for themselves lands they can inhabit and cultivate, are able to protect themselves, fend off any force, and live according to the common opinion of all.
>
> (*TP* 2 [15])

In other words, not only does the concept of natural right refer merely to something like a psychological, or phenomenological entity before the state is formed; as such it is constituted by the very right that we *imagine* handing over in establishing the state. This is to say that it is the constitution of civil – constructed – rights that makes the rights of nature become conceivable. Sovereignty, then, appears not only as a measurement of how well a state has managed to tie its subject to itself but also as an essential condition for the very idea of a rights discourse in the first place. Further evidence for this position can be inferred, I think, from the ambiguous use of the term *imperium* in *TP* 3 [16], where it is introduced as meaning and translated into sovereignty, as designating a kind of right, and later as referring to different forms of government (see Curley, 2016, 514, fn. 35).

With this, we have come a little way towards explaining the conceptual background to Spinoza's discussion of sovereignty in Chapter 3 of the *TP*. In sum, he first declares that it is in accordance with reason to live according to someone else's judgement despite the fact that reason apparently means nothing but determining one's actions by causes which can be understood through a person's own nature alone. Then, he states that civil order is naturally established to 'take away the common fear and relieve the common wretchedness' which make it aim at what 'everyone who is guided by reason would strive to do in the state of nature, but in vain' (*TP* 3 [6], G III/25–30). And so finally, he writes that 'no one, in so far as he does what he must according to the laws of the Commonwealth, acts contrary to the prescripts of his own reason' (ibid., G III/286/33–287/1).

After having laid out these internal aspects of sovereignty, Spinoza adds a few more things about the nature of the individuality of the state. To start off, he writes that the state is to be treated as an individual in so far as that state will be the most 'powerful and the most its own master [sovereign], if it is founded on and directed by reason' (*TP* 3 [7]). This is because 'the right of a Commonwealth is determined by the power of the multitude which is led as if by one mind' (ibid.). And, as mentioned previously, since there is no way such 'union of minds can be conceived unless the Commonwealth aims most at what sound reason teaches to be useful to all men', a state dictating through reason will be more powerful than those that govern according to dictates based on passive reactions (ibid.). In addition to this clarification, Spinoza also states that:

> [b]ecause the Commonwealth's Right is defined by the common power of a multitude, it's certain that its power and Right are diminished to the extent that it provides many people with reasons to conspire against it. Certainly the Commonwealth has some things it must fear for itself. Like each individual citizen, *or* like a man in the state of nature, the greater the reason for fear it has, the less it is its own master.
>
> (*TP* 3 [9])

Now, keeping in mind what I have said so far about the internal aspects of sovereignty, and before I move on to the question of the external effects of state sovereignty, I would like to pause for a brief digression. This digression concerns the fact that it seems to me that Spinoza's discussion in Chapter 2 of natural rights and how these are related to the state, qualifies the *Ethics*' representation of the human transformation of rights from the state of nature to a civil society.

It is apparent from the discussion in *TP* 2 that the natural right/power of the human being to do what she can to persevere in her present state of being is only practically defendable (and thus, existent) once a state has been formed, despite the fact that the state's very *raison d'être* is precisely to transform this natural right and power into something else. Thus, we find Spinoza confirming the human being as a 'social animal' (*TP* 2[15] in fine), in terms similar to those of Hobbes. To a certain extent, it would seem that civil society for Spinoza is nothing but a psychological precondition for our human ability to visualize our own nature and our natural way of being. So, the fact that human beings agree upon forming a greater individual and hand over to this individual their natural right and power to act and react to others' actions is what makes a) these rights detectable and defendable in the first place and b) the intrinsic connection visible between the maximization of these rights/powers and reason. This reflection will be important to keep in mind when we in the final section of this chapter return to the question of sovereignty in relation to how the problem of legitimacy in international law traditionally has been perceived as either an idealist or materialist scheme. Before that, however, I will briefly go through Spinoza's arguments in *TP* 3 about the state's external relations and recall Lauterpacht's critique of them.

TP 3 [11] is arguably one of the starting points for Lauterpacht's scepticism towards Spinoza's philosophy as a vantage point for a proper theory of international law. There, Spinoza states that because:

> the Right of the supreme power is nothing more than the Right itself of nature, it follows that two states are related to one another as two men are in the state of nature, with one exception. A Commonwealth can take precautions against being overpowered by another Commonwealth. But a man in the state of nature – a man burdened daily with sleep, often with illness or

> grief, and in the end with old age – that man can't provide security for himself against being overpowered by another man. Moreover, he is liable to other disadvantages from which the Commonwealth can make itself secure.

A little further down in the same chapter Spinoza accentuates the indication of a lawlessness among states which can be detected in this passage, as he writes that 'by nature two Commonwealths are enemies. For (by ii, 14) in the state of nature men are enemies' (*TP* 3 [13]). I opened this section by posing the question whether discovering the motives for Spinoza's peculiar treatment of legality would perhaps make us question the consistency of his philosophy as a whole. The just quoted passage gives evidence of precisely the kind of special treatment with respect to the state and legality in comparison with other modes that I highlighted in those introductory lines and that might set off suspicions of an arbitrary bifurcation within Spinoza's philosophical system. Because, considering the passages concerned with the internal and external effects of sovereignty in *TP* 3 it would seem as if there were two measurements of individuation at work simultaneously in Spinoza's philosophy. By separating the effects of being sovereign in terms of the individual vis-à-vis the state (where being sovereign means living according to the laws of the state) from the effects of being sovereign in terms of the state vis-à-vis other states (where being sovereign means living according to whatever means the state itself sees fit), Spinoza seems to be separating between kinds of individual. Such a separation, if indeed perceived correctly as such, is of course highly problematic from the perspective of Spinoza's commitment to substance monism, strict determinism, necessitarianism and philosophical naturalism. Does Spinoza really maintain a differentiation between the effects of two kinds of limited and determined mode – the human individual and the state – given that we know that he provides one and the same definition of being a mode? This question is especially warranted given Spinoza's repeated declaration of the principle of philosophical naturalism which stipulates that the same rules apply for all things and phenomena in nature and that the laws of nature are always and everywhere the same (cf. *E3* preface).

Now, I would suggest, based on what I have just highlighted about the *TP*'s (Chapters 2 and 3) inversion of the relationship between the order of natural and civil rights, that one possible way to tackle this question is to take that inversion as our point of departure. I said above that according to the discussion in those chapters of the *TP*, it seems as if the metaphysically true description of rights as purely descriptive and determined (natural rights) becomes perceptible and palpable only in the instance they are contrasted with a system of fictive prescriptive rules of living projecting a false sense of contingency to things. I have suggested elsewhere that, according to Spinoza, we ought to regard human civil laws as necessary psychological entities emerging out of a human limited and always partial outlook on the world. In the light of the *TP*'s discussion about natural right and sovereignty, stipulating that we need a fiction in order to see what is naturally installed, this means to say that civil laws appear to constitute one of the preconditions for a considered understanding of the human natural state of being and the highest human good. If we consider things this way, we begin to see how Spinoza actually can safeguard naturalism and its characteristic descriptiveness with respect to international law while simultaneously working with another description of that same law that confirms a kind of transcendental normative realm beyond the law. He allows for a dialectic language necessary for normative thought while rejecting that the state has neither more, nor a different kind of, sovereignty in relation to any other finite thing. To understand this argument, let us go through it step by step once more.

As we have seen, individual *sui iuris* vis-à-vis the state can for Spinoza be explained as the psychological product of a phenomenological experience which the individual does not adequately understand without recourse to certain inadequate and imaginary ideas. The idea of individual sovereignty as a kind of autonomy in decision-making appears to be of the same kind, then, as the necessary yet false idea of the free will, which I have discussed previously in this book. Indeed, the inverted constitutional relationship between sovereignty and right in the state of nature versus the civil state allows Spinoza to argue that the teleological aspect of sovereignty is something we must project onto the idea of a civil order in order to be able to perceive and appreciate the absolute non-teleological processes of nature, including such processes as govern our own behaviour like the ones we take to be the fundamental aspects of deliberate decision making.

Spinoza's twofold definition of sovereignty is in the light of this argument not necessarily arbitrary or inconsistent with his metaphysical commitment to naturalism, in so far as it only constitutes a recognition of the fact that the human being must posit a teleological order – must insert a purpose – into her life in order to be able to properly 'see' herself, and, in order to properly function in accordance with her own nature. This is to say that as long as the idea of the state is considered as a precondition for sovereignty (ethically speaking too, that is), then, there is no inconsistency in Spinoza's way of dealing with the concept. Human beings may need to rely upon an idea of a possible natural interaction between two ethically completely self-mastering beings – even if this is metaphysically erroneous – in order to be able to conceptualize and understand the natural mechanisms governing their own natural activity and interaction. Now, in so far as experience blocks the idea of human nature to take on the role as this model, the idea of a state which does not suffer from the limitations of being a finite mode may very well serve this purpose.

Governance as power and the problem of legitimacy in international law

Let us call the flip side of sovereignty governance. Both concepts are traditionally related to power and the ways in which power can be expressed. While sovereignty denotes the ability to master oneself, governance has to do with the conditions under which one can master another being. Traditionally, the discussion of what one can and what one has the right to do, both in terms of sovereignty and in terms of governance, are separated into two distinct but parallel discourses: one concerned with nature and the other with morality. As is familiar, Spinoza is by the principle of philosophical naturalism blocked from making such a separation.

Consequently, the *Ethics* states that right *is* power (*E*4d8). Normally, this is interpreted as meaning that one has the right to do what one can do in so far as an unregulated state of nature is concerned. However, I have argued in the previous sections of this chapter that it could be wise, at least with respect to sovereignty, to qualify our understanding of this proposition. To this end, I would like to suggest that Spinoza's discussion of sovereignty in the *TP* reveals that natural rights – undefendable as they are – become something, that is, are attributed meaning and sense, only in the instance that we juxtapose and contrast them with the natural right of another kind of individual who we may image as not suffering the same natural limitations as we do. Because of this, and this would be the second upshot of my argumentation in the previous section, the natural right to do what one can do becomes realizable or real only in a civil context where one's empirically measurable behaviour in fact is heavily constrained by another's power. Understanding sovereignty this way can explain why Spinoza holds the state to be situated in the state of nature with respect to other states without being afraid of this being an arbitrary digression from his definition of the individual as a naturally social animal. The state *is* an individual just like the human individual, indeed it appears in some senses to be the model for human individuality, constructed so that human interactions and social dealings may become visible, assessable and comprehensible for the human eye and mind.

So, what about governance? Can we make the understanding of the (sovereign) right of the state to master itself, which I have drawn out from Chapter 3 of the *TP*, relevant for understanding the external limits of the state's exercise of power?

Studying this issue will make us see once again, I believe, why Spinoza's political philosophy evades both the idealist and the materialist camp of explaining international law. In *TP* 4, Spinoza rhetorically asks one of the most frequently asked questions in the history of legal theory. 'But people commonly ask: is the supreme power bound by laws? and so can it sin?' (4 [4]). He answers his own question as follows:

> But since the words 'law' and 'sin' customarily apply, not only to the Laws of the Commonwealth, but also to the common rules of all natural things, and especially to the common rules of reason, we can't say, without qualification, that the Commonwealth isn't bound by any laws, *or* can't sin. For if a Commonwealth weren't bound by any laws *or* rules, ***without which the Commonwealth would not be a Commonwealth***, then we'd have to think of it, not as a natural thing, but as a fantasy.
>
> (Ibid., G III/292/25–293, last emphasis added)

I have placed emphasis on a small section of the quoted passage's last sentence as it nicely shows, in my view, how Spinoza attaches the human ability to understand to a fixed and arbitrary construction of rules and laws. Here again we see, then, the importance placed by Spinoza upon normativity for our ability to think and perceive things. In order for us to see a state *as* a state we must first think of it in terms of something that can be captured and held encased by laws and rules which determine its existence. Spinoza concludes his argument about the existence of an extra-constitutional or extra-legal norm of legality by saying that 'the Commonwealth sins, then, when it does, or allows to happen, what can be a cause of its ruin' (ibid. G III/293). Exemplifying this conclusion he adds that:

> [i]f I say, for example, that I can rightly do whatever I wish concerning this table, I surely don't mean that I have the right to make this table eat grass. *Similarly, even though we say that men are not their own masters, but are subject to the Commonwealth, we don't mean that they lose their human nature.* Nor do we mean that the Commonwealth has the right to make them fly, or (what is equally impossible) to make men honor those things which move them to laughter or disgust. What we mean is that when certain circumstances are present, the subjects respect and fear the Commonwealth and that when those circumstances are absent, this fear and respect are destroyed. When they're destroyed, so is the Commonwealth itself.
>
> (Ibid., G III/293/10–21, emphasis added)

No thing can be asked to do what it cannot do. Conversely, no thing has the right to do what it cannot do. Now, in addition to exemplifying the original – ethical – meaning of sin and justice, I read this passage in the light of what I have argued above deals with the relationship of mutual dependence between the human being and the state. When Spinoza writes that even if human beings are not *sui iuris* in so far as they have subjected themselves to the governance of the state, they still retain their nature as human beings, this seems to confirm that *sui iuris* (i.e. as self-determination) is part of human nature and not something that can be regulated by civil law even though it appears as a concept only when the idea of the state is in place. One way of reading this passage, then, is as stating that even if formally giving up their right to determine themselves and their actions when entering into the social contract, human beings cannot submit so much of their natural ability to act and think as to completely eliminate their own nature as humans. I think the passage most definitely says this. But I also think there is more to read out from it.

Considering the section of the passage that I emphasized together with the penultimate and the last sentence reveals something more, I think, about Spinoza's position with regard to governance. Because, through these sentences, Spinoza communicates that *if* circumstances are right for believing in the power of the state; if the state does not require impossible ideas from its subjects, then the state will continue in existence. If, on the contrary, the state requires ideas which block its subjects from believing in it (in its powers), then it will perish. So, if we were to generalize this, what we get is a position holding that when certain circumstances are present, then a given thing (or event, or concept) *is*, and when those circumstances are removed, so too is the thing. Now, turning this towards the human being and her ability/right to be her own master and the fact that this ability/right seems to be one of her defining qualities, it follows that if *sui iuris*, or self-mastering, is removed so too is the human being. We know from the previous section that *sui iuris* in the case of an individual human being depends on the existence of the idea of an existing civil state. Thus, the upshot of all this seems to be that if you remove the state you will have removed one of the fundamental aspects of human nature: her ability to determine actions and ideas – *sui iuris*. In short, eliminate the state and you have eliminated the human being.

At this moment, it becomes relevant to look at the concept of governance again. We know from the quoted passage that what destroys the state is a lack of human subjects' fear and respect of it; that is, a lack of subjects that believe in it and see it as a state. Creating impossible laws – like asking someone to honour a thing which fills that someone with disgust – will in the long run lead to the destruction of the state simply because it amounts to an activity that denies the nature of its own constituting components. Just as human natural rights depend on the idea of civil organization so too does the idea of the state and its powers depend on human beings fearing and respecting it as the organ for civil organization that it represents itself to be.

We then find Spinoza concluding that:

> We see, then, in what sense we can say that the Commonwealth is bound by laws and can sin. But if by law we understand the civil Law, which can be defended by the civil Law itself, and by sin what the civil Law prohibits us from doing – *i.e., if we take these terms in their proper meaning* – we can't say in any way that the Commonwealth is bound by laws or can sin. For the rules and causes of fear and respect the Commonwealth is bound, for its own sake, to observe don't concern the civil Law, but the Law of nature. By §4 they can't be defended by the civil Law but [only] by the Law of war.
>
> (*TP* 4[5], G III/293/29–294)

In this summary I think that Spinoza's position with regard to the issue of governance spreads some clear light on how he tackles the problem of legitimacy in international relations. The state is evidently not bound by any law in so far as we understand the concept of law in its proper sense, he writes. The state is a condition for lawmaking; therefore, it cannot also be bound by it. Spinoza's account of governance makes it obvious that he shares with Hobbes, and the materialist tradition in general, an idea of the state as an individual situated in nature abiding by the mechanical and descriptive 'laws' of nature only. However, it is equally obvious that this explanation does not exhaust the question of governance for Spinoza.

It should be kept in mind that in the paragraph preceding the quoted passage, Spinoza has declared that the word law also applies to 'common rules of all natural things, and especially to the common rules of reason' (*TP* 3[4]). This brings with it a necessary qualification of our conclusion that the state is bound by no law because, as I have already highlighted, in TP 3 [4] Spinoza states that '[f]or if a Commonwealth weren't bound by any laws *or* rules, without which the

Commonwealth would not be a Commonwealth, then we'd have to think of it, not as a natural thing, but as a fantasy' (ibid., G III/293, emphasis in original). What is important to underline here is that this passage reinforces the importance of the concept of law for the phenomenological experience which we perceive as the state.

So, just as in the case of sovereignty, Spinoza appears in the end to be affirming both a materialist and an idealist account of governance and, thereby, the law bound-ness of the state. This way, he not only manages to stay clear of the risk of creating a transcendent image of law which seems to be part and parcel of both materialist and idealist dialectical approaches to human nature. In doing so, he also sees to it that his account is consistent with his commitment to strict naturalism and causal determinism. My final words in this section will be dedicated to explaining how he manages this.

TP 4 [4 and 5] demonstrate, just as in the case of law and the aspect of *sui iuris* within the idea of sovereignty, that the state for Spinoza is *something* only to the extent that human nature depends on it to be that something. *TP* 4 [4] establishes that without laws or rules the state would not be a state. In short, the establishment of the state depends on meeting certain normative criteria.

However, Spinoza immediately clarifies that this establishment is a mental construct. To this end, he explicitly writes that the consequence of thinking about the state as law-less would be that 'we'd have to *think* of it, not as a natural thing, but as a fantasy'. Now, through *TP* 4[5] we see that the state and its governing power cannot be explained solely by either materialist or idealist concepts in so far as the state is only bound by laws which strictly speaking are laws only in the sense that they are necessary for our imagination of the state. Spinoza's understanding of governance eludes both kinds of dialectic regime in so far as he says that it is necessary to think in ideal terms about governance and the state's law bound-ness in order for us to grasp a completely law-less state of nature in which every single finite thing is situated and determined to act in a given way.

In effect, the state (just as civil law) appears as a psychological entity that is rendered necessary by human nature rather than as an object on its own, explainable either in material or idealist terms. Spinoza does not compromise with the commitment to naturalism when he says that the human being is governed by one kind of law (civil law) and the state by another kind (law of nature, or the law of war). Because the state appears to be a psychologically necessitated entity for the phenomenological explanation of human experiences; it seems to be consistent to hold both that the state belongs to the state of nature and that the human being belongs to organized society. In fact the two notions, that of the state of nature and that of the state, seem to be inseparable. The purely mechanical state of nature can only be played out or visualized according to a phenomenological experience of it as contrasted with the state and its ordered governance. Without the idea of the state and its sovereign power to make laws, our human ability to grasp the state of nature and the nature of things would be very limited.

How Spinoza's non-theory of international law can contribute to understanding international law

In the introduction to this chapter, after having presented Lauterpacht's critique of the usefulness of Spinoza's political philosophy as a foundation for a robust theory of international law, I posed the question whether this fact entirely disqualifies Spinoza as a thinker of international law. Now, having discussed how Spinoza represents sovereignty and governance throughout his accounts of natural right, the right of the state and other matters of the state (Chapters 2, 3 and 4 of the *TP*), I am in a position to motivate a negative answer to this question. To the question of *if* and, in that case, *how* Spinoza's non-theory of international law can aid our understanding of international law, my answer is the following.

According to Lauterpacht, the most troubling aspect of Spinoza's account of international relations is that it does not recognize a binding principle of contract or good faith beyond, as posited in *TP* 3[11], a brute state of nature among states. In *TTP* 16, Spinoza denies that contracts may have any kind of binding force beyond the imagined utility (its psychological effect) of the situation it stipulates. 'If this foundation [utility] should be removed', Spinoza writes, 'the contract is removed of itself' (*TTP* 16 [43–44], G III/196/23–29). Likewise, Spinoza dismisses the existence of a binding principle of good faith beyond utility. In the introductory chapter of the *TP*, he writes that 'a state whose well-being depends on someone's good faith, and whose affairs can't be properly looked after unless the people who handle them are willing to act in good faith, won't be stable at all' (1 [6]). Then, in *TP* 3 [11] he finally explicitly expresses that there is no law among states: 'the Right of the supreme power is nothing more than the Right itself of nature, it follows that two states are related to one another as two men are in the state of nature'. This, in turn, means that 'if one Commonwealth wants to make war on another, and will stop at nothing to bring it under its control, it has the Right to try this' (*TP* 3 [13], G III/290/3–5).

It may be correct to conclude, as does Lauterpacht, that these statements effectively annul the possibility of speaking of a robust theory of international law. This may be so at least in so far as we by such a theory mean an account making reference to an extra-legal element justifying the state's legality (such as for instance a principle of good faith or contract). However, I hope to have made it clear in this chapter that these statements cannot be read without making some qualifications to their apparent meaning. I believe that contrary to their apparent significance, the context in which Spinoza lets these statements operate makes it abundantly clear that the state of nature from which states allegedly never transcend is only conceptualized to the extent that it is a simultaneous production of, *and* responsible for producing a necessary yet 'false' idea of the civil legal order. Spinoza's rejection of law with respect to inter-state relations is therefore something more than an affirmation of a materialistic conception of the world as progressing towards its ideal state according to a principle of brute force and state power. In order to avoid the teleological end implicit in the idea of progression, Spinoza introduces an element of (qualified) idealism to his purely mechanical account of normativity. In other words, he makes the degree to which we can evaluate the laws of nature governing states' interactions depend on a less strict materialism; one that requires the idea of an *ideal* civil state.

So, responding to Lauterpacht's rejection I would therefore say that Spinoza most definitely is relevant as a thinker of international law. He is one of few in the history of philosophy who recognizes what could perhaps be denominated as *the problem of either/or* in normative and moral thought. He sees the danger of resorting to either a purely idealistic or materialistic explanation of the foundation of law and by extension international relations. What is more, he provides us with an explanation for why each explanation seems to be mutually exclusive yet impossible to completely refute from the perspective of the other. Each of them can be said to hold a grain of truth and each has a role to play in what for Spinoza is the most important lesson of them all with respect to normativity: namely, that law generally, as well as international law in particular, is a psychological product which human beings need in order to cope with the phenomenological experience that it implies to be alive.

We may use Spinoza's alternative explanation of sovereignty and governance in order to re-examine, not only our traditional idea of international law, but also Lauterpacht's claim that a considered understanding of this law requires a robust legal theory. Because, in my view, Spinoza's position renders visible two important things. First, that any attempt to formulate a general legal theory will necessarily fail to represent law's ontological nature because there is no natural normativity to theorize about. Second, that it is necessary, cognitively speaking, for human beings to organize their experiences in accordance with such a theory despite the fact that it does not truthfully represent the world because certain false representations are part and parcel of human nature and the human condition. To this end, superimposing a teleological structure and the idea of a natural progression onto any given legal order indubitably amounts to an erroneous ontological representation of that order, according to Spinoza's political philosophy. However, this alone does not negate the fact that human beings will benefit ethically from perceiving and interacting with a given legal order *as if* it was emerging from, or striving towards an abstract model.

Finally, it is important to point out how the image of the state and international law emerging from the statements in Chapter 16 of the *TTP* and Chapters 3 and 4 of the *TP* do not contradict Spinoza's strict commitment to philosophical and epistemological naturalism or determinism. This is important in as much as such a clash would cast some serious doubt over the consistency of Spinoza's philosophy at large. His entire philosophical structure would be affected by a contradiction between his metaphysical and normative accounts because it is a structure that makes claims of being both systematic and all-encompassing. A good place to start for construing an account that can save Spinoza's political philosophy from causing such a contradiction is the second half of the above-quoted passage from *TP* 3 [11].

After having stated that states relate to each other as two human beings would do would they ever regress to a state of nature, Spinoza adds an exception to the analogy:

> (by 3 [2]) A Commonwealth can take precautions against being overpowered by another Commonwealth. But a man in the state of nature – a man burdened with daily sleep, often with illness or grief, and in the end with old age – that man can't provide security for himself against being overpowered by another man. Moreover, he is liable to other disadvantages from which the Commonwealth can make itself secure.
>
> (*TP* 3 [11], G III/289/19–24)

This clearly seems to amount to an arbitrary bifurcation of the concept of the individual and hence a breach of the principle of naturalism as laid out in the preface to Part Three of the *Ethics*. How else can we motivate a differentiation between two things that share the same definition? Why would a state, to the extent that it is defined in the same way as an individual human being, not suffer from external impacts diminishing its forces to the same extent as all other individual things according to Spinoza's metaphysical and physical accounts? What kind of metaphysical explanation may warrant a metaphysical exception being made to the case of the state but not to that of the human individual? If Spinoza really intends to regard the state as almost, but not quite, an individual (and quite a lot of textual material supports this view) this indeed seems to amount to an internal inconsistency of Spinoza's philosophical structure.

There is, however, one possible way out of this dilemma. It consists in recalling once again the inverted relationship between the state of nature and that of civil law. In so far as a human individual can never really attain a considered understanding of her own natural powers and rights according to the state of nature, she needs to construe an image of it in her own mind based on its counter-image: that of civilized society. Now, even though this counter-image serves merely as the phenomenological starting point for achieving a further understanding of the natural conditions and terms for human existence, this does not take away the fact that it also amounts to something metaphysically real itself; as a psychological or phenomenological experience. It amounts to the image that humans must posit in order to allow their entirely natural and mechanical premises to function in their best possible ways. To this end, it makes complete sense to say, as Spinoza does, that two civil states are like two human beings in the state of nature with the exception that they do not suffer from the weaknesses of the human individual. This is because the state this way becomes a part of the human individual or at least her condition of existing. So, whereas two individuals, of course, must be treated metaphysically in identical ways in so far as they share the same definition (or natures), it seems rather unproblematic to say that a specific part of one individual may fill the function of appearing like an *almost* identical individual for the sake of that first individual's ethical striving. There is no contradiction of the metaphysical terms in this statement.

All in all, Spinoza's discussion of international relations is conducive of a productive confrontation of the problem of deficit in legitimacy with respect to international law. It does so in that it demonstrates that this is an unsolvable problem that stems, not so much from the idea of laws between states, but from the idea of human-made law and the erroneous epistemological perspective that the construction and maintenance of such an idea presumes. His discussion of international relations also demonstrates that both of the two most common ways of theorizing the problem of legitimacy in international law perform (as opposed to explain) a specific normative function. They effectively further an ideal image of human co-existence and international relations. This is an image that is metaphysically false yet fruitful for the overarching ethical goal of well-being in so far as it makes humans (individually or as represented by state powers) see the benefits of and strive towards mutual aid and cooperation rather than division, disruption and war.

References

Besson, S. 2011. 'Sovereignty, International Law and Democracy', in *European Journal of International Law* 22(2): 373–387.

Brierly, J.L. 1928. 'The "Lotus" Case', in *Law Quarterly Review* 44: 155–156.

Brownlie, I. 2003. *Principles of International Law*. Oxford: Oxford University Press.

Casullo, N. 1996. 'Karl Marx y Charles Baudelaire: Los Fantasmas de la Modernidad', in *Itenarios de la Modernidad: Corrientes del Pensamiento y Tradiciones intelectuales desde la Illustración hasta la posmodernidad*. Buenos Aires: Oficina de Publicaciones del CBC Universidad de Buenos Aires.

Curley, E. 2016. *The Collected Works of Spinoza*, vol. II. Princeton, NJ: Princeton University Press.

Friedmann, W. 1964. *The Changing Structure of International Law*. London: Steven and Sons.

Hall, W.E. 1895. *A Treatise on International Law* (4th edn). Oxford: Clarendon Press.

Kant, I. 1795 (1957). *Perpetual Peace*. White Beck, L. (ed. and trans.). Indianapolis, IN: Bobbs-Merrill Co.

Kelsen, H. 1934 (1992). *Introduction to the Problems of Legal Theory*. Litschewski Paulson, B. and Paulson, S.L. (trans.). Oxford: Oxford University Press.

Koskenniemmi, M. 2010. *From Apology to Utopia: The Structure of International Legal Argument*. Cambridge: Cambridge University Press.

Lauterpacht, H. 1927. 'Spinoza and International Law', in *British Yearbook of International Law*, vol. 8: 89–106. Oxford: Oxford University Press.

Permanent Court of International Justice (PCIJ). 1927. *The* Lotus Case *(France v Turkey)*, Ser. A, no. 10.

Shaw, M.N. 2003. *International Law* (5th edn). Cambridge: Cambridge University Press.

Spinoza, B. 2016. *Political Treatise (TP)*. Curley, E. (ed. and trans.), *The Collected Works of Spinoza*, vol. II. Princeton, NJ: Princeton University Press.

Spinoza, B. 2007. *Theological-Political Treatise (TTP)*. Israel, J. (ed.). Cambridge: Cambridge University Press.

Steinberg, J. 2009. 'On Being *Sui Iuris*: Spinoza and the Republican Idea of Liberty', in *History of European Ideas* 34(3): 239–249.

Waldron, J. 2006. 'The Rule of International Law', in *Harvard Journal of Law and Public Policy* 30(1): 15–30.

Waldron, J. 2011. 'Are Sovereigns Entitled to the Benefit of the International Rule of Law?', in *European Journal of International Law* 22(2): 315–343.

Walther, M. 2003–2004. 'Natural Law, Civil Law, and International Law in Spinoza', in *Cardozo Law Review* 25: 657–665.

6 The Reports and the normative implications of an eco-ethical approach inspired by Spinoza's philosophy

It has been one of the principal objectives of this book to demonstrate how the Reports' call for a new metaphysics and (by extension) new normative practices appear as a natural continuation of arguments visible within Spinoza studies as well as studies on environmental ethics for the use of Spinoza's philosophy as a possible foundation for a new kind of normative ethics. I argued initially that this goes to show how the Reports form part, consciously or unconsciously, of a discursive movement which is wider and more pervasive than is revealed by their expressed scope. Having dedicated the main thrust of this book to reviewing the principal features of Spinoza's philosophy, it is now time to return to the main objective of the investigation. Namely, to identify and analyse the impacts on international law following from turning towards Spinoza's philosophy as a means for responding to the normative challenges posed by the Anthropocene. It was argued initially that this objective presents itself through the fact that the Reports, on my understanding of them, suggest precisely this method as a solution to the global problem of nature.

A careful reflection on the impacts of turning to Spinoza's philosophy in the face of the Anthropocene implies considering the compatibility between the Reports' conceptualization of the normative consequences of the called-for new metaphysics with those consequences that my review of Spinoza's metaphysics reveals. In order to conduct this reflection, we must first connect the Reports' implicit reliance on Spinoza with a more elaborate and explicit reading of Spinoza, and then, analyse the explicated arguments produced by this connection in the light of the outline of Spinoza's philosophy that has been presented throughout Chapters 3 to 6 of this book. This chapter is therefore divided in two parts.

In the first, I will focus on the eco-ethical reading of Spinoza which appears in contemporary comments on Spinoza and nature and as developed from Arne Naess' initiative to connect the ecological ethical debate with Spinoza's metaphysics. In this part, and with the aim to render more explicit the Reports' arguments pointing to an alternative metaphysics and ethics, I will try to show *how* this eco-ethical reading must deduce normative consequences from Spinoza's metaphysics which are not present in his own political philosophy. Using this reading of Spinoza and, by extension, Spinoza's original works as the theoretical framework by which to interpret the Reports, is (as mentioned initially) motivated by two independent reasons.

The first reason is the semantic similarity between the Reports and Spinoza's formulations, in combination with the fact that Arne Naess and the deep ecology movement is one of the Reports' explicit theoretical sources of inspiration. Thus, as has been discussed in Chapter 1, the Reports themselves establish an affinity to Spinoza as they draw from a study of Spinoza's philosophy when explaining their claims. Now, Naess' attempt to extract a new environmental ethics from Spinoza's metaphysical structure has been carefully examined and critiqued (cf. Chapter 1 and de Jonge, 2004). Reading the Reports' claims through the newer eco-ethical reading of Spinoza is thus motivated by the fact that this reading, while aiming for the same goal as Naess, is sensitive to the weaknesses pointed out in Naess' reading by previous critiques. In other words, the eco-ethical reading that I will try to reconstruct in this chapter appears as a more considered and updated version of the same kind of theoretical basis from which the Reports draw when relying on Naess' work on deep ecology and Spinoza in support of their claims. The second reason consists in the fact that the eco-ethical reading within studies on Spinoza opens up a wider and more comprehensive discussion of the normative and political aspects of Spinoza's philosophical system. This reason is thus related to the second objective of the book to provide an independent reflection on Spinoza's responses to the philosophical issues underscored by the problem of nature taken on its own. A discussion of the normative and political consequences of Spinoza's understanding of the human–nature relationship is important in so far as it can contribute to the ongoing scholarly debate concerning the extent to which Spinoza's philosophy can be put to practical use in the service of different emancipatory projects.

When the preliminary issues of the first part have been settled, the chapter closes with a second part dedicated to the main problems sketched out at the beginning of this book. In this part, I will evaluate the theoretical consistency of the Reports' call for a new metaphysics in so far as this call indeed depends on an eco-ethical reading of Spinoza. In conclusion, I will discuss some of the general challenges attached to a practical use of Spinoza's political philosophy in the service of environmental protection, in light of the overarching goals and conditioning premises of that philosophy.

Part one: fleshing out the Spinozistic character of the Reports' arguments for a new metaphysics

Naess' reading of Spinoza

In Chapter 1, I showed how the Reports are linked theoretically to Spinoza via references to Norwegian eco-philosopher Arne Naess. I argued that the Reports make references to Naess in passages dedicated to explaining what kind of paradigmatic change they call for. They describe Naess' launch of the deep ecology movement as a reaction to the negative normative effects of having adhered to a supposedly superficial (shallow) understanding of nature. In the works referred to by the Reports, Naess explains his vision of the kind of metaphysical conception that is necessary for changing the way that we relate to nature. In doing so, Naess draws explicitly on Spinoza's doctrines. He argues that Spinoza's metaphysics can alter our understanding of desire and our construction of a sense of responsibility with respect to nature. The link between the Reports and Spinoza which is established by the references to Naess is weakened, however, by the fact that Naess' initiative has already been evaluated and correctly criticized for neglecting important components of Spinoza's metaphysics when constructing a new deep ecological ethics (cf. de Jonge, 2004).

In her book *Spinoza and Deep Ecology*, dedicated to the investigation of the viability of the deep ecology project to ground a new moral theory on Spinoza's metaphysics, Eccy de Jonge demonstrates how Arne Naess overlooks Spinoza's a-moralization of value as he argues for letting Spinoza's metaphysics form the basis for a moral theory that includes the perspective of nature. She argues that when Naess (and other deep ecologists) imagine Spinoza's substance monism and definition of value as pillars of a normative project aiming to bring about full consideration of nature *on its own* (Naess, 1977, 45–54), they do so in way that is inconsistent and problematic with substance monism as a metaphysical premise (de Jonge, 2004, 145). This is because, in order to couple Spinoza's substance monism with a moral theory based on nature, one must neglect the fact that Spinoza's non-anthropocentric metaphysics challenges not only the anthropocentric perspective on the issue of care for others, intrinsic value and so on, but also, the act of taking this perspective in defining nature as an object of morality in the first place (ibid.). Her conclusion is that Naess' ambition is problematic as it overlooks the explicitly expressed ethical consequences of Spinoza's metaphysical position. What Naess does not realize, she writes, is that alongside the metaphysics Spinoza establishes a moral relativism that is impossible to separate from his non-anthropocentrism. She argues that *if* Spinoza's critique of the dominion-within-a-dominion paradigm is seriously considered, we would not speak of a human responsibility to protect natural entities. In fact, we would not speak of any kind of moral responsibility at all (ibid.). In other words, if you remove the specialness attached to humanity on one side of the metaphysical/moral equation (positing that human beings do not hold a special value), you must also remove it on the opposite side (positing that human beings do not have a special responsibility for things' development since there is no special human power to affect that development).

In light of the review undertaken in Chapters 2–5, of the ethical and normative upshots of Spinoza's metaphysics, I see no reason for disagreeing with de Jonge when she writes that:

> deep ecologists seem to want to substantiate two contradictory positions: to develop a new type of environmentalism, based on a metaphysics of care, which makes environmental ethics redundant, *and* to develop a moral theory which tells us how we ought to act. It fails to do the former and in

> the latter case would be better served by turning to more traditional moral theory.
>
> (2004, 145)

According to de Jonge, Spinoza (unlike Spinoza according to the deep ecologists referred to in this quote) does not dodge the *a*moral consequences of an absolutely non-anthropocentric metaphysics. Thus, the core of de Jonge's charge against Naess and other deep ecologists is that they do not see that the ethics flowing from Spinoza's non-anthropocentric metaphysics, under no circumstances can be made into a sustainable basis for a non-anthropocentric morality. Spinoza's ethics reflects an *anti-anthropocentric* understanding of the world which gives rise to *amorality*, not a different kind of morality, like a species neutral or natural one. In other words, if we take Spinoza's critique of anthropomorphism as our starting point (see *E*3 preface), what must follow is a complete destruction of the idea of a *general and abstract morality* (cf. Della Rocca, 2008, 177–179). Replacing one moral standard (say, one resting on a principle of utilitarianism) with another, albeit non-anthropocentric, does not solve the problem of morality being necessarily perspectival.

According to de Jonge, the metaphysical position taken by Spinoza reveals how an anthropocentric explanation of the world – *including morality* – is a man-made fabrication caused by hubris in combination with the absence of an adequate understanding of things. Traditional moral theory, however, she emphasizes, does not constitute a metaphysical position on its own. It is merely a second-order organization of things and actions that, as such, *presumes* a philosophical outlook which rationalizes an anthropocentric understanding of things. In light of this clarification of objectives, it is pointless, she says, to appeal to Spinoza's metaphysics and ethics as an alternative basis for a moral order valuing nature as much as humans. It would imply collapsing Spinoza's philosophical outlook (metaphysics) into a moral theory which means turning it into a second-order organization of things which, as such, presumes an anthropocentric first-order philosophical perspective. In other words, it would be to turn a non-anthropocentric order into an anthropocentric one.

Developing this line of thought, I would add that traditional moral evaluation, for Spinoza, clearly is a tool developed by humans, for humans; it is a second-order tool that requires a first-order description of things according to a dominion-within-a-dominion perspective. On my understanding, a large part of his *Ethics* is a demonstration of what would be the case *if* we managed to live according to an adequate understanding of the world. Most of the ethical consequences sketched out therein are therefore to be understood as the moral attitude of someone who truly has managed to break the bounds of the limited human perspective that makes us treat things as if they were made for us, in a kingdom within a kingdom. This someone would cut her- or himself loose from the need protect things as if they could not protect themselves, since the idea of protection in itself is a reinforcement of the erroneous anthropocentric idea of us as godlike appearances.

Interestingly, all of this is explicated and highlighted by Spinoza himself in correspondence between him and some of his contemporary interlocutors. In response to Willem Van Blyenbergh, who at one point accuses Spinoza of depicting God in a way that blurs the line between virtue and vice, Spinoza emphasizes that the question of human nature, and its causes and effects with respect to the issue of wellbeing is a question that needs to be studied within the realms of physics and metaphysics, whereas the question of what we accept or not in terms of moral value, good and evil is another one entirely. The latter is a question that is posed only in so far as we are ignorant of what is good and bad in terms of our nature and for our perseverance. Morality is therefore a question the study of which should be referred to theology and political philosophy. Spinoza writes:

> I am bound to express astonishment at your saying that if God does not punish wrongdoing (that is, in the way that a *judge* inflicts punishment which is not entailed by the wrongdoing itself, for this alone is the point at issue), what consideration hinders me from plunging headlong into all sorts of crime? Surely, he who refrains from so doing by fear of punishment [...] in no way acts from love and by no means embraces virtue. For my own part I refrain, or try to refrain from such behaviour because it is directly opposed to my particular nature, and would cause me to stray from the love and knowledge of God.
>
> (*Ep.* 21)

Going back to de Jonge, she explains that Spinoza's clarification to Van Blyenbergh is relevant also in relation to our understanding of deep ecologists' initiative to make use of Spinoza's metaphysics as the basis of a new kind of eco-ethics and normativity. The crux of the matter now as well as then, for de Jonge, is that it does not matter for Spinoza's conclusion about non-anthropocentrism what kind of moral standard one opts for: *opting for any standard constitutes an anthropocentric move as such*. The fact that the standard in question may be motivated on more or less benevolent, or non-human specific, grounds does not affect the issue at stake, which is that an anthropocentric epistemology is needed in order for the standard to be formulated in the first place (cf. Della Rocca, 2008, 177–179). Concluding her critique, de Jonge shows how deep ecology, contrary to its claims, in the end turns out to be a variation of traditional moral theory: 'a set of "dos and don'ts" – more than a philosophical perspective on reality' (2004, 145).

De Jonge does not, however, reject all aspects of Naess' and other deep ecologists' reading of Spinoza. The aim, she says, of creating a new 'ethics of care' rather than 'an ethics of use' is commendable. Consequently, de Jonge leaves the possibility open for turning to Spinoza in order to find a suitable basis for a new 'ethics of care'. To this end she holds Naess to be correct in highlighting the fact that Spinoza's substance monism denies the attribution of an ontological specialness to humans. The fact that de Jonge does not reject Naess' ambition to formulate a new normative ethics creates an opening, on my understanding, for the Reports' call. This, in turn, provides us with a motive for moving on to consider a newer, more elaborate version of an eco-ethical reading of Spinoza formulated in the same spirit as the reading provided by Arne Naess.

A new generation of eco-ethical readings: lessons learned from Arne Naess and deep ecology

While deep ecology to a large extent emerged as a reaction to the first global ecological awakening in the 70s, which was underscored by seminal cultural interventions such as Rachel Carson's *Silent Spring*, the reading of Spinoza which is presently trending within discourses concerned with the problem of nature seems to respond instead to scientific findings. Nowadays, it is in connection to investigations about the causes and effects of the Anthropocene that we find Spinoza's philosophy being invoked. This approach, as discussed in Chapter 1, is also adopted by the Reports.

Presuming the imminent actualization of a set of serious and long-term negative effects of the Anthropocene, various kinds of eco-ethical reading of Spinoza's philosophy have been suggested as counter measures. Just as in the case of deep ecology, these readings refer to Spinoza's metaphysics as a potential basis for a politics able to include nature into its definitions of value, moral responsibility and human wellbeing (cf. Guilherme, 2011, 60–78; Kober, 2013, 43–66; Gamlund, 2007, 3–27; Sharp, 2011a, 185–220; 2011b, 48–68; 2016, 272–282; Mack, 2011). Apparently conscious of the mistakes made by Arne Naess in disregarding some of Spinoza's explicit statements about moral theory and normative ethics, these more recent eco-ethical readings seem to recognize, for instance, the tension pointed to by de Jonge between Spinoza's metaphysical commitment to philosophical naturalism and the philanthropic tendency in his political theory (cf. Sharp, 2011a, 4 and 174). To my knowledge, the most elaborate discussion of Spinoza's merits for ecology despite the existence of such a tension is Hasana Sharp's work on Spinoza's philosophy as a means towards a 'politics of renaturalization' (2011a).

According to Sharp, a 'politics of renaturalization' is a politics that aims at 'promot[ing] alternative conceptions of political activity that *connects us more palpably to nonhuman nature*' (2011a, 5, my emphasis). In a book dedicated to Spinoza and re-naturalization Sharp demonstrates her awareness of the risk of incommensurability following from drawing directly on Spinoza's metaphysics with respect to formulating a new political theory. She argues that notwithstanding the fact that Spinoza's metaphysical philosophy contains a strong 'warn[ing] [...] against turning nature into a norm' it may still guide us towards an alternative political practice (ibid.).

Sharp motivates settling on Spinoza for the task of formulating a new, more inclusive politics by pointing to two opposing critiques of the current mainstream conceptualization of the human–nature relationship. On the one hand, Sharp affirms what she calls 'the environmentalist and constructivist' critique (found for instance in the deep ecology platform) of representations of the human subject that 'promot[es] an anthropomorphic worldview in which everything appears to be a human artefact' (9). That this critique is endorsed by the Reports is clear from many of the passages that we studied in Chapter 1 (cf. Rep. III, paras29–30, see Ch. 2, 'Descriptions of the outdated metaphysics'). On the other hand, however, and in contrast to the Reports but in line with de Jonge, Sharp also recognizes the virtues of questioning that very critique for being responsible for re-establishing the same kind of dual relationship between nature and human culture which it sets out to reject in so far as that critique often merely switch places between man and nature (2011a, 9). Spinoza's philosophy, she argues, constitutes a suitable platform from which to start conceptualizing a new politics of nature because it has the sophistication to recognize the hierarchical and discriminatory elements built into Cartesian dualism without ending up affirming its conceptual opposite. She clarifies that:

> 'nature' must not be understood to imply whatever is non-human. It should already be clear that Spinoza challenges all of our usual distinctions between mind and body, 'man' and nature, culture and wilderness, artifice and adaptation. As long as we keep in mind that cyborgs, landfills and leviathans are just as natural as tides, forests, and flocks of birds, I hope to contribute to the ecopolitical ambition to rethink nature.
>
> (Ibid., quotation marks in original)

As is evident from this passage, Sharp is aware of the complexity of Spinoza's doctrine of naturalism and its effect on normative thought. However, it is equally evident that she is convinced that Spinoza's conception of nature indeed holds the potential to provide the basis for a new politics of nature just as argued by Naess.

This being the case, I will now continue with a brief overview of Sharp's eco-ethical reading of Spinoza's philosophy, before I juxtapose that reading with the previous review (Chapters 2–5) of those of Spinoza's doctrines that are relevant for understanding his take on the problem of nature. As mentioned initially, I do this as I believe that Sharp's eco-ethical reading constitutes an illustrative example of how the Reports' sometimes implicit ideas can be rendered explicit with the help of a more elaborate theorization of Spinoza's philosophy as a response to the Anthropocene. In short, the overview of Sharp's eco-ethical reading of Spinoza will provide us with an opportunity to seriously evaluate the normative implications of the Reports' argument.

Defending an eco-ethical reading of Spinoza from within Spinozism

Sharp demonstrates her familiarity with the complexity of Spinoza's philosophy by recognizing one of the more apparent problems in turning to Spinoza for support of an ecological ethics and politics. This is the problem of reconciling Spinoza's definition of virtue with the kind of abstract and universal moral standards that somehow seem to be part and parcel of normative structures. She writes that '[a] lthough Spinoza does not place any special metaphysical value on humanity, he urges us to prefer ourselves and one and another to other natural things', implying this way that Spinoza too saw normativity as something inherently coupled to abstract standards of evaluation (2011a, 186). Citing Spinoza, Sharp admits that even at the level of ethical arguments, his metaphysics leads to upshots which, while being completely value neutral, cannot be contextualized in any other way than from a given perspective:

> whatever there is in nature apart from men, the principle of seeking our own advantage [*utilitatis*] does not demand that we preserve it. Instead it teaches us to preserve or destroy it according to its use, or to adapt it to our use in any way whatever (*E*IV appXXXVI).
>
> (ibid., 191)

In order to evaluate the merits of Sharp's explication of the project to re-naturalize politics (or, to politicize nature if you will) along the Reports' line of argument, we need to look at how she understands Spinoza's conceptualization of virtue. In the previous review of Spinoza's metaphysics (Chapter 2), I established that moral value, according to Spinoza, is nothing but a comparative notion which requires both an ideal by which to measure things and a perspective from where the measurement can be made. As such, the term virtue (or value), understood according to its mainstream use, holds no positive significance in itself. From a Spinozistic perspective, evaluations of good and evil seem to require a particular subject, a specific context surrounding that subject, and a specific position taken by the subject in relation to both the context and its own capacities. All this is acknowledged by Sharp who implicitly admits a deficit in the textual support for the very view that she argues is compatible with Spinoza's ethics: namely, a being-neutral theory of value grounded in Spinoza's commitment to naturalism.

Thus, Sharp duly notes the discrepancy between Spinoza's definition of the universal use of moral terms as terms that can be expressed only from a particular perspective and her own ambition to use Spinoza's metaphysics as a ground for an extended definition of what amounts to a particular perspective – extending the self, as it were. As far as I can tell, she gives two different motives for re-reading Spinoza's political conclusions in response to this discrepancy so that they come to better fit with the metaphysical account of a neutral, yet inherently egoistic, human nature, even though such a re-reading is not immediately supported by the political texts themselves. The first is the internal complexity of Spinoza's political philosophy (2011a, 107–108; 158–160).[1] The other is the matter's urgency, which arguably warrants a digression from the literal and intended meaning of Spinoza's explicit representation of the relationship between metaphysics/ethics and normativity (2011a, 10–11).

With respect to the first motive, we should note that it is a well-attested conclusion that the relationship between Spinoza's metaphysical, physical and normative accounts is complex and opens up various interpretations of his political philosophy (cf. Moreau, 1996, 40–434).[2] It is for instance well known that one of the main reasons for the great debate caused by Spinoza's philosophy among German idealists in the seventeenth and eighteenth centuries stems from the fact that the metaphysical doctrines, if taken seriously and if considered as the most coherent account of human nature, lead to a complete disqualification of political, moral, religious and normative structures in so far as human reason is the true and *internal* substitute for all these (cf. Solé, 2011, 366; Walther, 2009, 25–40). So, in order to defend the idea of an interconnection between the metaphysical premises and a viable natural politics, Sharp does the following. She places the tension, between the arguably eco-ethical result of the metaphysics and the politically explicit expressions about human morality, within the philosophical system itself. To this end, she writes that Spinoza 'appears to authorize the exploitation of non-human nature, *even as he* excoriates those who fantasize about a God who might "direct the whole of Nature according to the needs of their blind desire and insatiable greed"' (2011a, 186, my emphasis, quotation marks in original). I read these critical words as a reflection of an inherent indecisiveness – vacillation – within Spinoza's writings as to how far one should apply his metaphysics. The fact that this indecisiveness exists is reason, then, according to Sharp, for interpreting his political philosophy in a way that creates coherence among the different doctrines.

In the same spirit, Sharp claims that 'even though his metaphysical system demands it, Spinoza himself does not seem altogether comfortable with the consequences of his metaphysics for human distinctiveness' (2011b, 50). Accordingly, we should understand Spinoza's position as ambivalent with respect to whether or not to follow through on the direct upshots of the metaphysics. Sharp later on develops this idea by saying that 'every time Spinoza mentions humans and animals, it is in the context of decrying the desire among some to reject human community in favour of a wild freedom in association with animals' (ibid., 55). So, whereas Spinoza clearly does not argue for a replacement of one exceptionalist paradigm (that of humans) with another (that of animals or nature), there is reason to believe, according to Sharp, that Spinoza did not intend for this to mean that we are not able to seek an alternative to the human dominion-within-a-dominion paradigm when it comes to creating a normative system out of the epistemology that follows from metaphysical naturalism.

Because Spinoza merely denounces the desire to live in 'wild freedom in association with animals' we are still permitted, she argues, to construe an extended moral theory of nature so long as this theory encourages us to embrace and to respect other beings' striving to persevere, and, as long as it does not stipulate a living in a state of 'wild freedom' alongside animals (Sharp, 2011a, 185–220).

The second motive for using Spinoza's metaphysical conclusions to construct a new natural politics revolves around downplaying Spinoza's conscious separation between the realms of metaphysics/ethics and morality/normativity because of our currently extreme living conditions, which were not actualized during Spinoza's own lifetime. Sharp opens a recent essay by defining the Anthropocene as 'the threat of ecological catastrophe [that] binds our fate palpably to non-human beings and powers' and claims that, as such, it 'puts *increasing pressure on the human provincialism* that has reigned for millennia in mainstream ethics and politics in the western world' (2016, 274, my emphasis). She also writes that we are facing a 'current horizon of mass extinction' and that 'climate change can better be understood as the failure of humanity to master nature' (ibid.). From these passages it is clear that she understands our failure to master nature, not as a failure of a feasible task but rather as a failure to understand that nature is not ours to master in the first place (ibid.). In short, her argument stipulates that our currently extreme living conditions, accentuated by climate change for instance, are so special that they justify questioning both the metaphysical portrait of ourselves as masters of nature, and the ethical and moral imperative which rewards co-operation among human beings alone. Whereas Spinoza seems to question the first position in his metaphysical investigations, he does not seem to question the second concerning political consequences.

Summarizing, we have seen how Sharp motivates her argument for grounding a 're-naturalized' politics in Spinoza's metaphysical definition of virtue and its immediate ethical consequences on the following two arguments. First, that there is an inherent tension within Spinoza's works that motivates a digression from his literal expressions about morality and political philosophy. The tension arguably concerns the correlation between the ethical propositions about virtue in the light of naturalism, and the moral and political propositions about co-existence and moral perspectival evaluation. The second argument is that we are now facing such extreme living conditions that it is doubtful that Spinoza would have insisted on his own apparently anthropocentric moral theory had he been aware of these new conditions. I will, in what follows, carefully analyse and respond to each of these arguments.

Conceptual conditions of Sharp's eco-ethical reading of Spinoza: monism, naturalism and desire

In order to facilitate a serious consideration of the feasibility of the Reports' call for a new metaphysics as a means for a new kind of normative thinking and politics, I will dedicate this part's last section to responding to Sharp's two motives for adapting Spinoza's philosophy to the conditions for a natural politics. In doing so, I will stress what has been established above: that the first motive stems from the view that an extended application of Spinoza's definition of value goes hand in hand with the overall purpose of Spinoza's philosophy although this purpose is sometimes overshadowed by the internal tension between the philosophy's metaphysical and normative aspects. And, that the second motive stems from the idea that it is possible to argue for a direct politicization of Spinoza's formal and species neutral moral theory because current living conditions warrant a new interpretation of this theory.

Is there an internal tension in Spinoza's philosophical structure enabling a moral and political naturalism?

Committing to substance monism obliges Spinoza, as we have seen, to hold that the human being is something other than merely a thing extrinsically produced by nature. Rather, she is, according to Spinoza an intrinsic aspect of nature and her true ontological nature can be revealed only by studying the same patterns and principles that must be studied in order to understand the rest of nature (*E3* preface). We know that Spinoza's rejection of human exceptionalism amounts to a harsh critique of the metaphysical idea of humanity as a dominion-within-a-dominion (Nadler, 2006, 122; Della Rocca, 2008, 18; Bennett, 1984, 35–36). Sharp picks up on this trait in Spinoza's thought and writes herself into a solid tradition of Spinoza scholarship which interprets his critique of human exceptionalism as a critique of the custom to fall back on human specifics for explaining our human nature when, in fact, the very same rules govern our behaviour that govern all of nature (cf. LeBuffe, 2010, 36; Della Rocca, 2008, 117; Nadler, 2006, 135; Bennett, 1984, 37).

The same tradition of scholarship, however, also affirms that even though it is correct to hold that Spinoza distances himself metaphysically from other modern rationalists, and perhaps especially Descartes, it is also abundantly clear that he considers the establishment of the metaphysical dominion-within-a-dominion realm as an inevitable result of the natural mechanisms of human cognition. This consideration on Spinoza's part is something that we have familiarized ourselves with in the previous discussion of the free will and the problem of human-made civil laws. My explanation of it in that discussion was as follows.

Spinoza's metaphysics impedes our recognition that as human beings we believe that we are constituted differently than other things in nature because of our relatively greater ability to register and reflect upon changes in our own states of being. The fact that the human being has a relatively greater cognitive ability does not contradict the idea of philosophical and causal naturalism in so far as it merely reflects a gradual difference and not a difference in kind. The relatively higher cognitive ability, therefore, in no way secures a perfectly adequate understanding of the things that we register about our nature and nature. Rather, as we saw in the discussion about law, this gradual difference between us and other modes is more than anything the reason Spinoza gives for why we – in contrast to other beings – perceive ourselves as authors of effects in cases where we do not completely grasp their true causes. In short, we grasp that we feel the necessity to act in a given way, but we do not grasp the true reason for this necessity which is why we place the reason in ourselves. Accordingly, the perception of our ontological position as one implying a dominion-within-a-dominion appears to be epistemologically erroneous albeit produced by the natural laws determining our cognitive mechanisms. It is related to Spinoza's explanation of human cognitive ability as being relatively greater yet still limited, in so far as it appears as the immediate effect of us perceiving 'the self' as primarily the result of external impacts and perceiving the external forces in question as especially concerned with the self's current state of being (cf. Della Rocca, 2008, 177).

It is in light of these considerations, then, that we must read Spinoza's critique of exceptionalism and his claim that he will treat human nature and its characteristics on exactly the same terms as those used to explain a stone's curved course towards Earth and its physical relation to another being's input of force. And it is in the light of some of these considerations that Sharp's reading of Spinoza appears problematic. She does not seem to remember, for instance, that the fact alone that human nature and human emotions *can* be explained according to the same natural principles and axioms as the rest of nature does not solve the problems caused by the natural tendency not to do so. A careful consideration of the ethical problems caused by our natural limitation to understand requires a careful consideration of how Spinoza ties normativity and politics to epistemology, not merely a study of his metaphysics.

According to Spinoza, it is in our interest, ethically speaking, to liberate ourselves from the natural tendency to perceive things, including ourselves, according to their effects rather than their causes. This is because such liberation corresponds to our highest sense of wellbeing and a maximization of our power to persevere (cf. *TdIE* [13]). Nowhere, however, does Spinoza imply that achieving an adequate understanding of our own natures – one that is couched in terms of lines, planes and bodies (*E*3 preface) – will have the additional effect of altering or extending the ethical basis for our use of moral terms or our practice of evaluating things in terms of good and evil. Quite the contrary conclusion is actually indicated by the very final proposition of the *Ethics* in which Spinoza states that 'blessedness *is not the reward* of virtue, but virtue itself' (*E*5p42, emphasis added). Now, if blessedness is taken to be mean wellbeing and virtue is understood as an increase in power (to understand in the case of the human being), then it follows from proposition 42 that understanding things adequately will not result in a sense of wellbeing different from the immediate sensation of understanding adequately. In what follows, I will try to explain why I find this conclusion to mark a point from where it is possible to a construe a consistent reading of Spinoza's metaphysics and political philosophy in contrast to Sharp's suggestion that there is an internal tension between the two. In order to situate my explanation in the context of the problem of protecting nature, I will first expand my outline of Sharp's arguments in favour of the existence of an internal tension and her response to it.

In one of her works Sharp discusses the negative effects of the Anthropocene. In that discussion, she clearly illustrates the components of her idea that Spinoza's metaphysics could assist us in moving towards a new kind of application of the notion of value if only the tension between metaphysical naturalism and normative anthropocentrism in his texts is done away with. Basically, I take this to be her position because of the way that she identifies Spinoza's critique of Cartesian metaphysics and epistemology as a possible starting point for the development of a new kind of practical relationship with nature. To this end, she writes that the emergence of the Anthropocene is caused by having adhered to Cartesian epistemology as this:

> aptly describes *an orientation to the world that has contributed to climate change*. We – or at least those born into national, racial, socioeconomic, and/or gender privilege – have been able to treat nonhuman nature as a mere resource for human projects. The near limitless exploitation and instrumentalization of nonhuman nature *is supported* by the metaphysical portrait of

> ourselves as uniquely minded, distinctively sensitive, and fundamentally different in kind from all other beings in nature.
>
> (Sharp, 2016, 276, my emphasis)

She continues by urging that 'if we want to do anything *more than diagnose* the pathologies of the Anthropocene, *we need to fight* the human exceptionalism it presupposes' (ibid., my emphasis). To me, this appears as an argument for remedying a practice (our exploitation of non-human nature) by way of attacking and reworking the metaphysics underpinning it (the Cartesian traditional metaphysical portrait of ourselves). Together, the two cited passages seem to constitute the view that if we want to properly address our vicious conduct with respect to nature, we must start in the metaphysical explanation of desire, as desire proceeds conduct (i.e. 'the human exceptionalism [that] it presupposes'). If I understand Sharp correctly, she suggests that a new metaphysical understanding of desire can make us experience wellbeing differently.

Given Spinoza's identification of wellbeing with an adequate understanding of metaphysics, it should not be surprising that Sharp turns to Spinoza in the search for an alternative understanding of desire (cf. Garrett, 1996, 281–282 and 290; Wilson, 1996, 90; Nadler, 2006, 227 and 229; Della Rocca, 2008, 186). It is, as we have seen, well attested Spinoza equates human virtue understood as an increase in power to persevere with an increase in rational understanding (cf. Lord, 2010, 113). We have also seen that Spinoza ultimately motivates the double identification (virtue with power and power with rational understanding), with the relatively complex corporal constitution of the human body together with the metaphysical premise of parallelism (cf. Della Rocca, 2008, 85, 116 and 181; LeBuffe, 2010, 100; Nadler, 2006, 226; Huenemann, 2014, 138; Bennett, 1984, 297).

So, Sharp relies upon this double identification in her argumentation for an empirically visible effect in favour of nature's perspective of a new conceptualization of desire. In order to succeed in this argumentation she must construe Spinoza's metaphysical definition of ethical wellbeing as implying that not only will we feel better about ourselves if we understand the world according to a true metaphysical representation of it (in so far as this will increase our number of adequate ideas i.e. power/virtue), we will also start to desire the wellbeing of other things and beings in nature since their sensation of wellbeing, in this scenario, will expand the object of our rational understanding. In short, I take her position to be that understanding the wellbeing of another being will make an individual desire to contribute to that wellbeing as if it were its own because such an understanding will constitute a parallel wellbeing in the thinking individual. We can see how this appears to be Sharp's position if we break open yet another of her statements. It reads: 'it is our ineluctable involvement with other beings that unite our fates and *redirects* our aims *well beyond* our intentions' (2016, 279, my emphasis). By positing that an adequate understanding of a given ontological fact (our ineluctable involvement with other things, for instance) is the cause of a given normative effect (the redirection of our aims), Sharp clearly accepts that we act upon the commands, not of natural laws, but of an independent intellectual faculty. Coming to terms with our own ontological status in the world will naturally cause a change in the way that we interact with it. In other words, understanding how and what we *are* can change the way we desire and act. In sum, then, her argument is that a result of appreciating the world and ourselves as we are (i.e. according to Spinoza's metaphysics for instance) will be that we find our desires being directed in ways we cannot anticipate while we are still in the grasp of an erroneous understanding. So, on my understanding of this argument, it presupposes that an adequate understanding of the causal mechanism behind human emotions will automatically alter, not only the human understanding of these mechanisms, but also their function.

To emphasize how this idea constitutes a general theme in Sharp's argumentation about Spinoza and nature, let us consider yet another passage:

> Climate change *reveals* the self-undermining effects of treating other beings as instruments and resources for human use. Surely human beings frequently *act* as if we are lords and masters of nature, but *the effects of our actions both exceed and undermine our intentions.*
>
> (Ibid., my emphasis)

It is possible to read this passage, I think, as a confirmation of the position that our misconceived (Cartesian) account of nature and ourselves constitutes the reason we act in ways that are detrimental to our own wellbeing. It is not due to something in nature or constitution, but rather due to an erroneous understanding of the metaphysical interconnectedness between non-human and human beings, that we desire things and ends that in fact are detrimental to our wellbeing.

It is my understanding, however, that Spinoza does not blame metaphysical explanations of any kind for any aspects of human behaviour. This is because metaphysics, according to Spinoza, can merely explain – in more or less adequate terms – what things are: including the 'things' that make us act, like desire, lust and emotions. Thus, no metaphysical explanation – however erroneous – can be blamed for the fact that we at times act against our own wellbeing. The only 'thing' to blame for this fact is human nature, correctly or erroneously perceived.

Taking this reminder with us back to Sharp's argumentation, it seems obvious that she does not appreciate the limitation of scope which I have just indicated with respect to Spinoza's metaphysics. Her argument is instead fuelled by the idea that there is a connection between understanding that things *are not* ontologically divided according to two kinds of substance and a desire to protect nature as naturally as one protects oneself. I am not alone, however, in finding the general conditions for this idea problematic in the light of Spinoza's metaphysical account. Jonathan Bennett makes, for instance, a similar reflection in his seminal study on the *Ethics* when he writes that Spinoza's metaphysics does not construe nature as capable of containing or expressing any pathologies at all (1984, 36). Following through on this line of thought leads us, I would argue, to precisely the conclusion that I have indicated here. Namely, that if there can be no pathologies in nature, there is no disease for us to cure – neither in nature as such nor in our relationship with it – since we constitute modes of its perfect being. There is only one substance: nature, and more or less adequate ways for us to create our understanding of it.

So, as discussed extensively in Chapter 2, as rehearsed in this section, and as affirmed by Sharp in her reading, ethical wellbeing for human beings is according to Spinoza intrinsically connected with achieving an adequate understanding of nature. I have pointed to various places in his works where this is stated in different terms. Now, my discussion of Spinoza's political philosophy has established, I hope, that achieving ethical wellbeing depends for Spinoza on a normative order that forces every one of a state's subjects to live according to one set of dictates (preferably the dictates of reason, if this is possible). My argument is that this implies that human wellbeing ultimately depends on the entertainment of inadequate ideas, notwithstanding the fact that the end goal of ethics amounts to a state of being where one does *not* depend on such ideas. Let me conclude my response to Sharp's first motivation for adapting Spinoza's philosophy to the necessities of nature by breaking down this argument a little further.

An adequate understanding depends on the availability of a conceptual space for developing ideas from within the mind itself. Such a conceptual space cannot be constructed in any other way than by a normative order curbing people's interaction by way of irrational ideas. This is because human beings are affective and social creatures by nature and because an idea's affective power is not the same as, and does not operate on the same plane as, the question of its truthfulness (cf. *E*4p14). The only way to curb the affective power of any given idea – true or false – is, as we have seen, by introducing a contrasting idea with a stronger affective power going in the opposite direction. Now, since the affective power of ideas is not related to their adequacy or truthfulness, to secure the domination of rational – adequate – prescripts of living a state must steer its people towards them by way of using ideas with great affective power, such as the inadequate ideas of hope and fear. A normative order which aims at increasing its subjects' level of adequacy and, by extension, freedom must therefore often further an erroneous idea of human nature in so far as this is the idea which is unconsciously upheld by the majority of its subjects.

On my understanding, a (for Spinoza) adequate understanding of nature implies hinging it upon a normative order that, paradoxical as it may sound, affirms an erroneous metaphysical perspective: one that portrays the human being as special and takes the human perspective to be the central one. The paradox is resolved once we consider that good and evil have no positive meaning in relation to nature beyond their comparative and perspectival significance, and that there is nothing ontologically special in the human being which makes us as receptive to inadequate ideas as adequate ones. Thus, in a normative order that does not incorporate inadequate, imaginative ideas in its structure, there is a risk of lacking affective power to hold back those less than perfectly rational people (everyone) from obstructing others' striving towards an adequate understanding and, by extension, ethical wellbeing. So, in terms of the function of the state as a means to the human highest end of freedom, it is clearly counterproductive to order its norms according to Spinoza's adequate definition of virtue directly.

To conclude, it would indeed seem that Spinoza's strict division between the metaphysical and the political realm contains no arbitrary cut or inherent inconsistency after all. Rather, when studied closely, it appears clear that a normative philosophy which affirms the necessity of inadequate and imaginary ideas is the best option available for achieving the ethical ends of Spinoza's metaphysical explanation of wellbeing and freedom. In other words, it does not seem to be in line with Spinoza's philosophical naturalism to postulate the metaphysical doctrines as normative ideals directly. To pursue an ideal, regardless if pursued individually or as a collective, implies for Spinoza to take a step away from a metaphysically adequate description of things. To close in on one's own truest metaphysical nature, that is, requires adhering to a normative order that presumes a less than completely adequate epistemology. In order to reach the level of adequate understanding that corresponds with one's highest expression of power to persevere – that is, wellbeing and freedom – it is inevitable that one will rely upon some form of irrational ideal.

Urgency of the matter – is there an adaptable object and purpose in Spinoza's normative theory?

Having demonstrated the problems attached to Sharp's first motivation for re-reading Spinoza, I will now focus on and discuss her second motive for doing so. This is the alternative motive of the urgency of the matter at hand. Judging by the way that Sharp describes our current state of being as a state where we face a 'threat of ecological catastrophe [that] binds our fate palpably to non-human beings and powers', it would seem as if there were indeed external circumstances impeding our re-thinking of Spinoza's normative structure. Constructed this way, this argument appears to presume that Spinoza would, were he to experience our current living conditions, admit the necessity of altering his political philosophy's anthropocentric and utilitarian focus for the benefit of the philosophical naturalism of his metaphysics.

This argument assumes the hypothetical position that *if* faced with the same state of affairs as we do today Spinoza would support a re-evaluation of the reasons for limiting the scope of his political and normative theories. To this end, it is an argument that appears similar to one of international law's principal norms of interpretation: the principle that a legal rule should be interpreted as a living instrument the object and purpose of which may evolve at the same pace as its context (cf. ICJ, 1997; United Nations, 1969, Art. 31.1). In order to evaluate Sharp's second motive for altering Spinoza's normative conclusions, I must therefore now consider whether Spinoza's political philosophy, and in particular his understanding of international law, contains an endorsement of such a norm.

For this reason, let me therefore briefly return to the previous chapter's review of Spinoza's position with respect to international law.

I concluded the previous chapter by arguing that the rather peculiar non-legal theory of international law, which seems to be implicit in Spinoza's political philosophy, holds unexpected potential to help us understand both the nature of the state and that of the individual. I said that because of his conceptualizations of international relations, the state and the law, Spinoza can be classified neither as a materialist nor as a pure idealist. His metaphysics in general and his strict commitment to determinism, philosophical naturalism and substance monism in particular block him from positing a teleological end of any kind in relation to the state, the law or international relations. Like any individual in Spinoza's metaphysics, the state can be explained as a given, mechanical striving to perseverance in being. This striving, I said, in relation to an individual like the state which metaphysically speaking is nothing more than a psychological entity necessary for ordering the human experience of existence, means a striving to keep providing for the explanations of the world and human experience that are necessary in order to make its presence motivated.

Thus, in order for a state to increase its power to persevere it must strive, not towards a state of being where no laws or governance are needed (which indeed is its overall object in so far as it ultimately is but a means to individual freedom) but towards a state of being where its apparatus of governance and its laws are considered necessary and useful for the purpose of peaceful coexistence and security. This means that a state of being in which the metaphysical truth about nature is fully realized and endorsed by everyone, is neither a natural nor a rational goal with respect to the state's ethical striving. Having this state of being as its goal would mean that the state was striving towards its own redundancy. And this would constitute, of course, a metaphysical impossibility according to Spinoza's definition of the essence of finite modes as a striving to persevere.

I believe that this conclusion can serve us well as a vantage point from where to analyse Spinoza's clear division between the metaphysical and the normative realms in light of the question of external changing conditions. The strict separation of metaphysics from normativity appears to this end neither as something accidental nor as resulting from a specific historical context and era; the strict separation is more than anything a carefully considered consequence of the metaphysics in so far as a limited and egoistic purpose of normative thought is a precondition for the achievement of the metaphysics' overarching ethical end.

With this consideration in place, it seems difficult to defend Sharp's indication that the urgency of the current state of affairs implores us to read another purpose and scope into Spinoza's recommendations for social interaction and moral responsibility. In so far as it is the function performed by the state with respect to the dissemination of metaphysical truth that explains its ontological nature, then this function is still the purpose and scope towards which all of its activities must be directed. Earlier, I pointed out that for the achievement of the explanatory function it is essential that the state and its laws are considered necessary. Now, upholding the idea that the nature of the state is necessary requires inadequate ideas, which is why it lies in the interest of the self-perseverance of the state *and*, by extension, in the interest of the ultimate ethical goal of an adequate metaphysical understanding, to not make laws that challenge the *false* metaphysics that upholds both the law itself and the state as such. What Spinoza's normative construction boils down to, then, I believe, is that the question of adequate understanding, and, by extension, highest virtue is a question that must be approached carefully and from a platform which itself does not question irrational ideas such as hope, fear, punishment and reward. A considered questioning of ideas like these, which indeed pertains to an ethical development, should never be forced upon a state's subjects because their affirmations function as a means to the end of coming to questioning them.

With this last remark, it is evident to me that neither one of the two motives envisioned by Sharp for a re-reading of Spinoza's philosophy in light of the normative problem of nature seems to hold up to closer scrutiny. In order, then, to provide for an exhaustive consideration of the implications of the call for a new metaphysics within the context of normative responses to the problem of nature, what remains is to look at one last hypothetical scenario. In the final part of this chapter I will therefore pose the question of what would be the implications for international law if the international community was to follow through on the Reports' call, presuming that this call amounts to a reliance on Spinoza's philosophy. In order to respond properly to this query, it is necessary to proceed in two steps. First, I will discuss the remaining conditions for understanding Spinoza's formal moral theory – after having rejected the Reports', Naess' and Sharp's attempts – in a way that connects this theory with a normative ethics extending to nature. And then, taking my cue from the analysis of international law in Chapter 5, I will explain why these remaining conditions render impossible an adaptation of Spinoza's normative ethics so as to include the intrinsic value of nature into our normative structures.

Part two: the implications for law of the Reports' call for a radical new metaphysics

To begin this final and concluding discussion about the normative implications of following through on the Reports' call, I would like to remind especially of one of the concepts with which I have tried to link the Reports to Spinoza's philosophy. Value is a central concept both to ethics and justice. From what we have seen in the review of the Reports, it would appear that their description of value shares important traits with Spinoza's metaphysical definition of the term. The Reports affirm that value is everywhere the same, in relation to human beings as well as in relation to any other thing in nature. They also posit value as something intrinsic to things and without a positive normative content in so far as it is merely a measurement of its host's natural tendency to strive towards perseverance in being. We have seen that this conceptual similarity is supported not only by formulations within the Reports but also by the fact that other eco-ethical readings of Spinoza formulated in much the same spirit as the Reports (like, for instance, Hasana Sharp's project of a renaturalization of politics) emphasize precisely Spinoza's definition of value (and virtue) as the key for a successful employment of his philosophy in the face of the problem of the Anthropocene. Let us keep this similarity in mind as I now turn to the concluding discussions of this book.

Can Spinoza's moral theory ground a normative ethics that includes nature?

Judging by the way they discuss the matter, it seems as if the Reports as well as the reading exemplified by Sharp's works, follow a line of reasoning according to which it is possible to combine Spinoza's definition of value with a new kind of normative structure: one that was not expressly recognized by Spinoza at the time of writing his political philosophy. However, my review of Spinoza's philosophical system points to a difficulty in adapting Spinoza's moral theory to any other normative structure than the one chiselled out by Spinoza himself. So, juxtaposing the Reports' argumentation concerning value with that of Spinoza, it becomes evident that the former constitutes a call for an entirely naturalistic and non-anthropocentric ontological understanding of value and moral theory which is not properly followed through in terms of the consequences this brings to normative ethics.

We have seen how the Reports, just like Sharp and other more theoretically focused studies supporting and expanding the Reports' basic arguments, indicate that Spinoza's metaphysics (or, a metaphysics inspired by Spinoza's doctrines at least) may function as a means to counter the ongoing ecological crisis due to its critique of Cartesian dualism. As I pointed out in Chapter 1, the Reports claim, among other things, that Cartesian dualism strips nature of essential human characteristics, like sentiments and desire, and that Spinoza, through his naturalistic definition of value, reinstalls these characteristics in nature. They also maintain that Descartes' erroneous understanding of nature in relation to value emerges from a fundamental misconception of human nature – as something ontologically different than the rest of nature. The review undertaken in Chapters 3 to 5 of this book of Spinoza's political philosophy has shown, however, that the Reports' understanding of Spinoza in this context is problematic.

Although it is true that Spinoza criticizes Descartes, the critique does not stem from an idea that nature holds human traits. According to Spinoza, it is justified to criticize Descartes' human/nature-division. Not because it explains nature erroneously, according to mechanical and material principles, and leaves out principles governing emotions, desires and affects, but because it does not include the human being (including those of her features which intuitively appear to us as especially 'human', like intuition, emotions and desires) into that mechanical explanation. In fact, Spinoza does not so much criticize Descartes for regarding nature as a thing without value, as he criticizes him for failing to see that the objects corresponding to value labels and other such notions that are typically employed for describing a human perspective should be understood and analysed according to the same principles as any another natural phenomenon: like lines, planes and bodies (*E3* preface). Spinoza is careful to emphasize, however, that this does not make our *phenomenological experiences* of the world – turning on such notions as mark our specialness, like desire and emotions – false, metaphysically speaking. We are naturally inclined to perceive the world this way despite the fact that the objects underpinning that perception – the objects of our desires and emotional changes – are not, ontologically speaking, how we perceive them to be from our limited human perspective. In a way, I think that it is this double recognition – a doubling of perspective if you will – that makes Spinoza's political philosophy radical and different to most other modern and rational explanations of the human condition. Spinoza's political philosophy is an anthropocentric philosophy in so far as it affirms anthropocentrism as necessary for the human condition and for a successful human orientation in a completely non-anthropocentric reality, ontologically speaking.

Let us keep this conclusion in mind while looking closer at one of the Reports' Spinozistic statements. The seventh Report states (as quoted in Chapter 1) that '"Earth rights" cannot be validly circumscribed or abrogated by *human* jurisprudence' (Rep. VII, para.36). We know from the overall configuration of the Reports' argumentation that this can be read as meaning that an adequate understanding of the world – one that reflects an entirely non-anthropocentric order of existence – leads to a rejection of an anthropocentric perspective on law and normativity. The same Report goes on to state that we should therefore 'include the rights of Nature into our governance systems', which clearly seems to confirm the validity of that reading (ibid.). In the light of what I have just stated about Spinoza's critique of the Cartesian explanation of human nature, these statements reflect a rejection of anthropocentrism in relation to normative thought that is not present in Spinoza's account of the state, law and international relations. Taking a Spinozistic perspective in response to the statements in the seventh Report, implies saying that being a mode implies taking one's own particular perspective. What is more, the law, in terms of being a means for organizing how to deal with the phenomenological experience of a complex ontology, necessarily implies affirming that our point of view is ontologically central.

Indeed, the preface to Part Five of the *Ethics* makes it reasonable to construe a Spinozistic answer along these lines to the problem of law and anthropocentrism being an erroneous metaphysical perspective. In this preface, Spinoza accuses Descartes of dodging the very point of departure that his own metaphysical premises produce.

> I cannot wonder enough that a Philosopher of his calibre – one who had firmly decided to deduce nothing except from principles known through themselves, and to affirm nothing which he did not perceive clearly and distinctly, one who had so often censured the Scholastics for wishing to explain obscure things by occult qualities – that such a Philosopher should assume a Hypothesis more occult than any occult quality. What, I ask, does he understand by the union of the Mind and Body? What clear and distinct concept does he have thought of so closely united to some little portion of quantity? Indeed, I wish he had explained this union by its proximate cause. But he had conceived the Mind to be so distinct from the Body that he could not assign any singular cause, either of this union or of the Mind itself. Instead, it was

necessary for him to have recourse to the cause of the whole Universe, i.e., to God.

(*E*5 preface, G II/279/20–280)

Descartes, Spinoza argues, turns to God in order to explain the final cause of the human mind and its apparent abilities even though he confesses to rationality and the principle of explainability. Having turned to God in order to explain the power of the mind, Descartes is already on the wrong path when it comes to formulating a moral theory according to Spinoza. Earlier in the same preface he connects the critique of Descartes' methodological inconsistency with the ethical question of wellbeing. He suggests in this discussion that instead of turning to an inexplicable divine power we should use 'the power of reason, showing what it can do against the affects, and what Freedom of the Mind, or blessedness is' (G II/277). So, there can be no doubt about the fact that even though Descartes, according to Spinoza, makes an arbitrary, brute and therefore erroneous reference to a providential God when grounding his moral theory, Spinoza himself recognizes both the naturalness by which we tend towards such a theory and the effect it may have with respect to the ethical goal of wellbeing.

The difference between the two philosophers' respective explanatory structures does not so much revolve around the notion of error, as such, as it does the fact that Spinoza considers his method – one that is not wrapped up around a transcendental or providential divinity – to be more *effective* with respect to the human striving towards wellbeing, that is, adequate understanding. Spinoza is clearly humble with regard to the fact that human beings must differentiate and evaluate although nature does not. By contrast, the Reports seem to focus on the fact that Descartes' metaphysical explanation of ourselves and nature is erroneous, as such, and that merely by correcting this we will be able to alter our human tendency to make biased ethical choices.

I have already established that I consider this to be a position which is very difficult to reconcile with Spinoza's take on morality and ethics. The seventh Report also, however, opens up a somewhat different view. This could be important in so far as it might bring us closer to a more plausible version of a Spinozistic approach to the contemporary problem of nature. As mentioned in Chapter 1, the seventh Report admits that the human position might necessitate an ethical relationship with nature that is not in conformity with an adequate ontological understanding of this relationship (Rep. VII, para.20). To this end, the seventh Report ties its position closer to the eco-ethical reading of Spinoza's philosophical structure which has been emerging recently within contemporary ethical and philosophical discourses. There is no doubt about the fact, however, that the underlying idea of the seventh Report – just as in Sharp's eco-ethical politics of 'renaturalization' – is to combine a more nuanced understanding of the perspectival aspect of value and a striving towards a normative order that includes all of nature and reflects the metaphysical understanding that everything is interconnected and unified.

In order to see if the formation of such a normative order can be sustained from a Spinozist perspective, that is, if it is possible to extend Spinoza's clearly anthropocentric normative focus to the rest of nature by way of extending the application of his definition of value, we must start with that definition and discuss how it affects his formulation of a formal moral theory.

For one thing, there are propositions about value in the *Ethics* that point to two very different understandings of the good. On the one hand, there are propositions that reveal a reductive definition of value, where the good is equated with whatever we associate with joy (cf. *E*3p9s; *E*3p39s; *E*4p8d). The scholium of proposition 39 in Part Three reads for instance:

> By good here I understand every kind of Joy, and whatever leads to it, and especially what satisfies any kind of longing, whatever that may be. And by evil every kind of Sadness, and especially what frustrates longing. For we have shown (in P9S) that *we desire nothing because we judge it to be good, but on the contrary, we call it good because we desire it.*
>
> (G II/170/12–20, my emphasis)

There are also, however, propositions about the good that point to an explanation of value as something absolute and constant (cf. *E*4p23 and *E*4p26, 27 and 28). So, *E*4p28d states that 'knowledge of God is the Mind's greatest good; its greatest virtue is to know God' (G II/228/7–10). Moreover, in the *Treatise on the Emendation of the Intellect*, Spinoza defines the human highest good as 'to arrive [...] at the enjoyment of' a 'special nature'. It follows that true good is 'whatever can be a means to his [man's] attaining' it. He then gives a hint of what this nature is, by stating:

> What that nature is we shall show in its proper place: that it is *the knowledge of the union that the mind has with the whole of Nature.* This, then, is the end I aim at: to acquire such a nature, and to strive that many acquire it with me. That is, it is part of my happiness to take pains that many others may understand as I understand, so that their intellect and desire agree entirely with my intellect and desire. To do this it is necessary, *first* to understand as much of Nature as suffices for acquiring such a nature; *next*, to form a society of the kind that is desirable, so that as many as possible may attain it as easily and surely a possible.
>
> (G II/8–9, emphasis in original)

A similar formulation can be found in the *Ethics* where the preface to Part Two states that:

> I pass now to explaining those things which must necessarily follow from the essence of God, or the infinite and eternal being – not, indeed, all of them, for we have demonstrated (IP16) that infinitely many things must follow from it in infinitely many modes, but only those that can lead us, by the

> hand, as it were, to the *knowledge of the human Mind and its highest blessedness.*
>
> (G II/84, my emphasis)

To judge by these propositions, it would seem that Spinoza endorses both a reductive account of value – for example *E*3p9s, *E*3p39s and *E*4p8d, which all equate value with joy-seeking, or desire-satisfaction – *and* a non-reductive account – for example the *TdIE*, *E*2 preface and *E*4p28, which affirm that there is *one* understanding of value which serves us better than others in the sense that it is more efficient than all others as a means to wellbeing. Indeed, Spinoza's formal theory of value, which is expressed in *E*4d1 and *E*4d2, seems to affirm the latter position by positing that the good is 'what we certainly know to be useful to us' (G II/209/12). If the highest sense of wellbeing (joy) is connected to a perfection of human nature, and Spinoza indeed dedicates Parts two and Three to demonstrate this, then there exists a way to evaluate whether one's particular understanding of value is detrimental or fruitful with respect to the aim of achieving such wellbeing.

In this light, the reductive accounts in Part Three appears rather as purely descriptive propositions about *how* humans use value terms, and the non-reductive accounts of the highest good become recommendations of the best means for evaluating which of our uses of the terms indeed brings us closer or further away from the goal to which all uses relate: wellbeing. It is important to note in this context, as Michael LeBuffe does, that Spinoza's formal theory of value – that good is what we certainly know to be useful for our striving to perseverance (i.e. wellbeing/power/rational understanding) (*E*4d1) – accommodates our use of value terms (according to a reductive account) better to our metaphysical and physical living circumstances than other common understandings of value terms do. It does not intend to explain why joy or wellbeing is good for us, but it gives us the key for understanding how to find its maximum expression given a) our nature and b) the nature of our use of value terms.

According to LeBuffe, the problem for Spinoza with moral theories establishing a universal and fixed understanding of value based on content and not function or use is that they often end up being counterproductive to the aim revealed by the human natural use of the terms, that is, wellbeing. Believing that the content of the good is something fixed, like something that a law giving, providential God determines, 'leads to bad consequences: people who understand value this way wind up with tortured understandings of nature, become overly involved in controversies about the good, and may, in the face of these problems, become moral sceptics' (LeBuffe, 2010, 161). So, not only is this kind of perception of the good detrimental to the ultimate end of wellbeing, it is also detrimental to the partial end of living in peace and security within a stable normative order.

So, Spinoza's moral theory is not really intended as a model for a fixed understanding of what is good. As LeBuffe correctly points out, there is according to Spinoza no universal understanding of value to be replaced by a true one – understandings will always differ as humans will differ in perspectives and rational capacities (ibid., 166). However, there is, as we have seen, a universal use of value terms: we relate to these terms – because of the principle of philosophical naturalism – in a way that is as predictable as a stone's reaction to the impact of a human hand letting it go. In other words, Spinoza's formal moral theory qualifies as a formal moral theory because it defines good as those means that are truly conducive to the end of our use of value terms: wellbeing.

This brings us back to Spinoza's discussion of the highest good. One way of understanding this discussion is to consider it as follows. If the only constant variable in our value judgements is our *use* of them, and if we usually do not have a clear idea of what wellbeing is, then Spinoza's statements about the highest good can be understood as an explanation of how we ought to understand wellbeing in order to make our understanding correspond as much as possible with our constant use of the terms. In LeBuffe's words: 'Spinoza provides his formal definitions [of value], then, at least in part because they are a more reliable guide to the attainment of value than a reductive explanation of value would be' (ibid., 168). In sum, the fact that human beings project values onto things reveals not only that they desire things, but also that they understand things to have value. This, in turn, opens up for discussion which understanding of a thing's value is the best. It 'inclines us to seek an explanation for value' which allows Spinoza to 'provide explanations of value that give a better account of what is valuable than the bare descriptions of the scholia of Part 3, "any kind of Laetitia" or "any object of longing"' (ibid., quotation marks in original). And in answer to the question of why Spinoza would feel inclined to provide such an understanding, we might say that it is because he has already demonstrated in previous parts of the *Ethics* that desires and passions are often inadequate and confused ideas of experiences. This is to say that when we desire something, we usually do this while misinterpreting both the thing and its effects on us. So, Spinoza's formal theory constitutes his attempt to provide us with a better, as in more effective (in terms of achieving wellbeing), definition of the good: one that 'builds upon his accounts of what desire and the affects really are, both insofar as we are aware of them and also insofar as we often are not' (LeBuffe, 2010, 168).

Formulated this way, the formal moral theory is thought to prepare the way for a normative basis apt 'to form a society of the kind that is desirable, so that as many as possible may attain it [perfected human nature/wellbeing] as easily and surely as possible' as called for early on in the *TdIE*. To this end, Spinoza's formal moral theory immediately conditions the normative ethics that follows from it by forcing it to be a practically useful guide concerned with accommodating our understanding of value to our universal and unchanging use of the terms better, so that we indeed may increase our level of wellbeing despite our tendency to understand desire, wellbeing and affects inadequately. In LeBuffes' words: 'Spinoza's normative ethics – his particular claims about what we should do, what the free man does, and the right way of living – are propositions designed to help us to attain' the things that bring joy (LeBuffe, 2010, 175). Now, because human beings subscribe to a wide range of traditional ethical views, share different experiences and have different beliefs as well as levels of rationality, the normative propositions formulated under the regime of Spinoza's idea of morality and ethics, must be formulated in many different ways.

Based on these considerations it seems justified to ask, as do the Reports, Naess, Sharp and others, if nature could not be included in what Spinoza defines as our most effective understanding of wellbeing so that it is covered automatically by Spinoza's formal moral theory. There certainly seems to be conceptual room for doing so in so far as our use of value terms reflects a universal and species-neutral desire to self-preserve. If caring for nature's wellbeing corresponds to an effective means for securing our own wellbeing, then it would seem as if their suggestion would be plausible. In other words, then there is a reason for holding that Spinoza's normative ethical propositions (about what we ought to always strive for, what the 'free man' would do and what the right way of living is) could be extended to include nature and other modes in nature. My answer to this question, however, is that it is not a plausible suggestion to make, and I will now explain why I reach this conclusion based on an analysis of Spinoza's normative ethics.

How does Spinoza's normative ethics condition domestic and international attempts to protect nature?

Just as the formal moral theory, Spinoza's normative ethics is rather evasive and difficult to get an overview of. There are propositions related to the normative aspects of ethics spread out at different places in Parts Four and Five of the *Ethics* and these are, although of course inter-related, ordered according to three slightly different normative categories (LeBuffe, 2010, 175). The difficulty of grasping the normative upshots of the moral theory also stems from the fact that this theory, as we have just seen, clearly lacks a transcendent structure where the content of the good is fixed at an abstract level and then passed down according to a chain of concretizations of events. This eliminates the aspect of natural prescriptiveness – like a natural law giving – to which ethical propositions are usually associated (cf. Bennett, 1984, 307; Rutherford, 2010; Deleuze, 1988, 17–29).

All three kinds of ethical norm in the *Ethics* are related to what Spinoza calls the 'Dictates of Reason' in so far as they all refer to (the formal moral theory's response to the question of) what reason requires of an individual who strives to persist in being. They all, in one way or another, relate to the double task of 'secur [ing] the means to perseverance' through resisting passions, in so far as reason dictates that resisting passions is the best means to secure perseverance (LeBuffe, 2010, 175). From the previous review of Spinoza's metaphysics (Chapter 2), we know that because joy (*laetitia*), or wellbeing, is directly related to our power to strive to persevere in being (*conatus*) which, in turn, is manifested by our ability to be active in mind and body, overcoming passive affects by way of actively forming our ideas about their causes marks our relative success in achieving ethical wellbeing (cf. LeBuffe, 2010, 175).

Now, since resisting passions is arguably an essential condition for securing the means to persevere,[3] it is natural that some of the dictates of reason (according to

Spinoza) relate to the task of overcoming the mental errors giving rise to passions (*E*5p4 and p10s) while others instead relate more directly to the main objective of persevering. LeBuffe provides a convincing explanation of this structure. He argues that Spinoza's normative ethics first and foremost should be regarded as a method for resisting passions insofar as this amounts to both the means and end of persevering in being. To this end, the normative ethics incorporate general advice to try to separate the ideas of a thing's effects from the affects it causes. However, since this task, straightforward as it seems, may not always be practically feasible for everyone, the normative ethics must be complemented by means which are directed towards the end of perseverance regarded as a practical endeavour, leaving the ultimate end of rational understanding aside. Sometimes, then, we need to rely on the imagination in order to find out what amounts to the best – that is, most rational – means to persevere without understanding why that is the best method or what the causes of our present state of being are (LeBuffe, 2010, 176). In short, because all human beings within one and the same social collective and context do not hold one and the same intellectual capacity, the dictates of reason must be divided into categories suitable to different stages of the ethical striving.

As mentioned, there is only one category of the dictates of reason in the *Ethics* (*E*5p4 and p10s) that relates directly to the unmediated connection between activity and ethical virtue/wellbeing. This category is therefore the only category consisting of universal and categorical imperatives. Since resisting passions is a matter of degree for Spinoza, these prescriptions are applicable always and to everyone (see LeBuffe, 2010, 175). Every human being – rational and irrational alike – always benefits from working towards understanding an affect clearly and distinctly and thinking and reflecting upon common human epistemological errors and fears (*E*5p4 and p10s). In this context, it is especially noteworthy that the prescripts' focus on epistemic exercises – separating a thing's cause from its effects and understanding fear and hate for instance – implies that the normative ethics already includes an entirely non-anthropocentric perspective. Thus, a call for adapting Spinoza's normative ethics to his non-anthropocentric metaphysics would surely then not affect this part since it already stipulates, as universal ethical advice, trying to perceive as adequately as possible a thing's causes and effects, including all of its interconnected relations with everything else in nature and nature as a whole. However, the practical implication for laws and law making of this conclusion may be very limited in so far as the prescripts in question are generally held and largely lack a concrete action guiding content (cf. Rutherford, 2010, 143–167).

According to LeBuffe, the other category of the dictates of reason (the majority of which we find in Part Four of the *Ethics*, starting with proposition 18) is different from the direct prescripts to try to control the passions in that these dictates relate to the task of perseverance without focusing on the causes obstructing that task. As such, they are composed of one sub group of norms prescribing different concrete means for perseverance (from *E*4p67 onward) and another sub group of theoretical tools aimed at helping us to diagnose our current ethical status in light of a model of a perfect human being: 'the free man' (2010, 175–176).

Characteristic of the first sub group is that they prescribe norms of action according to a description of the right way of living. They are formulated as concrete action guiding norms in contrast to the more general prescripts in Part Five. They are not formulated as having a universal applicability.

Whereas everyone's striving to persevere always, in every single circumstance, benefits from the general aim of separating the cause from its effect, the success of individual attempts to realize this aim does not depend on the same preconditions. Everyone's ability to rationalize and think adequately differ and so it follows that the right way of living – in relation to the end of becoming capable of separating an effect from its causes – must differ too. In order to understand which of the norms of perseverance one ought to adhere to, the first group of norms in Part Four (*E*4p18–p66 and *E*5p25 and *E*5p31s) creates a model for measuring and diagnosing one's ethical status. As LeBuffe puts it, 'knowing what a free person would do in a given situation can help people to understand which of their actions or proposed actions, as a kind, are free and which are unfree' (2010, 176).

People are not under an equal or constant influence of passions to begin with. Some of us are more affected by external inputs than others and one and the same person is not constantly predisposed to react to external things in one and the same way. This means that we have to adapt our striving to persevere according to the configurations and circumstances by which we happen to be surrounded. Among the norms in Part Four which are concerned with the means to perseverance, some are therefore directed to people who are relatively more rational and active in their interaction with external things and ideas, and others are more directed towards people who are less rational and more passive in their interactions. The group of dictates which is related to describing the 'free man' complements the first group of norms in that they can help us understand which of the perseverance norms we benefit by adhering to in a given circumstance. The 'free man' dictates describe a human being who holds a perfect rational understanding of nature and who, through this understanding, enjoys a maximum sensation of wellbeing and ability to persevere. In concrete terms, the dictates of reason describing the 'free man' are hypothetical descriptions of how a perfectly rational human being would react to and confront different situations in which external things require its attention. This fact, in my view, reveals that their function is less about creating a viable model for us to live strictly by than it is about helping us diagnose our own particular situation, by giving us a model of comparison. The ideal – a person who has perfect knowledge and therefore only experiences joy – appears to be a contradiction in terms with respect to the ontological status of modes as limited and externally caused things.

What it all boils down to, according to LeBuffe, is that the action guiding norms about perseverance together with the tools for diagnosing one's level of rationality in Part Four, in light of the formal moral theory, show that it may be 'useful for people with different backgrounds or in different situations to understand value in a number of different way' (2010, 182). If LeBuffe is correct in this observation, it means that even though there exists one way of understanding value that is metaphysically correct (in the sense that it leads more effectively than competing understandings to what corresponds to an adequate understanding of wellbeing), this does not mean that everyone is capable of appreciating it or living according to it. LeBuffe takes the norm of perseverance in *E*4p45s to be an illustrative example of precisely this effect. The scholium reads:

> It is part of a wise man to refresh himself and restore himself, in moderation, with good food and drink, with perfumes, with the beauty of lush plants, with decoration, with music, with sports, with the theatre, and with other things of this kind, which one can enjoy without harm to another.

LeBuffe juxtaposes this norm with Spinoza's description in Part Three of an individual overwhelmed by the sad passions of alcoholism or gluttony and explains that in such cases, the scholium should not be taken literally, as food and drink for these persons are bad means to wellbeing. This makes LeBuffe draw the conclusion that while it may be true that Spinoza's statement in *E*4p45s should be applied as a guideline for a reasonably rational individual or an individual mainly under the influence of positive passive affects, it should not be adhered to by a person under the influence of saddening passions. LeBuffe elaborates: '[p]eople in the wrong sets of circumstances, and especially people under the influence of the wrong sorts of passions, will not benefit from food and drink and so should not pursue them' (2010, 184).

With respect to the Reports' call for a new metaphysics, I suggest that this example shows that *if* it could be demonstrated that enjoying a pristine landscape, clean air and organic food, with certainty brings about an increased ability to persevere for a reasonably rational individual, then that demonstration in itself does not prove the generality necessary for a legal prescript stipulating the constant protection of those things. The example of food and drink above demonstrates that according to Spinoza's normative ethics, the intellectual understanding of how a means relates to the end it provides is a necessary condition for that end. The physical and chemical effects of the impacts of one being upon another will always be one and the same; the metaphysical effect however, in so far as this is the effect of the external being on the other's ability to understand, depends on how that other being understands the external being, its own being, and the mutual relationship between the two.

With these considerations in place, I think it is safe to say that the action guiding dictates concerning the right way of living in Part Four are not meant to perform a normative function on their own. The list of activities and behaviours, taken literally and by themselves, cannot help us in (and is not intended as a help for) accommodating our actions to the formal moral theory, which indeed seems to be entirely natural and species neutral. This means that even though some of these dictates can indeed be regarded as possible openings for a normative ethics of care (for nature),[4] LeBuffe's account of the relationship between the formal moral theory and the normative ethics reveals that we would do well to suspend our unqualified affirmation of this conclusion. A suspension of our judgement seems to be warranted considering how some of the goods listed in Part Four's account of the dictates of reason are expressly described as means to wellbeing only in specific circumstances.

We should not forget, however, that there are other action guiding norms within the category of dictates of reason in Part Four that do stipulate general and constant prescripts. Like, for instance, the norm to pursue all things that are conducive to 'the common society of men' and the norm to pursue all things that cause a conservation of the body's proportion of motion and rest (*E*4p39 and p40). The fact that these norms refer to goods that, according to Spinoza, are unconditionally beneficial for everyone's striving, invites us to consider whether nature could not be included into one of those goods.

However, if these generally held norms are read in the light of the overall motivation for proving a description of 'the right way of living' in the first place, we will once again come to qualify our understanding of their generality. Because, among the norms dedicated to providing concrete means to perseverance rather than means to the overall goal of understanding, there are two which can be described as maximization clauses (*E*4p65 and p66). These clauses establish that an individual ought to pursue not only those things that are always good, but in cases where two or more such are available (or, a greater future good is available at the expense of a lesser present one), the best of the two (or, in the opposite case of only poor alternatives available, the least harmful one) should be opted for.

So, LeBuffe takes the question of application reach of the generally formulated norms and connects it to the fact that there are so-called maximization clauses. 'Although some goods, such as society and the preservation of the body, may indeed be beneficial to all people in all circumstances, 4p65 suggests that not everyone should always pursue *any given good*' (2010, 185, my emphasis). This seems to suggest that in contrast to the prescripts concerning the epistemic treatment of passions in Part Five of the *Ethics*, none of the action guiding norms specifying certain goods and their effect on human wellbeing should *ever* be perceived as an unconditional and universally applicable rule. In fact, because the vast majority of us, to a significant degree at least, are always under the dominance of the passions, we must restrict and circumscribe the practical pursuit of the goods listed as means to wellbeing/perseverance in the dictates of reason. That this is the case with respect to individual ethical striving, in so far as the ethics of the *Ethics* largely functions as a psychological guide to self-help, is indisputable. More important, however, is that a carefully individualized approach to the means to perseverance is also warranted in the case of the state.

As I will discuss shortly, recent studies suggest that Spinoza considers a civil state rational to the extent that it adapts its laws to the *ingenium* (approximately: collective spirit) of its subjects, so that the circumstances necessary (peace and security) for advancing towards the ultimate ethical end of freedom can be obtained. An individual human being will often have to strive towards its ethical wellbeing by way of navigating between different inadequate ideas and passive affects confusing and blurring its perspective. Because of this, it would seem that a state sensitive to the *ingenium* of its people will create laws that are adapted to the general tendencies of irrational navigation rather than to a strict model of what is adequate and true.

Spinoza's normative ethics does not recommend that we try to attain a higher degree of rational understanding by way of just copying the behaviour of the truly rational human being as laid out in the norms describing 'the free man'. Instead, its advice for those of us (the majority it would seem) who have not attained a perfect ability to separate our passions from the external object with which we associate them, is to recognize our necessarily irrational approach to problems and choose the solution that inflicts the least harm on a peaceful co-existence with others. This is stated explicitly in *E*4p54:

> Because men rarely live from the dictates of reason, these two affects, humility and repentance, and also hope and fear, bring more advantage than harm. *Since men will sin, it is better to sin in that direction. For, if weak-minded men were all uniformly arrogant, ashamed of nothing, and afraid of nothing, what bonds could bring them together or control them?* The mob is terrifying unless it is afraid. No wonder, then, that the prophets, who cared about the common good and not that of the select few, commended humility, repentance, and reverence so much. Really, those who are subject to these affects can be led much more easily than others, so that, in the end, they can live under the guidance of reason, that is, they can be free and enjoy the life of the blessed.
> (My emphasis)

One of the overall conclusions we can draw from this is the following: harmful passions should be overcome by less harmful ones. Only in this way can we liberate enough power to perhaps eventually begin to create those active affects that amount to true ethical virtue by way of adequately understanding things, ourselves and our emotions. To this end, it is clear that *E*4p54 is underpinned by the civil state's *raison d'être*. The state must see to it that people driven by passive affects do not destroy each other and each other's natural abilities to actively pursue the means for increasing the level of adequate understanding. Because the human point of departure is one where passive interactions and reactions to things dominate; where we generally lack knowledge of thing's causes; and where we have a poorly developed ability to judge what things are good for us and what are bad, the state must use its *potestas* to create first of all a love for the community. This love, according to Spinoza, is the only available method for a successful path towards a common – yet individual – empowerment, and hence, ethical wellbeing. Another aspect highlighted by *E*4p54 is that none of the norms of the dictates of reason describing the fully rational person's means to perseverance (like *E*4p26 stating: 'from reason, we strive for nothing but understanding'), is configured so as to be applied in a social context incorporating human beings with differing levels of rationality. Rather, *E*4p54 tells us that even though we know that hope and fear are imaginative products and effects of inadequate ideas, and, in effect essentially contrary to wellbeing; it is virtuous (i.e. rational) for a state to utilize hope and fear to direct its citizens' thoughts and actions in so far as the state this way gets control over the external conditions determining each and everyone's ethical striving. Fear, despite being a passive affect, is paradoxically enough a rational good to pursue for the state in so far as it is a necessary means for it to use when making laws aiming at enabling a behaviour, on the part of its subjects, that is beneficial for achieving a state of being where active affects may be incentivized. Installing fear, and thus officially rejecting to some extent what is known to be the metaphysically true state of things, can therefore be seen as part and parcel of the adequate means towards the end of an intellectual activity amounting to the highest sense of wellbeing.

Based on all of the above reflections, I am inclined to hold that Spinoza's metaphysics as such cannot assist us in creating a normative ethics that includes nature's perspective into the human perspective. From what we have seen in this investigation of Spinoza's philosophy in the light of the problem of nature, it is problematic to read Spinoza's naturalistic definition of value as directly leading to a normative ethics capable of embodying that same naturalistic perspective. From what we have seen in this chapter about Spinoza's normative ethics, the point of intersection between metaphysics, ethics and political theories can in his philosophy be localized to the idea that it is not always truly good (rational) to do what objectively, or rationally, is the good. In the previous discussion of Spinoza's conception of law (Chapter 3), I mentioned the apparent paradox between Spinoza's statements in the *TTP* about how following the law can be regarded as always being an action in accordance with reason, and the fact that a state can create laws clearly going against reason. Justin Steinberg argues that it is possible to resolve this paradox by emphasizing the pragmatic position that Spinoza takes in understanding 'the good' in one sense when regarded *per se* and another sense when it is regarded *in situ* (2014, 183). According to this explanation, it is correct, metaphysically speaking, to hold that the good (i.e. rational) for a human being is always what corresponds to an adequate understanding of things. However, taking into consideration the fact that human beings will always find themselves in surroundings where the pursuit of an adequate understanding may be blocked or hampered by other obstacles than those related to their own natural intellectual capacity, the adequacy criterion alone with respect to the understanding of the good is not sufficient, ethically speaking. Therefore, there is conceptual room for justifying a definition of the good as whatever within each and every particular situation (*in situ*) constitutes the best means for approaching a position from where one is better off than before with respect to increasing one's number of adequate ideas. The *Ethics*' maximization clause, which happens to be reiterated in the *TTP* with respect to the purpose of the state, thus appears as a key for understanding how to deduce advice on what constitutes good law-making from the perspective of Spinoza's normative ethics.

Using Steinberg's terminology, it seems quite clear to what category of the *per se/in situ* division we should refer law. Laws are, generally speaking, means installed to decide on concrete problems of co-existence, taking into account concrete and changing social conditions. Their objectives may be formulated as abstract and general purposes but their applicability and elasticity to differing and changing contexts are regularly considered a measurement of their success, especially so within the context of international environmental law (Craig et. al., 2017). There is no room for doubt with respect to the fact that Spinoza affirms this position when it comes to laws. In fact, as we have seen, it is possible to understand Spinoza as identifying the ontological status of the state with the function of resolving changing social problems. He opens his last political treatise with the words that unlike those who 'conceive of men not as they are, but as they would like them to be', he formulates his advice on political organization based on certain ideas about human nature, which, of course, includes accounting for and taking into consideration the tendency to perceive things confusedly and inadequately.

According to these ideas, in order for the state to function as a practical and preliminary step towards the ultimate end of maximizing its subjects' collective power/freedom, it must pay attention to 'the actual capacities of the relevant agents' when it legislates (Steinberg, 2014, 184). For Steinberg this means that laws according to Spinoza should be tailored so as to suit the 'actual social psychological conditions of a given context' (ibid.). Steinberg elaborates by writing that laws according to Spinoza must be tailored in accordance with 'the general features of human psychology as expressed within a particular social arrangement and the specific *ingenium* or *cast of mind* of a people shaped by socio-historical circumstance' (2010, 184, my emphasis).

On my understanding, what this argument boils down to is that laws, for Spinoza, should be elastic and adaptable enough to meet the actual intellectual capacity (to understand things, phenomena and emotional changes) of the particular group of individuals whose social interactions the laws are meant to regulate. Even if it is, for obvious reasons, difficult to think about international law through the concept of *ingenium*, I believe that there are motives for letting Spinoza's general reflections on the purpose of civil law spill over onto our evaluation of the feasibility of creating an international law that places care for nature first, notwithstanding local variations and cultural contexts. To this end, we could, for instance, apply the concept of *ingenium* as an effective limit on how we can think about states' prioritization of the means available with respect to their limited yet principal goal of perseverance.

Now, considering all the aspects of this chapter, my final position with respect to the feasibility of the Reports' call is this: even *if* it can be argued that some (at least one) of the norms postulated by Spinoza as dictates of reason with respect to the human striving to perseverance, indeed posit, as a normative claim, understanding everything's connectedness and value, there are other aspects of the normative ethics that encourage a cautious approach towards using it directly as a guide for law making – domestic as well as international. Here is my motivation for taking this position.

Those action guiding norms of the dictates of reason which are directed towards a situation based evaluation of the means for perseverance do not, on their own, form a basis of normative evaluation. We have seen in this last section of the book that Spinoza complements his formal moral theory with a normative ethics that is adaptable, relative and always context-sensitive for a specific purpose. This is so, in order to never lose sight of the principal goal of understanding that every normative phenomenon is merely a means to the highest human end of freedom. To this end, it is sometimes required, as we have seen, that we rely upon an inadequate worldview and episteme even though it is in order to combat such an episteme we create normative structures in the first place. So, again, even *if* an ethical norm of care for nature could be successfully inserted into one of Spinoza's norms for perseverance (and probably already can be said to be included in the universal prescripts for the control of passions), the review of the connection between the political philosophy and the metaphysics that I have undertaken in this book shows that the aim of freedom cannot be understood, that is, achieved, unless coupled to the anthropocentric tendencies within human nature.

It is not a truthful understanding of the world as such – like a painting on a canvas that reflects a given external object – that holds the ethical power to liberate us. To this end, changing our behaviour, according to my understanding of Spinoza, is not only a matter of coming to our senses, or truly understanding the effects of our activities. Rather, it is our abilities to activate our own approximation towards such a truthful understanding of the things around us – understood as a practical ability to produce adequate ideas – that matters. Spinoza's metaphysics appears in this sense as a curiously pragmatic construction. In so far as his representation of what there is to know – the complex system of the modal/substance relationship – requires access to a wide affective register, the metaphysics becomes impossible to appreciate without engaging with the very concrete and particular conditions according to which each of us perceives the world. His political philosophy has a related but much more limited goal. Its goal is to provide the means for a collective approximation of a state of being where the individual, generally speaking, is better off in terms of developing his or her ability to *produce* the representation given in the metaphysics. The goal is not to establish a collective image of the content of that representation as such. Political (including legal) theory must therefore focus on assimilating the various and differing variables of our different affective registers so that the task of producing adequate ideas about ourselves and our contexts becomes less overwhelming and a little bit more manageable.

In other words, the law for Spinoza is ontologically explainable as the means by which to create a practical situation where the inherently normative aspects of the metaphysics become visible: normative aspects that might very well include caring for nature. So, an adequate and 'true' law – that is, a law that best fulfills its own ontological essence or nature – is focused on installing certain affective relationships *among* its subjects so that the normativity inherent to the metaphysics becomes palpable, rather than communicating this normativity as such. If legal regulations are used as means for installing the content of a specific metaphysics – including the outlines of the best affective relationships among the law's subject – then, to judge by Spinoza's political philosophy in light of the overall purpose of his metaphysics and ethics, the state will be considerably less effective as a means to the highest human good of freedom, as well as, to the more limited end, establishing peace and security among its subjects. The result would be both an increased risk for a general misunderstanding of what a non-anthropocentric care for nature is, and, more importantly, a weakened ability on the part of the state to force its subject to protect nature based on any kind of motive (anthropocentric or other).

Notes

1 More specifically, Sharp envisions the fundaments of Spinoza's political theory as combinable with feminist and queer theorist Elizabeth Grosz's prescription to 'renaturalize ourselves as corporal forces striving to actualize our power within nature' and to 'abandon the "regime of recognition"' as this results in yet another 'investment in a humanistic politics of identity' (Sharp, 2011a, 158, quotation marks in original).

2 See for instance the discussion in the introduction to Chapter 3 of this book.

3 In fact, it is the only means that amounts to the end of ethical wellbeing as we have seen in the discussion in Chapter 2 about how Spinoza connects epistemological error to ethics.

4 Like for instance proposition *E*4p28 which states that the greatest good is to know God and the fact that this knowledge implies knowing as much as possible of any kind of modal condition in nature, which, in turn, seems to imply the ethical wellbeing *qua* perseverance for as many things as possible of nature's infinite expressions.

References

Bennett, J. 1984. *A Study of Spinoza's Ethics.* Indianapolis, IN: Hackett Publishing Company.

Craig, R.K., Garmestani, A.S., Allen, C.R., Arnold, C.A., Birgé, H., DeCaro, D.A., Fremier, A.K., Gosnell, H., and Schlager, E. 2017. 'Balancing Stability and Flexibility in Adaptive Governance: An Analysis of Tools Available in U.S. Environmental Law', *Ecology and Society* 22(2): 3. https://doi.org/10.5751/ES-08983-220203, accessed on 28 April 2018.

Deleuze, G. 1988. *Spinoza: Practical Philosophy.* San Francisco, CA: City Lights Books.

Della Rocca, M. 2008. *Spinoza.* New York: Routledge.

International Court of Justice (ICJ). 1997. *Gabčíkovo-Nagymaros Project, Hungary v Slovakia*, Judgement, Merits, Rep 7. 25 September 1997.

Gamlund, E. 2007. 'Who Has Moral Status in the Environment? A Spinozistic Answer', in *The Trumpeter* 23(1): 3–27.

Garrett, D. 1996. 'Spinoza's Ethical Theory', in *The Cambridge Companion to Spinoza*, Garrett, D. (ed.): 267–314. Cambridge: Cambridge University Press.

Guilherme, A. 2011. 'Metaphysics as a Basis for Deep Ecology, An Equiry into Spinoza's System', in *The Trumpeter* 27(3): 60–78.

Huenemann, C. 2014. *Spinoza's Radical Theology: The Metaphysics of the Infinite.* Durham, UK: Acumen Publishing.

de Jonge, E. 2004. *Spinoza and Deep Ecology: Challenging Traditional Approaches to Environmentalism.* Aldershot, UK: Ashgate Publishing.

Kober, G. 2013. 'For They Do Not Agree in Nature: Spinoza and Deep Ecology', in *Ethics and the Environment* 18(1): 43–66.

LeBuffe, M. 2010. *From Bondage to Freedom: Spinoza on Human Excellence.* Oxford: Oxford University Press.

Lord, B. 2010. *Spinoza's Ethics*. Bloomington: Indiana University Press.

Mack, M. 2011. *Spinoza and the Specters of Modernity*. London: Continuum.

Melamed, Y. 2017. 'The Causes of Our Belief in Free Will: Spinoza on Necessary, "Innate," yet False Cognition', in *Spinoza's Ethics: A Critical Guide*, Melamed, Y. (ed.): 121–141. Cambridge: Cambridge University Press.

Moreau, P-F. 1996. 'Spinoza's Reception and Influence', in *The Cambridge Companion to Spinoza*, Garrett, D. (ed.): 408–434. Cambridge: Cambridge University Press.

Nadler, S. 2006. *Spinoza's Ethics: An Introduction*. Cambridge: Cambridge University Press.

Naess, A. 1977. 'Spinoza and Ecology', in *Philosophia* 7(1): 45–54.

Rutherford, D. 2010. 'Spinoza's Conception of Law: Metaphysics and Ethics', in *Spinoza's Theological-Political Treatise: A Critical Guide*. Melamed, Y. and Rosenthal, M. (eds): 143–167. Cambridge: Cambridge University Press.

Sharp, H. 2011a. *Politics of Renaturalization*. Chicago: The University of Chicago Press.

Sharp, H. 2011b. 'Animal Affects: Spinoza and the Frontiers of the Human', *Journal for Critical Animal Studies* 9(1/2): 48–68.

Sharp, H. 2016. 'Endangered Life: Feminist Posthumanism in the Anthropocene?', in *Feminist Philosophies of Life*, Sharp, H. and Taylor, C. (eds): 272–281. Quebec/Kingston: McGill-Queen's University Press.

Solé, M. J. 2011. *Spinoza en Alemania (1670–1789): Historia de la santificación de un filósofo maldito*. Buenos Aires: Editorial Brujas.

Spinoza, B. 1985. *Ethics; Treatise on the Emendation of the Intellect*. Curley, E. (ed. and trans.), *The Collected Works of Spinoza*, vol. I. Princeton, NJ: Princeton University Press.

Spinoza, B. 2016. *Theological-Political Treatise (TTP); Political Treatise (TP) and Letters* (*Ep.*). Curley, E. (ed. and trans.), *The Collected Works of Spinoza*, vol. II. Princeton, NJ: Princeton University Press.

Steinberg, J. 2014. 'Following a *Recta Ratio Vivendi*: The Practical Utility of Spinoza's Dictates of Reason', in *Essays on Spinoza's Ethical Theory*, Kisner, M.J. and Youpa, A. (eds): 178–196. Oxford: Oxford University Press.

Walther, M. 2009. 'Suppress or Refute? Reactions to Spinoza in Germany around 1700', in *The Use of Censorship in the Enlightenment*, Laerke, M. (ed.): 25–40. Leiden: Brill.

Wilson, S. 1996. 'Spinoza's Theory of Knowledge', in *The Cambridge Companion to Spinoza*, Garrett, D. (ed.): 89–141. Cambridge: Cambridge University Press.

United Nations. 1969. *Vienna Convention on the Law of Treaties*. United Nations, Treaty Series, vol. 1155, p. 331. www.refworld.org/docid/3ae6b3a10.html, accessed on 21 March 2018.

United Nations Secretary General (UNSG). 2010–2015. *Harmony with Nature: Report of the Secretary General I–VI*. Report II: UNGA Res A/66/302; Report VII: UNGA Res A/71/266.

Index

For Product Safety Concerns and Information please contact our EU representative GPSR@taylorandfrancis.com
Taylor & Francis Verlag GmbH, Kaufingerstraße 24, 80331 München, Germany

www.ingramcontent.com/pod-product-compliance
Ingram Content Group UK Ltd.
Pitfield, Milton Keynes, MK11 3LW, UK
UKHW011014180926
475701UK00004B/732
* 9 7 8 0 3 6 7 6 6 5 5 1 7 *